INSTANT POT
COOKBOOK #KETO 500 RECIPES

Delicious, Quick & Easy Keto Instant Pot Recipes with 30-Day Meal Plan

Emma Peterson

© Copyright 2019 by Emma Peterson

All rights reserved.

ISBN: 978-1797667812

No part of this book may be reproduced or transmitted in any form or by any means, electronic or mechanical, including photocopying, recording or by any information storage and retrieval system, without written permission from the publisher, except for the inclusion of brief quotations in a review.

Warning-Disclaimer

The purpose of this book is to educate and entertain. The author or publisher does not guarantee that anyone following the techniques, suggestions, tips, ideas, or strategies will become successful. The author and publisher shall have neither liability or responsibility to anyone with respect to any loss or damage caused, or alleged to be caused, directly or indirectly by the information contained in this book.

CONTENTS

INTRODUCTION 9

GOING KETO 10

BREAKFAST & BRUNCH 13

- Cauli Grits 13
- Giant Pancakes 13
- Egg, Sausage & Cheese Bundt 14
- Salmon Veggie Cakes 14
- Poached Eggs on Heirloom Tomatoes ... 15
- Bacon & Sausage Omelet 15
- Spanish Zucchini Tortilla 16
- Cheesy Spinach Casserole 16
- Very Berry Ricotta Pancakes 16
- Spinach and Tomato Cheesy Braise 17
- Delicious Scallions and Eggs 17
- The Easiest Eggs with Mushrooms 18
- Healthy Artichokes with Eggs 18
- Classic Eggs with Cheese and Bacon 18
- Ricotta Cheese with Eggs 19
- Fresh Veggies Mix 19
- Hot Scrambled Eggs 19
- Eggs Chicken Casserole 20
- Creamy Egg Casserole 20
- Mexican Chili Eggs 20
- Chili Egg Cubes 21
- Basil-Flavored Spinach & Bacon Eggs ... 21
- Vanilla Cheesecake Pancakes 22
- Quick and Easy Breakfast Porridge 22
- Egg Cups with Broccoli and Mushrooms 22
- Basil and Parsley Scramble 23
- Two-Cheese Almond Bagels 23

LUNCH AND DINNER RECIPES 24

- Feta and Cauliflower Rice Stuffed Bell Peppers 24
- Shrimp with Linguine 24
- Mexican Cod Fillets 25
- Simple Mushroom Chicken Mix 25
- Squash Spaghetti with Bolognese Sauce 25
- Healthy Halibut Fillets 26
- Clean Salmon with Soy Sauce 26
- Simple Salmon with Eggs 26
- Easy Shrimp 27
- Scallops with Mushroom Special 27
- Delicious Creamy Crab Meat 27
- Creamy Broccoli Stew 28
- No Crust Tomato and Spinach Quiche ... 28
- Ratatouille 28
- Steamed Artichokes 29
- Creamed Savoy Cabbage 29
- Tilapia Delight 30
- Spinach Tomatoes Mix 30
- Spinach Almond Tortilla 30
- Zucchini Noodles in Garlic and Parmesan Toss 31
- Lemoned Broccoli 31
- Keto Carrot Cake 31
- Asparagus Gremolata 32
- Beets with Yogurt 32
- Vegetarian Faux Stew 32
- Egg Fried Cauli Rice 33
- Vegetable en Papillote 33
- Keto Coconut Almond Cake 34
- Faux Beet Risotto 34
- Broccoli Rice with Mushrooms 34
- Stuffed Cabbages 35
- Garlic Buttered Sprouts 35

STEW, SOUPS & CHILI 36

- Butternut Cauliflower Soup 36
- Chicken Turnip Soup 36
- Healthy Taco Soup 37
- Veggie Brisket Stew 37
- Hot Beef Chili 38
- White Chicken Chili 38
- Chicken and Green Onion Soup 38
- Mixed Veggie Stew 39
- Veggie Walnut Chili 39
- Cauliflower Soup 40
- Green Beans and Spinach Soup 40
- Baby Spinach Green Soup with Asparagus ... 40

Coriander and Spinach Soup 41	Garlic Chicken and Egg Soup 45
Shrimp Soup... 41	Beef and Broccoli Stew 45
Sausage and Seafood Stew 42	Spinach Soup 46
Creamy Chicken Mushroom Stew 42	Delicious Full Chicken Soup 46
Pork Chunk Chili.. 43	Squash Soup 46
Sweet and Sour Tomato Soup...................... 43	Baby Spinach Soup 47
Vegetable Soup 44	Butter Squash Soup 47
Pumpkin Soup 44	Creamy Asparagus Soup.............................. 47
Crème de la Broc... 44	Mushroom Soup 48

KETO POULTRY RECIPES 49

Creamy Basil Chicken Breasts 49	Chicken with Sweet Potatoes 64
Lemon Chicken.. 49	Bell Pepper and Egg Tortilla 65
Coq Au Vin 50	Chicken with Avocado Cream....................... 65
Coconut Chicken Curry 50	Chicken and Turnip Stew.............................. 66
Chicken Taco Bowls 51	Chicken Mushroom Mix 66
Sweet Spicy Shredded Chicken 51	Chicken Meatballs with Parmesan 66
Chicken in Tomato Sauce 52	Tasrty Fried Chicken.................................... 67
Spinach Feta Stuffed Chicken 52	Curried Chicken Patties................................ 67
Meatballs Primavera.................................... 53	Turkey Stew with Veggies 68
Buffalo Chicken Soup 53	Turkey Breasts in Italian Sauce 68
Balsamic Chicken.. 54	Simple Chicken Soup 68
Tuscan Chicken 54	Worcestershire Turkey Cubes 69
Barbecue Chicken 55	Chicken Enchilada Soup 69
Quick Chicken Fajitas 55	Perfected Butter Chicken.............................. 70
Stuffed Full Chicken 56	Sweet and Chili Goose Breasts..................... 70
Chicken Wings 56	Chicken Zoodle Soup 70
Whole Chicken 57	Crack Chicken 71
Broccoli Chicken 57	Creamy Garlic Tuscan Chicken Thighs 71
Simple Chicken Wings................................. 57	Creamy Duck with Spinach 72
Asian-Style Chicken Thighs......................... 58	Creamy Chicken with Broccoli 72
Chicken with Sesame oil 58	Chicken Taco Filling 72
Hot Garlic Chicken Breasts 58	No Cream Chicken and Broccoli 73
Chicken Tenders with Garlic........................ 59	Buffalo Chicken Meatballs 73
Tropic Shredded Chicken 59	Ranch and Lemon Whole Chicken 74
Hot Butter Chicken 59	Chicken Thighs with Bacon and Cheese....... 74
Egg and Carrot Spread 60	Hot Chicken Stew... 74
Roasted Eggs Gravy 60	Chicken Breasts with Mushrooms and Coconut .. 75
Squash with Eggs.. 60	Chicken Soup with Veggies 75
Tomato Eggs 61	Greek Chicken Casserole............................. 76
Zucchini Eggs 61	Easy and Cheesy Chicken and Cauliflower... 76
Tomato and Coconut Chicken 61	Mexican Chicken 76
Pepperoni Pizza Egg 62	Chicken Carnitas 77
Poached Eggs 62	Cajun Drumsticks 77
Asian Style Steamed Eggs 62	Chicken Daikon and Cabbage Soup 78
Jalapeno and Cheddar Chicken 63	Mexican Risotto with Turkey......................... 78
Cream Chicken with Tomatoes and Zucchini 63	Chicken Lazone... 79
Sour Cream Chicken with Cauliflower........... 63	Butternut Squash with Turkey Chili................ 79
Hot Chicken Chili 64	Lemon and Olive Ligurian............................. 80
Chicken Breast with Green Onions 64	Tarragon and Mushroom Chicken 80

Leftover Chicken in Spicy Tomato Sauce 81
Simple Alfredo Shredded Chicken 81
Shredded Chicken Pizza Casserole 81
No Beans Chicken Chili 82
Lemon Garlic Chicken 82

KETO RED MEAT RECIPES 83

Beef and Broccoli Sauce 83
Homemade Beef Stew 83
Beef, Tomato & Cabbage Soup 84
Beef Stroganoff 84
Swedish Meatballs with Mushroom Gravy 84
Beef Stuffed Grape Leaves 85
Beef Short Ribs 85
Beef and Zoodle Soup 86
Texas Beef Chili 86
Beef Curry Stew 86
Mocha Rubbed Pot Roast 87
Plain Beef Broth Stew 87
Beef and Broccoli 88
Beef Hoagies 88
Pepper Rolled Beef 89
Dairy Free Beef Stew 89
Beef Brisket in Red Curry 90
Pot Roast 90
Bell pepper Beef Mix 91
Beef and Beer Stew 91
Unstuffed Cabbage Roll Soup 92
Spicy Beef Stew 92
Green Beans Beef Soup 92
Beef Taco Soup 93
Meatballs in Spaghetti Sauce 93
Balsamic Beef Pot Roast 94
Italian Pepperoncini Beef 94
Minute Steak and Cheese Stuffed Mushrooms 94
Bacon Wrapped Beef with Green Beans 95
Coconut Beef Roast 95
Sliced Meat with Mixed Mushrooms 95
Beef Celeriac Soup 96
Beef with Haricots vert 96
Ground Beef with Peppers 96
Cauliflower Meat 97
Ground Beef with Flax Seeds 97
Beef Meat with Shallots 98
Tamari Steak with Tomatoes 98
Meatloaf with Cheddar 98
Beef with Cauliflower Pilaf 99
Sesame Tamari Flank Strips 99
Cauliflower Rice with Ground Beef 100
Shredded Mexican Beef 100
Beef Tenderloin with Tarragon Sauce 100
Keto Beef Chili 101
Beef Casserole with Veggies 101
Creamy Cauli & Beef Soup 102
No Carb Lasagna 102
Lamb Leg 102
Minty Lamb "Rice" 103
Lamb Curry 103
Goulash Soup 104
Lamb Shanks 104
Lamb Stew 104
Greek Style Lamb Shoulder 105
Lamb Kofta in Tomato Sauce 105
Chipotle Braised Lamb Shank 106
Cinnamon and Cocoa Lamb Shoulder 106
Butter Lamb 106
Lamb Chops 107
Braised Oxtail 107
Oxtail Soup 108
Easy Osso Buco 108
Oxtail Ragout 108
Rosemary Veal Stew 109
Spicy Pulled Pork 109
Brown Gravy Pork Roast 110
Pork Strips with Tomatoes 110
Bangers and Mash with Onion Gravy 111
Herby Cuban Pork Roast 111
Pork Stew 112
Lemony Pork Belly 112
Ham with Collard Greens 112
Pork in Mushroom Gravy 113
Pork Tenderloin with Ginger Soy Sauce 113
Beef Bourguignonne 114
Beef Burger 114
Pork Carnitas Lettuce Cups 115
Easy BBQ Ribs 115
Braised Pork Neck Bones 116
Pork Roast Sandwich 116
Balsamic Pork Tenderloin 117
Tender Greek Pork 117
Pork in Vegetable Sauce *118*
Creamy Pork with Bacon 118
Pulled Pork in Lettuce Wraps 119
Coconut Ginger Pork 119
Sweet Spicy Pork Chops 120
Green Chile Pork Carnitas 120
Pork in Peanut Sauce 121

Carrot and Pork Stew 121	Bacon Onion Jam 125
Kalua Pork 122	Pork and Tofu Toscana Soup 126
Coconut Pork Shoulder 122	Coconut Ginger Pork 126
Prosciutto Wrapped Asparagus Canes 122	Pork Meatballs 126
Hot Shredded Pork 123	Southern Pork Roast 127
Bacon Brussel Sprout Dish 123	Bacon Cheddar Egg Bites 127
Spicy Pork Chops 123	Tandoori BBQ Pork Ribs 128
Sausage and Pepper Sauce 124	Sweet Chipotle Pork 128
Pork Roll Soup 124	Creamy Ranch Pork Chops 128
Easy Pork Ribs 124	Pork Roast with Mushroom Gravy 129
Fall-Apart Pork Butt with Garlic Sauce 125	No-Pressure Cumin Pork Chops 129

FISH AND SEAFOOD 130

Sweet & Spicy Mahi Mahi 130	Steamed Shrimp with Asparagus 138
One Pot Monk Fish with Greens 130	Stewed Shellfish 139
Fennel Alaskan Cod with Turnips 131	Creamy Prawn Scampi 139
Salmon with Lime Sauce 131	Lobster Tails with Dill Butter Sauce 140
Scottish Seafood Curry 132	One Pot Tuna & Veggies Dish 140
Carolina Crab Soup 132	Simple Steamed Clams 141
Seared Scallops with Butter Caper Sauce .. 133	Lemon Pepper Salmon 141
Oyster Stew 133	Shrimp in Coconut Milk Sauce 141
Fish Soul-Satisfying Soup 134	Simple Fish Curry 142
Fish Tamarind Gravy 134	Haddock in Creamy Tomato Broth 142
Salmon with Broccoli 134	Spicy Herbed Tuna 143
Teriyaki Salmon with Ginger 135	Ginger Steamed Scallion Fish 143
Fish with Coconut and Cauliflower Rice 135	White Fish Stew 144
Duo Seafood Medley 136	Hot Anchovies 144
Tilapia with Chia Seeds 136	Sea Bass in Tomato Sauce 144
Steamed Crab Legs 136	Dill Spiced Salmon 145
Cheesy Tilapia 137	Cod Fish Packets 145
Crab Quiche 137	Simple Steamed Cod 146
Salmon in Spicy Lime Sauce 138	Mackerel Packets 146
Gingery and Orange Mackerel 138	Chili Black Mussels 147

VEGETABLES, VEGAN & SIDE DISHES 148

Cauli Rice Stuffed Peppers 148	Tofu and Swiss Chard Bowl 154
Creamy Broccoli Mash 148	Peppery and Cheesy Pizza 154
Easy Spaghetti Squash 149	Spinach Ricotta Pie 155
Basic Steamed Asparagus 149	Smoked Paprika Cauliflower Cakes 155
Coconut Cauli Rice 149	Three-Cheese Stuffed Peppers 156
Spicy Zoodle and Bok Choy Soup 150	Beet and Pecan Bowl 156
Leafy Green Sauté 150	Broccoli with Tomatoes 156
Greek-Style Eggplant Lasagne 151	Asparagus Zoodles with Pesto & Boiled Eggs 157
Tofu Soup 151	Squash Spaghetti with Mint and Almond Pesto . 157
Winter Vegetable Soup 152	Radish Hash Browns 158
Creamy Kale Soup 152	Cheese Sandwich with Chimichurri 158
Mini Pesto Cake 152	Cheesy Jalapeno Lunch 'Waffles' 159
Mediterranean Pasta with Avocado 153	Fake Mac and Cheese 159
Feta-Stuffed Mushrooms with Walnuts 153	Mushroom Cream Soup 159

Kale and Cauliflower Stew 160	Low Carb Taco Soup 168
Flax and Swiss Chard Patties 160	Cauliflower Bacon Soup 168
Portobello Burgers 160	Broccoli Soup 169
Dill and Artichoke Salad 161	Broccoli "Slaw" 169
Eggplant and Parmesan Burgers 161	Chili and Zesty Brussel Sprouts 170
Tomato Soup with Goat Cheese Topping 162	Squash and Zucchini Soup 170
Pumpkin Chipotle Soup 162	Herbed Portobellos 170
Soft Cabbage with Garlic and Lemon 162	Tomato & Celery Okra 171
Winter Vegetable Soup with Shirataki Rice . 163	Cheesy Cauliflower 171
Creamy Gingery Coconut "Rice" 163	Creamed Kale with Bacon 172
Cheesy Green Beans 164	Herbed Zucchini Flatbread 172
Mock Grilled Onions 164	Cabbage Soup 172
Kale "Pita Bread" 164	Fried Parmesan Cauliflower 173
Caramelized Peppers and Onions 165	Broccoli Lemongrass and Cilantro Soup 173
Soft and Cheesy Keto "Bread" 165	Spiced Radishes 174
Squash Side 166	Onion Soup 174
Chili Green Beans with Coconut 166	Mixed Vegetable Soup 174
Soft Cumin Cabbage 166	Pumpkin Puree 175
Turmeric Squash Cubes 167	Carrot Ginger Soup 175
Curried Eggplant 167	Creamed Spinach Soup 175
Creamy Spinach 167	Celeriac Pumpkin Soup 176
Tofu & Tomatoes 168	Stuffed Mushrooms with Parmesan 176

SNACKS & APPETIZERS 177

Barbecue Chicken Wings 177	Sausage Weenies 186
Buffalo Chicken 177	Tropic Cauliflower Manchurian 186
Bacon Wrapped Cheese Bombs 178	Tropic Sweet Potato Gravy 187
Cheesy Chicken Dip 178	Pumpkin Pie Mini Pancakes 187
Tomato Basil Dip 178	Prosciutto Wrapped Asparagus 188
Avocado Paste Snack 179	Bacon Cheeseburger Dip 188
Eggs in Sausage 179	Garlic Fried Mushrooms 188
Stir Fried Garlic Zest Spinach 179	Pao de Queijo 189
Sweet Potato Wedges 180	Mini Biscuits 189
Fried Mushrooms 180	Ham & Cheese Puffs 190
Easy Cauliflower Hummus 180	Broccoli & Cheddar Nuggets 190
Carrot Broccoli Stew 181	Basil Cheese Balls 190
Creamy Pumpkin Puree Soup 181	Chili Tortilla Chips 191
Instant Pot Creamy Mushrooms 181	Chili Party Meatballs 191
Tomatoes Mix Recipe 182	Carrot and Pumpkin Stew 192
Hot Stir-Fried Chili Pepper 182	Zucchini Ham and Cheese Rolls 192
Lemonade Pilaf 182	Pepperoni Pizza Bites 192
Spiced Zucchini Fingers 183	Mini Quesadillas 193
Zucchini Chips 183	Cream Cheese & Salami Snack 193
Asparagus Chowder 183	Stuffed & Wrapped Meaty Jalapenos 193
Ground Beef Zucchini Zoodles 184	Gorgonzola Chicken Dip 194
Cauliflower Tots 184	Cheddar Crisps 194
Stir Fried Vegetables 184	Sausage and Cheese Dip 194
Caulicheese Mini Bowls 185	Prosciutto Wrapped Chicken Sticks 195
Stuffed Mini Peppers 185	Green Devilled Eggs 195
Egg Brulee 186	Simple Almond-Buttered Walnuts 195

Eggplant Spread 196
Mushroom Pate 196
Mini Haddock Bites 197
Au Jus Dip 197
Chicken Ranch Dip 197
Cauliflower Alfredo Dip 198
Spicy Chicken Dip 198
Spicy Queso Dip 198
Veggie Tomato Dip 199
Homemade Ricotta Cheese 199
Beef and Bacon Dip 199

BROTH, STOCK & SAUCES 200

Chicken Broth 200
Mixed Seafood Broth 200
Mixed Bone Broth 201
Mushroom and Pork Broth 201
Perfect Hard Boiled Eggs 201
Octopus Broth 202
Lemon Flavored Fish Broth 202
Anchovy Stock 202
Strawberry Jam 203
Pressure-Cooked Coconut Milk 203
Keto Porridge 203
Cauliflower Mash 204
Barbecue Sauce 204
Gouda Cheesy Vegan Sauce 204
Starfruit Sauce 205
Homemade Marinara Sauce 205
Keto Choc Mousse 206
Bolognese Beef Sauce 206
Homemade Ketchup 207
Homemade Tabasco Sauce 207

DESSERTS 208

Chocolate Cheesecake 208
Easy Crème Brulee 209
Hot Lava Cake 209
Vanilla Pudding 210
Blackberry Smash 210
Fruit Mix Dessert 210
Pumpkin Cake 211
Vanilla Bean Cheesecake 211
Lemon Ricotta Cheesecake 212
Lemony Ricotta Cake 212
Very Chocolate Cheesecake 213
Chocolate Mini Cakes 213
Strawberry Cobbler Mock 214
Lemon Curd 214
Cocoa Walnut Cake 214
Lavender and Apple Cake 215
Pistachio Cake 215
Chocolate Squares with Chia Seeds 216
Rum Mug Cake 216
Orange-Flavored Cake 217
Chocolate and Applesauce Pudding Cake .. 217

30-DAY MEAL PLAN 218

INTRODUCTION

Following a strict diet such as the Ketogenic one can be truly challenging. And while it is true that this eating plan can transform our physical and mental health tremendously, when life's obligations have us in a constant rush, sticking to the no-carb rule can be pretty overwhelming. But not if you know the easiest way to maintaining the Keto lifestyle.

Combining the most revolutionary kitchen appliance - the instant pot, with one of the most popular and super successful diets today - the ketogenic diet, this book will reveal to you the secrets of easy Keto cooking, weight losing, and taste-bud-pleasing.

Quick, healthy, and without having to spend hours in front of the stove, Instant Keto cooking is the best guarantee that you will reap out the Ketogenic benefits without sacrificing meal satisfaction.

Providing you with 500 carefully selected delightful recipes, this cookbook is a definite must-have for those who own an Instant Pot, want to enter or maintain Ketosis, and ideally, both.

Now, jump to the first recipe and see how delicious low-carb meals can be when cooked under pressure.

GOING KETO

The Ketogenic diet is undoubtedly the most controversial one today. And while there are tons of successful stories that prove to us that the secret to healthy living and weight maintaining indeed lies in ditching the carbs, many people are scared to approach such a strict eating plan.

*Won't all that fat raise my cholesterol levels? Won't butter and bacon widen my waist? Will I hurt my health if I enter ketosis? The answer? A definite **NO**.*

Does It Really Work?

Definitely! Ask anyone who has been motivated enough to stick to this diet's guidelines and you will get the same answer – the Keto diet will help you lose or maintain weight in the healthiest way possible without sacrificing your full tummy or your satisfied taste buds.

The main point of the Ketogenic diet is to steer clear of carbohydrates and instead, train your body to run on fat. It may seem impossible at this point, but this is very achievable.

Think of your body as a car with a backup tank. When the petrol runs out, your car will use the fuel from the gas tank to keep on moving. Your body works in a similar way. Once you empty your glucose reserves (as we know that carbohydrates get broken down into glucose), your body will turn to your reserved fat for energy.

What Is Ketosis and Is It Dangerous?

The moment that your body starts to use fat for energy, it enters the state of ketosis. During the food conversion fat gets broken down into ketones (hence the name ketogenic), and the goal of this diet is to use the ketones for energy instead of glucose.

Many confuse the state of ketosis with diabetic ketosis, which is something else entirely, and think that it is dangerous. Instead, it is just an indicator that your carb ditching has not been in vain and that you are on the right path to weight loss and lasting health.

How to Know if It's Working?

If you have reached ketosis, that means that you have been following the right Ketogenic guidelines. You will know that you are in the state of ketosis if you are experiencing fatigue, rapid weight loss, or bad breath.

These symptoms may not sound appealing but they will only bother you for about 2 weeks or so, since that is the average time that the human body needs in order to adapt to the new source of energy.

What Are the Ketogenic Guidelines?

The Ketogenic diet has gotten the bad reputation for being hard to follow thanks to its strict macro recommendation:

65 – 70% **Fat**

25 – 30% **Protein**

5% **Carbohydrates**

But even though this may seem impossible to accomplish on daily basis, if you know which ingredients to use and which will only cause your weight to rise, the Ketogenic diet is pretty straightforward and easy plan to follow.

WHAT TO EAT:

- eat (fresh and processed meat)
- Seafood
- Eggs
- All Dairy Products (milk, cheeses, heavy cream, sour cream, yogurt, butter, etc.)
- Avocados (low in carbs, high in healthy fats)
- Non Starchy Veggies (broccoli, leafy greens, cauliflower, asparagus, Brussel sprouts, zucchini, cabbage, tomatoes, etc.)
- Lower-in-carbs Fruits (Berries, watermelon, citrus fruits, etc.)
- Seeds
- Nuts
- Oils (aim for the healthiest kind such as olive oil, coconut oil, flaxseed oil, etc.)

WHAT NOT TO EAT:

- Grains
- Beans and Legumes
- Sugar
- Trans Fats

- Fruit Juices
- Starchy Veggies (corn, potatoes, peas, parsnips, etc.)
- Diet Soda
- Refined Gats and Oils (such as margarine)

How Can the Instant Pot Help?

If you own an Instant Pot, you are already familiar with everything that this revolutionary kitchen appliance can do. It works as a:

1. A Saute Pan
2. A Pressure Cooker
3. A Rice Cooker
4. A Steamer
5. A Slow Cooker
6. Warming Pot
7. A Yogurt Maker

It multiple buttons allow hassle-free cooking and it is kind of obvious that this is one extremely valuable gadget to have. But how can it help during your Ketogenic experience?

Since the Ketogenic diet is quite restrictive, it is of utmost importance that the nutrient intake is balanced. And what better way to ensure that than to cook your food in an Instant Pot? The Instant Pot will not cause your food to lose its vitamins and minerals during cooking, unlike the conventional cooking appliances. And besides ensuring proper nutrition, the Instant Pot also ensures quick cooking without sacrificing your free afternoon. Doesn't that sound like a good reason to give these yummy recipes a try?

BREAKFAST & BRUNCH

Cauli Grits

Prep + Cook Time: 20 minutes | Servings: 4

INGREDIENTS:

4 small Heads Cauliflower
2 tsp Olive oil
Salt and Black Pepper
½ cup Water
½ cup Milk, full fat
1 ½ cups grated Cheddar Cheese

DIRECTIONS:

With a knife, cut off every leaf and cut the cauliflower into 6-8 large florets. Grate with a grater into fine cauli rice while discarding the stems. Pour half of the water in the Instant Pot.

Add the cauli rice, and olive oil. Stir using a spoon. Seal the lid, select Multigrain mode on High pressure for 5 minutes. After 5 minutes, do a quick pressure release and open the lid. Add milk, salt, and pepper. Stir with a spoon while breaking any hard lump and mashing the cauli rice into a smoother consistency. Seal the lid and set on Multigrain on High for 5 minutes.

Once ready, do a quick pressure release, and immediately add the cheddar cheese and give the pudding a good stir using the same spoon. Dish the cauli grits into serving bowls and serve with toasted low carb bread.

Nutrition facts per serving: Calories 132, Protein 5.8g, Net Carbs 1g, Fat 9.6g

Giant Pancakes

Prep + Cook Time: 30 minutes | Servings: 4 to 6

INGREDIENTS:

3 cups Almond flour
¾ cup Stevia Sugar
5 Eggs
⅓ cup Olive oil
⅓ cup Sparkling Water
⅓ tsp Salt
1 ½ tsp Baking Soda

To Serve:
2 tbsp Monk Fruit Syrup
Dollop of Whipped Cream

DIRECTIONS:

Start by pouring the almond flour, stevia sugar, eggs, olive oil, sparkling water, salt, and baking soda into the food processor and blend until smooth. Pour the resulting batter into the Instant Pot and let sit for 15 minutes. Seal the lid, select Multigrain on Low pressure for 15 minutes.

Once ready, press Cancel, release the pressure quickly. Stick in a toothpick and once it comes out clean, the pancake is done. Gently run a spatula around the pancake to let loose any sticking. Then, slide the pancakes into a serving plate.

Top with whip cream and drizzle with monk syrup. Serve as an add up to the breakfast table.

Nutrition facts per serving: Calories 271, Protein 13g, Net Carbs 3.1g, Fat 16g

Egg, Sausage & Cheese Bundt

Prep + Cook Time: 25 minutes | Servings: 4 to 5

INGREDIENTS:

8 Eggs, cracked into a bowl
8 oz Breakfast Sausage, chopped
3 Bacon Slices, chopped
1 large Green Bell pepper, chopped
1 large Red Bell pepper, chopped
1 cup chopped Green Onion
1 cup grated Cheddar Cheese
1 tsp Red Chili Flakes
Salt and Black Pepper to taste
½ cup Milk, full fat
4 slices Low Carb Bread, cubed
2 cups Water

DIRECTIONS:

Add sausage, bacon, green pepper, red pepper, onion, chili flakes, cheddar, salt, pepper, and milk to a bowl and use a whisk to beat them together.

Grease the bundt pan with cooking spray and pour the egg mixture into it. After, drop the bread slices in the egg mixture all around while using a spoon to push them into the mixture. Open the Instant Pot, pour the water in, and fit in the trivet. Place the bundt pan on top, seal the lid, select Steam mode for 8 minutes on High pressure.

Once ready, press Cancel and do a quick pressure release. Use a napkin to gently remove the bundt pan onto a flat surface. Run a knife around the egg in the bundt pan, place a serving plate on the bundt pan, and turn the egg bundt over. Slice and serve.

Nutrition facts per serving: Calories 267, Protein 20g, Net Carbs 2g, Fat 16.9g

Salmon Veggie Cakes

Prep + Cook Time: 40 minutes | Servings: 4

INGREDIENTS:

2 (5 oz) packs Steamed Salmon Flakes
1 Red Onion, chopped
Salt and Black Pepper to taste
1 tsp Garlic Powder
2 tbsp Olive oil
1 Red Bell pepper, seeded and chopped
4 tbsp Butter, divided
3 Eggs, cracked into a bowl
1 cup Low Carb Breadcrumbs
4 tbsp Mayonnaise
2 tsp Sugar Free Worcestershire Sauce
¼ cup chopped Parsley

DIRECTIONS:

Heat half of the butter and the oil on Sauté. Add the onions and the bell peppers. Cook for 9 minutes, stirring occasionally. Press Cancel.

In a bowl, mix salmon flakes, bell pepper, onion, breadcrumbs, eggs, mayo, Worcestershire sauce, garlic, salt, pepper, and parsley. Mix well while breaking the salmon into the smallest possible pieces. Use your hands to mold 4 patties out of the mixture and set them on a plate.

Press Sauté and melt the remaining butter. Fry the patties in the butter until golden brown. Remove onto a wire rack to rest for 2 minutes. Serve with a side of lettuce and radish salad with a mild drizzle of herb vinaigrette.

Nutrition facts per serving: Calories 264, Protein 16.4g, Net Carbs 2g, Fat 15.5g

Poached Eggs on Heirloom Tomatoes

Prep + Cook Time: 10 minutes | Servings: 4

INGREDIENTS:

4 large Eggs
2 cups Water
2 large Heirloom Tomatoes, halved crosswise
Salt and Black Pepper to taste
1 tsp chopped Fresh Herbs
2 tbps grated Parmesan Cheese

DIRECTIONS:

Pour the water into the Instant Pot and fit in a trivet. Grease 4 ramekins with cooking spray and crack an egg into each of them. Place the ramekins on the trivet.

Seal the lid, select Steam and cook for 3 minutes on High. Once ready, press Cancel, do a quick pressure release, and open the pot.

Use a napkin to remove the ramekins onto a flat surface. In serving plates, share the halved heirloom tomatoes and toss the eggs in the ramekin over on each tomato half. Sprinkle with salt and pepper, Parmesan, and garnish with herbs. Serve at a brunch table.

Nutrition facts per serving: Calories 123, Protein 6.3g, Net Carbs 2g, Fat 4.9g

Bacon & Sausage Omelet

Prep + Cook Time: 40 minutes | Servings: 3

INGREDIENTS

1 Onion, diced
6 Eggs
6 Sausage Links, chopped
6 Bacon Slices, cooked and crumbled
½ cup Milk
¼ tsp dried Parsley
Salt and Pepper, to taste
1 ½ cups Water

DIRECTIONS

Pour the water in and lower the trivet. Crack the eggs in a bowl and pour the milk over. Beat the eggs and milk along with some salt and pepper until well-incorporated and smooth. Stir in the parsley, onion, bacon, and sausage. Grab a baking dish and grease it with cooking spray. Pour the egg mixture over. Place the baking dish on top of the trivet.

Close the lid of the Instant Pot and turn it clockwise to seal. Select the MANUAL/PRESSURE COOK mode. Set the cooking time to 25 minutes on HIGH pressure.

When the timer goes off, release the pressure naturally by allowing the valve to drop down on its own. Open the lid carefully and remove the baking dish from the pot. Serve and enjoy!

Nutrition facts per serving: Calories 220, Protein 17g, Net Carbs 3.5g, Fat 15g

Spanish Zucchini Tortilla

Prep + Cook Time: 15 minutes | Servings: 3

INGREDIENTS:

3 Eggs
1 large Zucchini
1 Onion, chopped
½ tbsp Thyme, chopped
¼ tbsp Salt
¼ tbsp white Pepper
2 tbsp Olive oil
Chopped Parsley, for garnish

DIRECTIONS:

Cut the zucchini into thin strips and set aside. Crack the eggs in a medium bowl and whisk for 1 minute. Add the zucchini strips, onion, thyme, salt, and pepper, mix well.

Add 2 cups of water into the Instant Pot and place a trivet inside. Spray a medium-sized baking dish with olive oil, transfer the eggs mixture into a pan and place on the trivet.

Seal the lid and cook on Manual mode for 10 minutes on High pressure. Once ready, do a quick release. Garnish the tortilla with parsley.

Nutrition facts per serving: Calories 233, Protein 10.3g, Net Carbs 4.1g, Fat 19.4g

Cheesy Spinach Casserole

Prep + Cook Time: 30 minutes | Servings: 6

INGREDIENTS:

1 cup Spinach, chopped
½ lb Cheddar cheese
½ lb Mozzarella cheese
1 Onion, chopped
4 Eggs, whisked
I yellow Bell Pepper, chopped
¼ tbsp Salt
¼ tbsp black Pepper
2 tbsp Olive oil

DIRECTIONS:

In a bowl add the eggs, spinach, mozzarella cheese, cheddar cheese, bell pepper, and onion, mix well. Season with salt and pepper. Grease the Instant Pot with olive oil.

Transfer the spinach mixture to the pot and seal the lid. Cook for 15 minutes on High pressure.

Once ready, let the pressure release naturally for 10 minutes.

Nutrition facts per serving: Calories 531, Protein 31g, Net Carbs 6.1g, Fat 43.4g

Very Berry Ricotta Pancakes

Prep + Cook Time: 55 minutes | Servings: 4

INGREDIENTS

1 tbsp chopped Blackberries
2 tbsp Blueberries
1 tbsp mashed Strawberries
¾ cup Ricotta
4 Eggs
1 cup Almond flour
¼ cup Milk
½ tsp Stevia
½ cup Flaxseed Meal
1 tsp Baking Powder
½ tsp Vanilla Extract
A pinch of Sea Salt
1 ½ cups Water

DIRECTIONS

Pour in water and lower the trivet. Place the strawberry mash, ricotta, stevia, milk, eggs, and vanilla extract in a blender. Blend the mixture until smooth.

In a bowl, stir together the flaxseed meal, almond flour, baking powder, and salt. Stir the dry mixture into the wet one until well incorporated. Finally, fold in the berries.

Grease a baking dish with cooking spray and pour the pancake batter inside it. Place the dish on top of the trivet and seal the lid. Cook on Low pressure for 45 minutes.

When the timer goes off, do a quick pressure release and open the lid carefully. Remove the dish from the Instant Pot. Divide the pancake into 4 servings.

Nutrition facts per serving: Calories 390, Protein 19g, Net Carbs 6.5g, Fat 24g

Spinach and Tomato Cheesy Braise

Prep + Cook Time: 20 minutes | Servings: 3

INGREDIENTS:

- 1 cup baby Spinach, sliced
- 2 Tomatoes, chopped
- 1 cup Mushrooms, sliced
- 1 tbsp Ginger powder
- 1 tbsp Garlic paste
- ¼ lb Parmesan cheese, shredded
- ½ lb Mozzarella cheese, shredded
- 2 Eggs, whisked
- ¼ pinch Salt
- ¼ tbsp Thyme
- ¼ tbsp black Pepper
- 2 tbsp Butter, melted

DIRECTIONS:

In the Instant Pot, add the butter and garlic; cook for 30 seconds on Sauté mode.

Then, add spinach, tomatoes, thyme, salt, black pepper, eggs, ginger, mozzarella and mushrooms; mix well. Seal the lid and cook on High pressure for 15 minutes.

Once ready, do a quick release. Sprinkle with the grated Parmesan and serve.

Nutrition facts per serving: Calories 424, Protein 51g, Net Carbs 8.9g, Fat 21g

Delicious Scallions and Eggs

Prep + Cook Time: 10 minutes | Servings: 2

INGREDIENTS:

- 2 Eggs
- 1 cup Water
- ½ lb Scallions, chopped
- ½ cup Sesame seeds
- ½ tbsp Garlic powder
- Salt and Pepper, to taste

DIRECTIONS:

Mix water and eggs in a bowl. Add scallions, sesame seeds, garlic powder, and salt and pepper in the instant pot. Pour in the egg mixture. Set on Manual mode for 5 minutes on High pressure. When the timer goes off, quick release the pressure.

Nutrition facts per serving: Calories 348, Protein 15.7g, Net Carbs 6.2g, Fat 27g

The Easiest Eggs with Mushrooms

Prep + Cook Time: 15 minutes | Servings: 2

INGREDIENTS:

1 cup Mushrooms, sliced
4 Eggs
2 Tomatoes, chopped
1 cup Basil, chopped
1 tbsp Butter
Salt and Pepper, to taste

DIRECTIONS:

Whisk eggs in a bowl. Add salt and pepper, tomatoes, basil and mushrooms. Mix well.

Grease a baking tray and pour the mixture into it. Pour 2 cups of water into the pot, then lay a trivet inside. Place the tray on top of the trivet. Seal the lid and cook for 10 minutes on High pressure. When done, do a quick pressure release and serve.

Nutrition facts per serving: Calories 173, Protein 13g, Net Carbs 5.6g, Fat 11g

Healthy Artichokes with Eggs

Prep + Cook Time: 15 minutes | Servings: 2

INGREDIENTS:

2 cups artichokes, cut off stems
1 tbsp fennel
2 tbsp Cream
3 Eggs
4 Garlic cloves, minced
1 tbsp Nutmeg powder
Salt and Pepper, to taste
Nonstick cooking spray

DIRECTIONS:

Whisk the eggs in a bowl. Add fennel, cream, nutmeg powder, salt and pepper. Blend well and then add artichokes. Grease a round baking tray with cooking spray.

Pour the mixture into the tray. Add 2 cups of water into the pot and place a trivet. Place the tray on the trivet. Seal the lid and cook for 15 minutes on Manual mode on High pressure. When ready, let the pressure release naturally for 10 minutes.

Nutrition facts per serving: Calories 209, Protein 14.7g, Net Carbs 8.1g, Fat 9.3g

Classic Eggs with Cheese and Bacon

Prep + Cook Time: 14 minutes | Servings: 4

INGREDIENTS:

5 Eggs
½ tsp Lemon Pepper seasoning
3 tbsp Cheddar cheese, grated
2 green Onions, chopped
3 slices bacon, crumbled

DIRECTIONS:

Whisk the eggs in a bowl and put them in the Instant pot. In a separate bowl, mix the cheddar cheese, green onions and bacon. Add the mixture to the eggs and seal the lid.

Cook on Manual for 10 minutes on High pressure. When the timer goes off, quick release the pressure. Carefully open the lid, and season with lemon pepper and enjoy!

Nutrition facts per serving: Calories 185, Protein 11.5g, Net Carbs 2.2g, Fat 13.7g

Ricotta Cheese with Eggs

Prep + Cook Time: 15 minutes | Servings: 4

INGREDIENTS:

4 Eggs
½ cup Stevia
2 ½ cups Ricotta cheese
1 cup Vanilla Yogurt
2 tbsp Vanilla extract
½ cup Almond flour
1 tbsp Baking powder
Salt to taste

DIRECTIONS:

Mix well eggs, stevia, vanilla extract and flour in a bowl. Transfer the mixture into the Instant pot and mix with vanilla yogurt along with salt. Stir well. Add baking powder.

Seal the lid, press Manual mode and cook on high pressure for 10 minutes. When the pot beeps, do a quick pressure release. Serve and enjoy!

Nutrition facts per serving: Calories 377, Protein 25.3g, Net Carbs 7.2g, Fat 24.5g

Fresh Veggies Mix

Prep + Cook Time: 20 minutes | Servings: 2

INGREDIENTS:

½ cup Almond Milk
6 oz. chopped Spinach
1 cup Cheddar cheese, shredded
½ Onion, chopped
½ Bell Pepper, chopped
4 Eggs
Salt and Pepper, to taste
½ cup Mint, chopped
1 tbsp Olive oil
2 cups water

DIRECTIONS:

Whisk eggs in a bowl. Add milk, cheese, spinach, onion, bell pepper, salt and pepper, and mint. Grease the round baking tray with the olive oil. Pour the mixture into a tray.

Add water into the Instant Pot and place a trivet. Put a tray on the trivet. Seal the lid and cook for 14 minutes on Manual mode on High. When ready, let the pressure release naturally for 10 minutes.

Nutrition facts per serving: Calories 510, Protein 43g, Net Carbs 8.8g, Fat 35g

Hot Scrambled Eggs

Prep + Cook Time: 15 minutes | Servings: 2

INGREDIENTS:

4 Eggs, whisked
¼ tbsp Salt
1 cup Chicken broth
¼ tbsp black Pepper
¼ tbsp fresh Dill, chopped
2 tbsp Olive oil

DIRECTIONS:

Heat oil on Sauté and pour the whisked eggs. Crumble the eggs using a fork and add the chicken broth. Season with salt and pepper. When the chicken broth is dried out, transfer the scrambled eggs to a serving dish and top with dill.

Nutrition facts per serving: Calories 247, Protein 11g, Net Carbs 0.5g, Fat 22.3g

Eggs Chicken Casserole

Prep + Cook Time: 30 minutes | Servings: 4

INGREDIENTS:

¼ lb Chicken breast, cut into small pieces
3 Eggs, whisked
1 Onion, chopped
3-4 Garlic cloves, minced
½ lb Mozzarella cheese, shredded

2 oz. Parmesan cheese
¼ tbsp Salt
¼ tbsp black Pepper
¼ tbsp Thyme
2 tbsp Butter

DIRECTIONS:

Melt butter on Sauté mode. Fry onion and garlic for 2 to 3 minutes, until translucent. Add the chicken and fry until golden brown. Add salt, black pepper, thyme and mix well.

Add the eggs, Parmesan cheese, mozzarella cheese and mix thoroughly. Seal the lid and cook on High pressure for 20 minutes. When ready, do a quick release.

Nutrition facts per serving: Calories 286, Protein 33g, Net Carbs 5.1g, Fat 14g

Creamy Egg Casserole

Prep + Cook Time: 15 minutes | Servings: 3

INGREDIENTS:

4 Eggs, whisked
1 Onion, sliced
1 green Chili, chopped
1 red Bell Pepper, chopped
½ lb Mozzarella cheese, shredded

¼ tbsp Salt
¼ tbsp black Pepper
¼ tbsp dried Basil
2 tbsp Butter
¼ cup fresh Parsley leaves, chopped

DIRECTIONS:

Melt butter on Sauté mode, add the onion and sauté for 2 to 3 minutes, until tender. Add the bell pepper and fry for 2 minutes. Add the eggs, mozzarella cheese, green chilies, and season with basil, salt and pepper.

Seal the lid, press Manual and cook on High pressure for 10 minutes. Once ready, let the pressure release naturally for 10 minutes. Sprinkle with the fresh parsley.

Nutrition facts per serving: Calories 246, Protein 32g, Net Carbs 2.3g, Fat 12.1g

Mexican Chili Eggs

Prep + Cook Time: 30 minutes | Servings: 4

INGREDIENTS

1 cup shredded Cheddar Cheese
1 cup Heavy Cream
4 Eggs
⅓ cup chopped canned Chilies
2 tbsp chopped Cilantro
1 tbsp chopped Parsley

¼ tsp Garlic Powder
¼ tsp Onion Powder
¼ tsp Cumin
Salt and Pepper, to taste
1 ½ cups Water

DIRECTIONS

Pour the water in and lower the rack. In a bowl, beat the eggs and stir in the remaining ingredients. Grease a baking dish with cooking spray and pour the egg mixture inside. Place the baking dish on top of the trivet.

Seal the lid, cook on HIGH pressure for 20 minutes. After the beep, release the pressure naturally by allowing the valve to drop down on its own. Remove the dish. Cut into 4 pieces and serve.

Nutrition facts per serving: Calories 270, Protein 14g, Net Carbs 4.5g, Fat 19g

Chili Egg Cubes

Prep + Cook Time: 14 minutes | Servings: 6

INGREDIENTS

⅔ tsp Chili Powder
¼ tsp Sea Salt
¼ tsp Garlic Powder

6 Eggs
1 ½ cups Water

DIRECTIONS

Grab a baking dish that fits inside your Instant Pot and grease it with cooking spray. Crack the eggs into the dish and scramble them with a whisk. Sprinkle with all the spices.

Pour the water in the pot and lower the trivet. Place the baking dish on top of the trivet and seal the lid. Cook on High pressure for 4 minutes.

When the timer goes off, turn the pressure handle to "Venting" to release the pressure quickly and remove the dish from the Instant Pot. Transfer the eggs to a cutting board and cut into cubes.

Nutrition facts per serving: Calories 80, Protein 5g, Net Carbs 0g, Fat 4g

Basil-Flavored Spinach & Bacon Eggs

Prep + Cook Time: 25 minutes | Servings: 4

INGREDIENTS

½ cup chopped Spinach
4 Bacon Slices, diced
2 tbsp chopped Basil
3 tbsp Heavy Cream

8 Eggs, beaten
Salt and Pepper, to taste
1 ½ cups Water

DIRECTIONS

Turn the Instant Pot on and set to SAUTÉ. Add the bacon and cook until crispy, about 2-3 minutes. Transfer the bacon to a bowl and stir in the rest of the ingredients, except the water.

Grab a dish that fits in your Instant Pot and grease it with cooking spray. Pour the egg mixture into the dish. Add the water to the pot and insert the trivet. Lower the baking dish on top.

Seal the lid and cook for 8 minutes on High pressure. When the timer goes off, turn the pressure handle to "Venting" for a quick pressure release. Serve immediately.

Nutrition facts per serving: Calories 275, Protein 7g, Net Carbs 2g, Fat 21g

Vanilla Cheesecake Pancakes

Prep + Cook Time: 15 minutes | Servings: 2

INGREDIENTS

4 ounces Cream Cheese
¼ tsp Vanilla Extract
2 tsp Butter

2 Eggs
1 tsp Granulated Sweetener
A pinch of Cinnamon, optional

DIRECTIONS

In a blender, place the eggs, cream cheese, sweetener, and cinnamon. Blend until the mixture becomes smooth and well-combined.

In the Instant Pot, melt half of the butter on Sauté. Add half of the pancake batter and cook for about 3 minutes. When set, flip the pancake over and cook for another 2 minutes.

Melt the remaining butter and repeat the same process with the remaining batter. You should have two fluffy and delicious cream cheese pancakes. Serve with strawberry jam to enjoy.

Nutrition facts per serving: Calories 345, Protein 17g, Net Carbs 3g, Fat 29g

Quick and Easy Breakfast Porridge

Prep + Cook Time: 10 minutes | Servings: 1

INGREDIENTS

2 tbsp Ground Almonds
1 tbsp Chia Seeds
1 tbsp Flaxseed Meal
2 tbsp Hemp Seeds
2 tbsp Shredded Coconut

¼ tsp Granulated Stevia
½ tsp Vanilla Extract
A pinch of Salt
½ cup Water
Fresh raspberries for topping

DIRECTIONS

Place all ingredients inside your Instant Pot. Give the mixture a good stir and seal the lid. Press MANUAL/PRESSURE COOK and cook on High pressure for 4 minutes.

When the timer goes off, do a quick pressure release and open the lid carefully. Stir before serving. The porridge should be smooth and thick. Top with fresh rasberries and serve.

Tip: *You can also cook this porridge on Sauté mode. Just keep stirring and keep an eye on the porridge until it reaches your desired consistency.*

Nutrition facts per serving: Calories 335, Protein 15g, Net Carbs 1.5g, Fat 29g

Egg Cups with Broccoli and Mushrooms

Prep + Cook Time: 25 minutes | Servings: 6

INGREDIENTS

⅓ cup Heavy Cream
1 cup Pecorino Cheese, grated
10 Eggs
½ head Broccoli, broken into florets
1 Onion, chopped

1 cup sliced Mushrooms
1 tbsp chopped Parsley
Salt and Pepper, to taste
1 ½ cups Water

DIRECTIONS

Pour in the water and lower the trivet. In a bowl, beat the eggs along with the cream. Stir in the remaining ingredients well. Grab smaller jars and divide the egg and veggie mixture among them. Seal the jars and place them on top of the trivet.

Seal the lid and cook on HIGH pressure for 5 minutes. When the Instant Pot reads 00:00, turn the pressure handle from "Sealing" to "Venting" for a quick pressure release and open the lid carefully. Using tongs or mittens, remove the jars from the Instant Pot.

Nutrition facts per serving: Calories 130, Protein 9g, Net Carbs 2.9g, Fat 10g

Basil and Parsley Scramble

Prep + Cook Time: 15 minutes | Servings: 4

INGREDIENTS

8 Eggs
¼ cup chopped Parsley
3 tbsp chopped Basil
¼ tsp Garlic Powder
¼ tsp Salt
¼ tsp Pepper
¼ cup Milk
1 tbsp Butter

DIRECTIONS

Melt butter on Sauté. Meanwhile, beat the eggs in a bowl and stir in the remaining ingredients. Pour the egg mixture into the Instant Pot and stir for about 5 minutes with a spatula, until the eggs are set. When set, divide the eggs among 4 plates. Serve and enjoy!

Nutrition facts per serving: Calories 295, Protein 12g, Net Carbs 4.2g, Fat 15g

Two-Cheese Almond Bagels

Prep + Cook Time: 30 minutes | Servings: 3

INGREDIENTS

1 Egg
1 tbsp Butter, melted
¾ cup Almond flour
1 tsp Xanthan Gum
1 ½ cups grated Mozzarella Cheese, melted
2 tbsp Cream Cheese
A pinch of Salt
1 ½ cups Water

DIRECTIONS

Pour in water and lower the trivet. In a bowl, beat the egg along with the xanthan gum. Add the remaining ingredients, except the butter, and whisk until the mixture becomes well-combined.

Transfer the dough to a lightly floured surface and shape into a long log. Divide the log into 3 equal pieces. To make the bagels, flatten the pieces of dough, making a ring-like bagel form. Cut out the center with a small cookie cutter or a shot glass. Brush the bagels with the butter.

Grease a baking dish with cooking spray and arrange the bagels in it. Place the dish on top of the trivet and seal the lid.

Cook on High pressure for 15 minutes. After the beep, do a quick release and serve.

Nutrition facts per serving: Calories 370, Protein 20g, Net Carbs 3.5g, Fat 29g

LUNCH AND DINNER RECIPES

Feta and Cauliflower Rice Stuffed Bell Peppers

Prep + Cook Time: 30 minutes | Servings: 3

INGREDIENTS:

1 green Bell Pepper
1 red Bell Pepper
1 yellow Bell Pepper
½ cup Cauliflower rice
1 cup Feta cheese
1 Onion, sliced

Yogurt Sauce:
1 clove Garlic, pressed
1 cup greek Yogurt
kosher Salt, to taste

2 Tomatoes, chopped
1 tbsp black Pepper
2-3 Garlic clove, minced
3 tbsp Lemon juice
3-4 green Olives, chopped
3-4 tbsp Olive oil

juice from 1 Lemon
1 tbsp fresh Dill

DIRECTIONS:

Grease the Instant Pot with olive oil. Make a cut at the top of the bell peppers near the stem. Place feta cheese, onion, olives, tomatoes, cauliflower rice, salt, black pepper, garlic powder, and lemon juice into a bowl; mix well.

Fill up the bell peppers with the feta mixture and insert in the Instant Pot. Set on Manual and cook on High pressure for 20 minutes. When the timer beeps, allow the pressure to release naturally for 5 minutes, then do a quick pressure release.

To prepare the yogurt sauce, combine garlic, yogurt, lemon juice, salt, and fresh dill.

Nutrition facts per serving: Calories 388, Protein 13.5g, Net Carbs 7.9g, Fat 32.4g

Shrimp with Linguine

Prep + Cook Time: 20 minutes | Servings: 4

INGREDIENTS:

1 lb Shrimp, cleaned
1 lb Linguine
1 tbsp Butter
½ cup white Wine
½ cup Parmesan cheese, shredded
2 Garlic cloves, minced

1 cup Parsley, chopped
Salt and Pepper, to taste
½ cup Coconut Cream, for garnish
½ Avocado, diced, for garnish
2 tbsp fresh Dill, for garnish

DIRECTIONS:

Melt the butter on Sauté. Stir in linguine, garlic cloves and parsley. Cook for 4 minutes until aromatic. Add shrimp and white wine; season with salt and pepper, seal the lid.

Select Manual and cook for 5 minutes on High pressure. When ready, quick release the pressure. Unseal and remove the lid. Press Sauté, add the cheese and stir well until combined, for 30-40 seconds. Serve topped with the coconut cream, avocado, and dill.

Nutrition facts per serving: Calories 412, Protein 48g, Net Carbs 5.6g, Fat 21g

Mexican Cod Fillets

Prep + Cook Time: 20 minutes | Servings: 3

INGREDIENTS:

3 Cod fillets
1 Onion, sliced
2 cups Cabbage
Juice from 1 Lemon
1 Jalapeno Pepper

½ tsp Oregano
½ tsp Cumin powder
½ tsp Cayenne Pepper
2 tbsp Olive oil
Salt and black Pepper to taste

DIRECTIONS:

Heat the oil on Sauté, and add onion, cabbage, lemon juice, jalapeño pepper, cayenne pepper, cumin powder and oregano, and stir to combine. Cook for 8-10 minutes.

Season with salt and black pepper. Arrange the cod fillets in the sauce, using a spoon to cover each piece with some of the sauce. Seal the lid and press Manual. Cook for 5 minutes on High pressure. When ready, do a quick release and serve.

Nutrition facts per serving: Calories 306, Protein 21g, Net Carbs 6.8g, Fat 19.4g

Simple Mushroom Chicken Mix

Prep + Cook Time: 18 minutes | Servings: 2

INGREDIENTS:

2 Tomatoes, chopped
½ lb Chicken, cooked and mashed
1 cup Broccoli, chopped
1 tbsp Butter

2 tbsp Mayonnaise
½ cup Mushroom soup
Salt and Pepper, to taste
1 Onion, sliced

DIRECTIONS:

Once cooked, put the chicken into a bowl. In a separate bowl, mix the mayo, mushroom soup, tomatoes, onion, broccoli, and salt and pepper. Add the chicken.

Grease a round baking tray with butter. Put the mixture in a tray. Add 2 cups of water into the Instant Pot and place the trivet inside. Place the tray on top. Seal the lid, press Manual and cook for 14 minutes on High pressure. When ready, do a quick release.

Nutrition facts per serving: Calories 561, Protein 28.5g, Net Carbs 6.3g, Fat 49.5g

Squash Spaghetti with Bolognese Sauce

Prep + Cook Time: 15 minutes | Servings: 3

INGREDIENTS

1 large Squash, cut into 2 and seed pulp removed
2 cups Water

Bolognese Sauce to serve

DIRECTIONS

Place the trivet and add the water. Add in the squash, seal the lid, select Manual and cook on High Pressure for 8 minutes. Once ready, quickly release the pressure. Carefully remove the squash; use two forks to shred the inner skin. Serve with bolognese sauce.

Nutrition facts per serving: Calories 37, Protein 0.9g, Net Carbs 7.8g, Fat 0.4g

Healthy Halibut Fillets

Prep + Cook Time: 15 minutes | Servings: 2

INGREDIENTS:

2 Halibut fillets
1 tbsp Dill
1 tbsp Onion powder
1 cup Parsley, chopped
2 tbsp Paprika
1 tbsp Garlic powder
1 tbsp Lemon Pepper
2 tbsp Lemon juice

DIRECTIONS:

Mix lemon juice, lemon pepper, garlic powder, and paprika, parsley, dill and onion powder in a bowl. Pour the mixture in the Instant pot and place the halibut fish over it.

Seal the lid, press Manual mode and cook for 10 minutes on High pressure. When ready, do a quick pressure release by setting the valve to venting.

Nutrition facts per serving: Calories 283, Protein 22.5g, Net Carbs 6.2g, Fat 16.4g

Clean Salmon with Soy Sauce

Prep + Cook Time: 35 minutes | Servings: 2

INGREDIENTS:

2 Salmon fillets
2 tbsp Avocado oil
2 tbsp Soy sauce
1 tbsp Garlic powder
1 tbsp fresh Dill to garnish
Salt and Pepper, to taste

DIRECTIONS:

To make the marinade, thoroughly mix the soy sauce, avocado oil, salt, pepper and garlic powder into a bowl. Dip salmon in the mixture and place in the refrigerator for 20 minutes.

Transfer the contents to the Instant pot. Seal, set on Manual and cook for 10 minutes on high pressure. When ready, do a quick release. Serve topped with the fresh dill.

Nutrition facts per serving: Calories 512, Protein 65g, Net Carbs 3.2g, Fat 21g

Simple Salmon with Eggs

Prep + Cook Time: 10 minutes | Servings: 3

INGREDIENTS:

1 lb Salmon, cooked, mashed
2 Eggs, whisked
2 Onions, chopped
2 stalks celery, chopped
1 cup Parsley, chopped
1 tbsp Olive oil
Salt and Pepper, to taste

DIRECTIONS:

Mix salmon, onion, celery, parsley, and salt and pepper, in a bowl. Form into 6 patties about 1 inch thick and dip them in the whisked eggs. Heat oil in the Instant pot on Sauté mode.

Add the patties to the pot and cook on both sides, for about 5 minutes and transfer to the plate. Allow to cool and serve.

Nutrition facts per serving: Calories 331, Protein 38g, Net Carbs 5.3g, Fat 16g

Easy Shrimp

Prep + Cook Time: 9 minutes | Servings: 2

INGREDIENTS:

1 lb Shrimp, peeled and deveined
2 Garlic cloves, crushed
1 tbsp Butter.
A pinch of red Pepper
Salt and Pepper, to taste
1 cup Parsley, chopped

DIRECTIONS:

Melt butter on Sauté mode. Add shrimp, garlic, red pepper, salt and pepper. Cook for 5 minutes, stirring occasionally the shrimp until pink. Serve topped with parsley.

Nutrition facts per serving: Calories 245, Protein 45g, Net Carbs 4.8g, Fat 4g

Scallops with Mushroom Special

Prep + Cook Time: 25 minutes | Servings: 2

INGREDIENTS:

1 lb Scallops
2 Onions, chopped
1 tbsp Butter
2 tbsp Olive oil
1 cup Mushrooms
Salt and Pepper, to taste
1 tbsp Lemon juice
½ cup Whipping Cream
1 tbsp chopped fresh Parsley

DIRECTIONS:

Heat the oil on Sauté. Add onions, butter, mushrooms, salt and pepper. Cook for 3 to 5 minutes. Add the lemon juice and scallops. Lock the lid and set to Manual mode.

Cook for 15 minutes on High pressure. When ready, do a quick pressure release and carefully open the lid. Top with a drizzle of cream and fresh parsley.

Nutrition facts per serving: Calories 312, Protein 31g, Net Carbs 7.3g, Fat 10.4g

Delicious Creamy Crab Meat

Prep + Cook Time: 15 minutes | Servings: 3

INGREDIENTS:

1 lb Crab meat
½ cup Cream cheese
2 tbsp Mayonnaise
Salt and Pepper, to taste
1 tbsp Lemon juice
1 cup Cheddar cheese, shredded

DIRECTIONS:

Mix mayo, cream cheese, salt and pepper, and lemon juice in a bowl. Add in crab meat and make small balls. Place the balls inside the pot. Seal the lid and press Manual.

Cook for 10 minutes on High pressure. When done, allow the pressure to release naturally for 10 minutes. Sprinkle the cheese over and serve!

Nutrition facts per serving: Calories 443, Protein 41g, Net Carbs 2.5g, Fat 30.4g

Creamy Broccoli Stew

Prep + Cook Time: 50 minutes | Servings: 4

INGREDIENTS:
1 cup Heavy Cream
3 oz. Parmesan cheese
1 cup Broccoli florets
2 Carrots, sliced
½ tbsp Garlic paste
¼ tbsp Turmeric powder
Salt and black Pepper, to taste
½ cup Vegetable broth
2 tbsp Butter

DIRECTIONS:
Melt butter on Sauté mode. Add garlic and sauté for 30 seconds. Add broccoli and carrots, and cook until soft, for 2-3 minutes. Season with salt and pepper.

Stir in the vegetable broth and seal the lid. Cook on Meat/Stew mode for 40 minutes. When ready, do a quick pressure release. Stir in the heavy cream.

Nutrition facts per serving: Calories 239, Protein 8g, Net Carbs 5.1g, Fat 21.4g

No Crust Tomato and Spinach Quiche

Prep + Cook Time: 40 minutes | Servings: 3

INGREDIENTS
14 large Eggs
1 cup Full Milk
Salt to taste
Ground Black Pepper to taste
4 cups fresh Baby Spinach, chopped
3 Tomatoes, diced
3 Scallions, sliced
2 Tomato, sliced into firm rings
½ cup Parmesan Cheese, shredded
Water for boiling

DIRECTIONS
Place the trivet in the pot and pour in 1 ½ cups of water. Break the eggs into a bowl, add salt, pepper, and milk and whisk it. Share the diced tomatoes, spinach and scallions into 3 ramekins, gently stir, and arrange 3 slices of tomatoes on top in each ramekin.

Sprinkle with Parmesan cheese. Gently place the ramekins in the pot, and seal the lid. Select Manual and cook on High Pressure for 20 minutes. Once ready, quickly release the pressure.

Carefully remove the ramekins and use a paper towel to tap soak any water from the steam that sits on the quiche. Brown the top of the quiche with a fire torch.

Nutrition facts per serving: Calories 310, Protein 12g, Net Carbs 0g, Fat 27g

Ratatouille

Prep + Cook Time: 20 minutes | Servings: 4

INGREDIENTS
1 cup Water
3 tbsp Olive oil
2 Zucchinis, sliced in rings
2 Eggplants, sliced in rings
3 large Tomatoes, sliced in thick rings
1 medium Red Onion, sliced in thin rings
3 cloves Garlic, minced
2 sprigs Fresh Thyme
Salt to taste
Black Pepper to taste
4 tsp Plain Vinegar

DIRECTIONS

Place all veggies in a bowl, sprinkle with salt and pepper; toss. Line foil in a spring form tin and arrange 1 slice each of the vegetables in, one after the other in a tight circular arrangement.

Fill the entire tin. Sprinkle the garlic over, some more black pepper and salt, and arrange the thyme sprigs on top. Drizzle olive oil and vinegar over the veggies.

Place a trivet to fit in the Instant Pot, pour the water in and place the veggies on the trivet. Seal the lid, secure the pressure valve and select Manual mode on High Pressure for 6 minutes. Once ready, quickly release the pressure. Carefully remove the tin and serve ratatouille.

Nutrition facts per serving: Calories 152, Protein 2g, Net Carbs 4g, Fat 12g

Steamed Artichokes

Prep + Cook Time: 25 minutes | Servings: 3

INGREDIENTS

2 medium Artichokes
3 Lemon Wedges (for cooking and serving)
1 ½ cup Water

DIRECTIONS

Clean the artichokes by removing all dead leaves, the stem, and top third of it. Rub the top of the artichokes with the lemon. Set aside. Place a trivet to fit in the Instant Pot, pour in water.

Place the artichokes on the trivet, seal the lid. Select Manual mode on High Pressure for 9 minutes. Once the timer ends, keep the pressure valve for 10 minutes; then quickly release the remaining pressure. Remove artichokes and serve with garlic mayo and lemon wedges.

Nutrition facts per serving: Calories 47, Protein 3.3g, Net Carbs 6g, Fat 0.2g

Creamed Savoy Cabbage

Prep + Cook Time: 20 minutes | Servings: 3

INGREDIENTS

2 medium Savoy Cabbages, finely chopped
2 small Onions, chopped
2 cups Bacon, chopped
2 ½ cups Mixed Bone Broth, see recipe above
¼ tsp Mace
2 cups Coconut Milk
1 Bay Leaf
Salt to taste
3 tbsp Chopped Parsley

DIRECTIONS

Set on Sauté. Add the bacon crumbles and onions; cook until crispy. Add bone broth and scrape the bottom of the pot. Stir in bay leaf and cabbage. Cut out some parchment paper and cover the cabbage with it.

Seal the lid, select Manual mode and cook on High Pressure for 4 minutes. Once ready, press Cancel and quickly release the pressure. Select Sauteé, stir in the milk and nutmeg. Simmer for 5 minutes, add the parsley.

Nutrition facts per serving: Calories 27, Protein 4g, Net Carbs 3.1g, Fat 3g

Tilapia Delight

Prep + Cook Time: 16 minutes | Servings: 4

INGREDIENTS:

4 Tilapia fillets
4 tbsp Lemon juice
2 tbsp Butter
2 Garlic cloves
½ cup Parsley
Salt and Pepper, to taste

DIRECTIONS:

Melt butter on Sauté, and add garlic cloves, parsley. Season with salt and pepper; stir well. Cook for 2 to 3 minutes. Then, add tilapia and lemon juice and stir well.

Seal the lid and set on Manual mode. Cook for 10 minutes on High pressure. When the timer beeps, allow the pressure to release naturally, for 5 minutes.

Nutrition facts per serving: Calories 135, Protein 23.7g, Net Carbs 1.3g, Fat 4.4g

Spinach Tomatoes Mix

Prep + Cook Time: 14 minutes | Servings: 2

INGREDIENTS:

2 tbsp Butter
1 Onion, chopped
2 cloves Garlic, minced
1 tbsp Cumin powder
1 tbsp Paprika
2 Tomatoes, chopped
2 cups Vegetable broth
1 small bunch of Spinach, chopped
Cilantro for garnishing

DIRECTIONS:

Melt the butter on Sauté mode. Add onion, garlic, and cumin powder, paprika, and vegetable broth; stir well. Add in tomatoes and spinach. Seal the lid, press Manual and cook on High pressure for 10 minutes. When ready, do a quick pressure release.

Nutrition facts per serving: Calories 125, Protein 7.7g, Net Carbs 8.3g, Fat 5.5g

Spinach Almond Tortilla

Prep + Cook Time: 15 minutes | Servings: 3

INGREDIENTS:

1 cup Almond flour + extra for dusting
1 cup Spinach, chopped
¼ tbsp Chili flakes
¼ cup Mushrooms, sliced
½ tbsp Salt
2 tbsp Olive oil

DIRECTIONS:

In a bowl, combine flour, mushrooms, spinach, salt, and flakes; mix well. Add ¼ cup of water and make a thick batter. Roll out the batter until is thin. Heat oil on Sauté mode.

Cook the tortilla for 5 minutes until golden brown. Serve with cilantro sauce and enjoy.

Nutrition facts per serving: Calories 165, Protein 5g, Net Carbs 2.1g, Fat 9g

Zucchini Noodles in Garlic and Parmesan Toss

Prep + Cook Time: 20 minutes | Servings: 4

INGREDIENTS

3 large Zucchinis, spiralized
2 tbsp Olive oil
3 cloves Garlic, minced
1 Lemon, zested and juiced

Salt to taste
Black Pepper to taste
5 Mint Leaves, chopped
6 tbsp Parmesan Cheese, grated

DIRECTIONS

Set on Sauté. Heat the oil, and add lemon zest, garlic, and salt. Stir and cook for 30 seconds. Add zucchini and pour lemon juice over. Coat the noodles quickly but gently with the oil.

Cook for 10 seconds, press Cancel. Sprinkle the mint leaves and cheese over and toss gently.

Nutrition facts per serving: Calories 15, Protein 10g, Net Carbs 2g, Fat 2g

Lemoned Broccoli

Prep + Cook Time: 15 minutes | Servings: 3

INGREDIENTS

1 lb Broccoli, cut in biteable sizes
3 Lemon Slices
¼ cup Water

Salt to taste
Pepper to taste

DIRECTIONS

Pour the water into the Instant Pot. Add the broccoli and sprinkle with lemon juice, pepper, and salt. Seal the lid, secure the pressure valve, and Manual in Low Pressure mode for 3 minutes. Once ready, quickly release the pressure. Drain the broccoli and serve as a side dish.

Nutrition facts per serving: Calories 34, Protein 2.8g, Net Carbs 5.6g, Fat 0.4g

Keto Carrot Cake

Prep + Cook Time: 70 minutes | Servings: 6 to 8

INGREDIENTS

5 Eggs
1 ¼ cup Almond flour
½ cup Swerve Sweetener
1 tsp Baking Powder
1 ½ tsp Apple Pie Spice

⅓ cup Coconut Oil
½ cup Heavy Cream
1 ½ cup Carrots, shredded
⅓ cup Walnuts, chopped
2 cups Water

DIRECTIONS

Grease an 8-inch cake tin; set aside. Place all ingredients in a bowl, and mix evenly with a cake mixer. Pour the batter into the cake tin and cover the tin with foil. A pinch the edges of the pan to tighten the foil. Pour the water into the Instant Pot and fit in a trivet with handles.

Place the tin on top. Seal the lid, select Cake mode for 40 minutes on High. Once ready, do a natural release for 10 minutes; then quickly release the pressure. Let cool before slicing.

Nutrition facts per serving: Calories 301, Protein 9g, Net Carbs 2g, Fat 29g

Asparagus Gremolata

Prep + Cook Time: 20 minutes | Servings: 2

INGREDIENTS

1 lb Asparagus, hard ends cut off

Gremolata:
2 Lemons, zested
2 Oranges, zested
4 cloves Garlic, minced

1 cup Water

½ cup Chopped Parsley
Salt to taste
Pepper to taste

DIRECTIONS

Mix all gremolata ingredients in a bowl; set aside. Pour water in the pot and fit a steamer basket. Add asparagus to the basket, seal the lid and cook on Steam for 4 minutes on High.

Once ready, quickly release the pressure. Remove asparagus and serve with gremolata.

Nutrition facts per serving: Calories 125, Protein 3g, Net Carbs 2g, Fat 3.4g

Beets with Yogurt

Prep + Cook Time: 50 minutes | Servings: 3 to 4

INGREDIENTS

1 lb Beets, washed
1 Lime, zested and juiced
1 cup Plain Full Milk Yogurt
1 clove Garlic, minced
Salt to taste

1 tbsp Fresh Dill, chopped
1 tbsp Olive oil to drizzle
Black Pepper to garnish
1 cup Water

DIRECTIONS

Pour the water in the Instant Pot and fit in a steamer basket. Add the beets, seal the lid, secure the pressure valve and select Manual mode on High Pressure mode for 30 minutes.

Once ready, do a natural pressure release for 10 minutes, then quickly release the remaining pressure. Remove the beets to a bowl to cool, and then remove the skin. Cut into wedges.

Place beets in a dip plate, drizzle the olive oil and lime juice over; set aside. In a bowl, mix garlic, yogurt and lime zest. Pour over the beets and garnish with black pepper, salt, and dill.

Nutrition facts per serving: Calories 102, Protein 5.7g, Net Carbs 8.2g, Fat 3.8g

Vegetarian Faux Stew

Prep + Cook Time: 30 minutes | Servings: 3

INGREDIENTS

1 ½ cups Diced Tomatoes
4 cloves Garlic
1 tsp Minced Ginger
1 tsp Turmeric
1 tsp Cayenne Powder
2 tsp Paprika
Salt to taste

1 tsp Cumin Powder
2 cups Dry Soy Curls
1 ½ cups Water
3 tbsp Butter
½ cup Heavy Cream
¼ cup Chopped Cilantro

DIRECTIONS

Place the tomatoes, water, soy curls and all spices in the Instant Pot. Seal the lid, secure the pressure valve and select Manual mode on High Pressure mode for 6 minutes.

Once ready, do a natural pressure release for 10 minutes. Select Sauté, add the cream and butter. Stir while crushing the tomatoes with the back of the spoon. Stir in the cilantro and serve.

Nutrition facts per serving: Calories 143, Protein 4g, Net Carbs 2g, Fat 9g

Egg Fried Cauli Rice

Prep + Cook Time: 20 minutes | Servings: 3

INGREDIENTS

2 heads Cauliflower, cut in big chunks
8 Eggs, beaten
3 tbsp Butter
5 cloves Garlic, minced
1 large White Onion, chopped

2 tsp Olive oil
2 tsp Soy Sauce
Salt to taste
½ cup Water

DIRECTIONS

Pour water in the Instant Pot and fit in a steamer basket. Place the cauli chunks in the basket. Seal the lid and cook on High Pressure for 1 minute. Once ready, quickly release the pressure.

Remove the cauli chunks onto a plate. Discard the water in the pot and clean dry. Select Sauté, and melt olive oil and butter. Add the eggs and stir frequently to break as they cook.

Add onions and garlic, stir and cook for 2 minutes. Add cauli chunks, and use a masher to break the chunks into a rice-like consistency. Stir in soy sauce and salt, and cook for 3 more minutes. Serve cauli rice as a side dish.

Nutrition facts per serving: Calories 47, Protein 4g, Net Carbs 2g, Fat 2.8g

Vegetable en Papillote

Prep + Cook Time: 20 minutes | Servings: 3

INGREDIENTS

1 cup Green Beans
4 small Carrots, widely julienned
¼ tsp Black Pepper
A pinches Salt
1 clove Garlic, crushed
2 tbsp Butter

2 slices Lemon
1 tbsp Chopped Thyme
1 tbsp Oregano
1 tbsp Chopped Parsley
17 inch Parchment Paper

DIRECTIONS

Add all ingredients, except lemon slices and butter, in a bowl and toss. Place the paper on a flat surface and add the mixed ingredients at the center of the paper. Put the lemon slices on top and drop the butter over. Wrap it up well.

Pour 1 cup of water in and lower the trivet with handle. Put the veggie pack on the trivet, seal the lid, and cook on High Pressure for 2 minutes. Once ready, do a quick release. Carefully remove the packet and serve veggies in a wrap on a plate.

Nutrition facts per serving: Calories 60, Protein 3g, Net Carbs 1g, Fat 3g

Keto Coconut Almond Cake

Prep + Cook Time: 65 minutes | Servings: 6

INGREDIENTS

1 ½ cups Almond flour
1 cup Shredded Coconut, unsweetened
½ cup Truvia
1 ½ tsp Baking Powder

1 ½ tsp Apple Pie Spice
4 Eggs
½ cup Melted Butter
1 cup Heavy Cream

DIRECTIONS

Pour all the dry ingredients into a bowl and mix well. Add the wet ingredients one after the other, mixing until fully incorporated. Grease an 8-inch cake tin and pour the batter into it.

Cover the tin with foil and A pinch the edges of the tin to tighten the foil. Pour 2 cups of water into the Instant Pot and fit in a trivet with handles. Place the cake tin on the trivet.

Seal the lid, select Cake mode for 40 minutes on High. Once ready, do a natural pressure release for 10 minutes; then release the remaining pressure. Cool the cake, slice and serve.

Nutrition facts per serving: Calories 235, Protein 2.9g, Net Carbs 2g, Fat 6.5g

Faux Beet Risotto

Prep + Cook Time: 20 minutes | Servings: 2

INGREDIENTS

4 Beets, tails and leafs removed
2 tbsp Olive oil
1 big head Cauliflower, cut into florets
4 tbsp cup Full Milk

2 tsp Red Chili Flakes
Salt to taste
Black Pepper to taste
½ cup Water

DIRECTIONS

Pour the water in the Instant Pot and fit a steamer basket. Place the beets and cauliflower in the basket. Seal the lid, and cook on High Pressure mode for 4 minutes.

Once ready, do a natural pressure release for 10 minutes, then quickly release the pressure. Remove the steamer basket with the vegetables and discard water. Remove the beets' peels.

Place veggies back to the pot, add salt, pepper, and flakes. Mash with a potato masher. Hit Sauté, and cook the milk for 2 minutes. Stir frequently. Dish onto plates and drizzle with oil.

Nutrition facts per serving: Calories 153, Protein 3.6g, Net Carbs 2.5g, Fat 9g

Broccoli Rice with Mushrooms

Prep + Cook Time: 30 minutes | Servings: 3

INGREDIENTS

2 tbsp Olive oil
1 small Red Onion, chopped
1 Carrot, chopped
2 cups Button Mushrooms, chopped
½ Lemon, zested and juiced
Salt to taste

Pepper to taste
2 cloves Garlic, minced
½ cup Broccoli rice
½ cup Chicken Stock
5 Cherry Tomatoes
Parsley Leaves, chopped for garnishing

DIRECTIONS

Set on Sauté. Heat oil, and cook the carrots and onions for 2 minutes. Stir in mushrooms, and cook for 3 minutes. Stir in pepper, salt, lemon juice, garlic, and lemon zest.

Stir in broccoli and chicken stock. Drop the tomatoes over the top, but don't stir. Seal the lid, and cook on High pressure for 10 minutes. Once ready, do a natural pressure release for 4 minutes, then quickly release the remaining pressure. Sprinkle with parsley and stir evenly.

Nutrition facts per serving: Calories 160, Protein 6g, Net Carbs 10g, Fat 2g

Stuffed Cabbages

Prep + Cook Time: 1 hour 40 minutes | Servings: 4

INGREDIENTS

- 1 medium Cabbage, cut into halves
- 1 ½ cups Cauliflower, riced
- ½ lb Ground Beef
- ¼ Chopped Parsley
- 2 cloves Garlic, minced
- 1 Egg, beaten
- Salt to taste
- Black Pepper to taste
- 1 tsp Oregano
- ½ cup Tomato Sauce
- ¼ cup Sour Cream
- 1 tbsp Swerve Sweetener

DIRECTIONS

Pour 1 cup of water in the pot and lower a steamer basket. Place the halves of the cabbage on the basket. Seal the lid, select Manual mode and cook on High pressure for 5 minutes.

Once ready, quickly release the pressure. Remove the cabbage, let it cool and remove as many large leaves off it as possible. Set aside.

In a bowl, add garlic, salt, beef, egg, and cauli rice; mix well. In another bowl, mix the sour cream, tomato sauce, swerve and ¼ cup of water. Pour half of the tomato sauce in a casserole.

Set aside. Lay each cabbage leaf on a flat surface, scoop 2 tbsp of the beef mixture onto each leaf and roll. Arrange the rolls in the casserole dish and pour the remaining tomato sauce over the rolls. Bake it in an oven at 350 F for 1 hour. Flip the cabbages 30 minutes into baking.

Nutrition facts per serving: Calories 290, Protein 2g, Net Carbs 1g, Fat 13g

Garlic Buttered Sprouts

Prep + Cook Time: 15 minutes | Servings: 2

INGREDIENTS

- ½ lb Brussels Sprouts, trimmed and washed
- ½ cup Water
- 3 tbsp Butter
- 4 clove Garlic, minced
- ½ cup Parmesan Cheese, grated

DIRECTIONS

Pour the water in the Instant Pot and fit a steamer basket. Add the brussels sprouts to the basket. Seal the lid and cook on High Pressure mode for 3 minutes.

Once ready, quickly release the pressure, open the lid and remove the basket. Discard the water and clean dry. Select Sauté, melt the butter and cook the garlic for 1 minute. Add the brussel sprouts; toss evenly. Press Cancel. Serve sprouts and garnish with Parmesan.

Nutrition facts per serving: Calories 38, Protein 3g, Net Carbs 0g, Fat 2g

STEW, SOUPS & CHILI

Butternut Cauliflower Soup

Prep + Cook Time: 30 minutes | Servings: 4

INGREDIENTS:

2 tsp Olive oil
1 large White Onion, chopped
4 cloves Garlic, minced
2 Butternut Squash, chopped and frozen
2 heads Cauliflower, cut in florets and frozen

3 cups Chicken Broth
3 tsp Paprika
Salt and Black Pepper to taste
1 cup Coconut Milk, full fat

Topping:

Low Carb Croutons
Sour Cream
Grated Cheddar Cheese

Crumbled Turkey Bacon
Chopped Chives
Pumpkin Seeds

DIRECTIONS:

Heat olive oil on Sauté, and sauté the white onion for about 3 minutes. Add the garlic and cook until fragrant for 3 minutes. Pour in butternut squash, florets, broth, paprika, pepper, and salt.

Stir the ingredients with a spoon. Seal the lid, select Soup and cook on High pressure for 10 minutes. Once ready, do a quick pressure release. Top the ingredients with milk and use a stick blender to puree. Adjust the seasoning, apply the topping, and dish into serving bowls.

Nutrition facts per serving: Calories 390, Protein 12.2g, Net Carbs 5.2g, Fat 32.1g

Chicken Turnip Soup

Prep + Cook Time: 35 minutes | Servings: 8

INGREDIENTS:

2 lb Turnips, peeled and thinly sliced
4 Chicken Breasts, skinless and Boneless
1 large White Onion, chopped
8 Bacon Slices, chopped
4 cloves Garlic, minced
Salt and Black Pepper to taste

2 medium Carrots, sliced
2 cups sliced Celery
½ cup chopped Parsley
1 ½ tsp Dried Thyme
8 cups Chicken Broth

DIRECTIONS:

Fry bacon for 5 minutes until crispy, on Sauté. Add onion and garlic, and cook for 3 minutes. Remove the mixture with a slotted spoon on a plate and set aside; discard the grease.

Pour the bacon mixture back into the pot and add chicken breasts, turnips, carrots, celery, broth, thyme, salt, and pepper. Seal the lid, select Soup mode on High pressure for 15 minutes.

Once ready, do a quick pressure release; leave on Keep Warm. Use a wooden spoon to remove the chicken on a plate, and stir the soup while breaking the turnips into smaller units.

Shred the chicken with 2 forks and add it back to the soup. Stir with a wooden spoon. Season to taste, and dish into serving bowls. Sprinkle with cheddar and serve with low-carb bread.

Nutrition facts per serving: Calories 419, Protein 25g, Net Carbs 3g, Fat 9g

Healthy Taco Soup

Prep + Cook Time: 30 minutes | Servings: 4

INGREDIENTS:

2 tbsp Coconut Oil
6 Green Bell peppers, diced
2 Yellow Onion, chopped
3 lb Ground Beef
Salt and Black Pepper to taste
3 tbsp Chili Powder
2 tbsp Cumin Powder
2 tsp Paprika

1 tsp Garlic Powder
1 tsp Cinnamon
1 tsp Onion Powder
6 cups chopped Tomatoes
½ cup chopped Green Chilies
3 cups Bone Broth
3 cups Coconut Milk

Topping:

Chopped Jalapenos
Sliced Avocados
Chopped Cilantro

Chopped Green Onions
Lime Juice

DIRECTIONS:

Heat coconut oil on Sauté, add the yellow onion and green bell peppers. Sauté them until soft for 5 minutes. Add ground beef, stir, and cook the beef for 8 minutes until browned.

Add chili, cumin, black pepper, paprika, cinnamon, garlic, onion, and chilies. Give it a good stir using a wooden spoon. Top with tomatoes, coconut milk, and bone broth; stir well.

Seal the lid, select Soup mode and cook on High pressure for 20 minutes. Once ready, do a quick pressure release. Adjust the seasoning. Dish the taco soup into serving bowls and add the toppings.

Nutrition facts per serving: Calories 447, Protein 18.5g, Net Carbs 0g, Fat 45.3g

Veggie Brisket Stew

Prep + Cook Time: 70 minutes | Servings: 4

INGREDIENTS:

2 lb Brisket, cut into 2-inch pieces
2 cups Beef Broth
Salt and Black Pepper to taste
1 tbsp Dijon Mustard
1 tbsp Olive oil
1 lb Rutabaga, quartered
¼ lb Carrots, cut in 2-inch pieces

1 Red Onion, quartered
3 cloves Garlic, minced
1 Bay Leaf
2 fresh Thyme sprigs
¾ cup Brewed Coffee
2 tbsp Xanthan Gum
3 tbsp chopped Cilantro to garnish

DIRECTIONS:

Pour the beef broth, xanthan gum, Dijon mustard, ½ tsp salt, and ½ tsp pepper in a bowl. Mix with a whisk and set aside. Season the beef strips with salt and pepper.

Heat the olive oil on Sauté, add the beef strips and cook until browned. Turn the beef halfway through the cooking, for a total of 8 minutes. Stir in the coffee.

Add rutabaga, carrots, onion, garlic, thyme, mustard mixture, and bay leaf. Stir once more. Seal the lid, select Meat/Stew mode and cook on High pressure for 45 minutes.

Once ready, do a quick pressure release. Stir and remove the bay leaf. Season with pepper and salt.

Nutrition facts per serving: Calories 235, Protein 18.3g, Net Carbs 2.6g, Fat 10.2g

Hot Beef Chili

Prep + Cook Time: 40 minutes | Servings: 4

INGREDIENTS:

2 lb Ground beef
2 tbsp Olive oil
1 Red Bell pepper, seeded, chopped
1 Yellow Bell pepper, seeded, chopped
1 White Onion, Chopped
2 cups Chopped Tomatoes
2 Carrots, chopped in little bits
2 tsp Onion Powder

2 tsp Garlic Powder
5 tsp Chili Powder
2 tbsp Worcestershire Sauce
2 tsp Paprika
½ tsp Cumin Powder
2 tbsp chopped Parsley
Salt and Black Pepper to taste

DIRECTIONS:

Heat olive oil on Sauté and brown the beef, stirring occasionally, for 8 minutes. Stir in onion, bell peppers, tomatoes, carrots, onion powder, garlic powder, chili powder, Worcestershire sauce, paprika, cumin powder, parsley, salt, and pepper.

Seal the lid, select Meat/Stew mode and cook on High pressure for 20 minutes. Once ready, do a quick pressure release. Stir and dish into serving bowls. Serve with low carb crackers or with spaghetti squash.

Nutrition facts per serving: Calories 225, Protein 23g, Net Carbs 0g, Fat 6g

White Chicken Chili

Prep + Cook Time: 50 minutes | Servings: 4

INGREDIENTS:

3 Chicken Breasts, cubed
3 cups Chicken Broth
1 tbsp Butter
1 White Onion, chopped
Salt and Black Pepper

1 Cauliflower, cut in small florets
1 tsp Cumin Powder
1 tsp dried Oregano
½ cup Heavy Whipping Cream
1 cup Sour Cream

DIRECTIONS:

Melt the butter on Sauté, and add the onion and chicken. Stir and cook for 6 minutes. Stir in the florets, cumin powder, oregano, salt, and pepper. Pour in the broth, stir, and seal the lid.

Select Meat/Stew and cook on High pressure for 20 minutes. Once ready, do a quick pressure release. Add the whipping and sour creams. Stir well and dish the sauce into serving bowls. Serve warm with a mix of steamed bell peppers, broccoli, and green beans.

Nutrition facts per serving: Calories 102, Protein 16.7g, Net Carbs 0g, Fat 33g

Chicken and Green Onion Soup

Prep + Cook Time: 20 minutes | Servings: 3

INGREDIENTS:

1 lb Chicken breast, shredded
2 cups Chicken stock
1 tbsp Ginger

2 tbsp Sesame oil
Salt to taste
2 green Onions, chopped

DIRECTIONS:

Heat sesame oil on Sauté mode. Mix in the stock, chicken breast, ginger, salt and green onions. Seal the lid and cook on High pressure for 10 minutes. When done, allow the pressure to release naturally for 10 minutes.

Nutrition facts per serving: Calories 294, Protein 32g, Net Carbs 0.9g, Fat 18g

Mixed Veggie Stew

Prep + Cook Time: 35 minutes | Servings: 4

INGREDIENTS:

3 tbsp Olive oil
2 White Onions, chopped
8 oz Pepperoni, sliced
2 Eggplants, cut in half moons
2 cloves Garlic, minced
¾ lb Brussels Sprouts, halved
Salt and Black Pepper to taste
1 ½ lb Tomatoes, chopped
3 Zucchinis, quartered
¾ lb Green Beans

DIRECTIONS:

Heat 1 tbsp of oil on Sauté, and stir-fry garlic and pepperoni for 8 minutes. Add the remaining oil, eggplants, Brussel sprouts, tomatoes, zucchinis, beans, salt, and pepper. Stir with a spoon.

Seal the lid, select Meat/Stew mode and cook on High pressure for 15 minutes. Once ready, do a quick pressure release. Dish into serving bowls and serve with braised bamboo shoots.

Nutrition facts per serving: Calories 134, Protein 6.3g, Net Carbs 0.1g, Fat 2.3g

Veggie Walnut Chili

Prep + Cook Time: 30 minutes | Servings: 4

INGREDIENTS:

4 Celery Stalks, chopped
2 (15 oz) cans Diced Tomatoes
1 tbsp Olive oil
3 Carrots, chopped
2 cloves Garlic, minced
2 tsp Smoked Paprika
2 Green Bell peppers, diced
1 tbsp Cinnamon Powder
1 tbsp Cumin Powder
1 Sweet Onion, chopped
2 cups Tomato Sauce
1.5 oz sugar-free Dark Chocolate, chopped
1 small Chipotle, minced
1 ½ cups Walnuts, chopped + extra to garnish
Salt and Pepper to taste
Chopped Cilantro to garnish

DIRECTIONS:

Heat the oil on Sauté, and add the onion, celery, and carrots. Sauté for 4 minutes. Add the garlic, cumin, cinnamon, and paprika. Stir and let the sauce cook for 2 minutes.

Then, stir in the bell peppers, tomatoes, tomato sauce, chipotle, and walnuts. Seal the lid, select Meat/Stew and cook on High pressure for 15 minutes. Once ready, do a quick pressure release. Pour in the chopped chocolate and stir until well-incorporated.

Season with salt and pepper. Dish the chili into a serving bowl, garnish with the remaining walnuts and cilantro. Serve with zoodles.

Nutrition facts per serving: Calories 260, Protein 15g, Net Carbs 0g, Fat 5.7g

Cauliflower Soup

Prep + Cook Time: 35 minutes | Servings: 4

INGREDIENTS:

1 cup Cauliflower florets
1 tbsp Ginger paste
1 red Bell Pepper chopped
2 cups Vegetable broth
2 tbsp Vinegar
1 Lemon, sliced
1 green Chili, chopped
4 Garlic cloves, minced
½ tbsp black Pepper
¼ tbsp Salt
1 tbsp Olive oil
Fresh Parsley for garnish

DIRECTIONS:

Heat oil, add the ginger paste and cook for 1 minute on Sauté mode. Add cauliflower and cook for 5 minutes. Add bell pepper, salt, pepper, vinegar, chilies, and lemon slices.

Mix well and pour in the vegetable broth. Seal the lid and cook on High pressure for 15 minutes. When ready, allow the pressure to release naturally for 10 minutes.

Divide between serving bowls, top with fresh parsley and serve.

Nutrition facts per serving: Calories 97, Protein 1g, Net Carbs 2.2g, Fat 5.4g

Green Beans and Spinach Soup

Prep + Cook Time: 15 minutes | Servings: 4

INGREDIENTS:

1 cup baby Spinach
1 cup Green Beans
2 cups Vegetable broth
½ cup Almond Milk
4-5 Garlic cloves, minced
1 cup Heavy cream
½ cup Tofu
½ tbsp Chili flakes
¼ tbsp Salt
2 tbsp Olive oil
Fresh Dill, to garnish

DIRECTIONS:

Heat oil and cook garlic cloves for 1 minute on Sauté. Add broth, spinach, beans, tofu, cream, chili and salt, mix well. Seal the lid and cook on High pressure for 10 minutes.

When done, do a quick pressure release. Carefully open the lid. Pour in the milk and cook for 5 minutes on Sauté mode without the lid. Serve in bowls topped with fresh dill.

Nutrition facts per serving: Calories 239, Protein 4g, Net Carbs 7.3g, Fat 21g

Baby Spinach Green Soup with Asparagus

Prep + Cook Time: 30 Minutes | Servings: 5

INGREDIENTS

2 Zucchinis
A handful Kale
2 celery sticks
4 Asparagus spears
¼ lb baby Spinach
1 small Onion
A ¼ quarter of deseeded Chili
2 Garlic cloves, minced
2 tbsp Coconut oil
A pinch of Salt
A pinch of ground black Pepper
1 cub Vegetable stock
2 tsp spirulina
½ cup fresh Parsley, chopped

DIRECTIONS

Start by peeling and chopping the onion. Mix with garlic, and chili; and set aside for 10 minutes. Finely chop the parsley and the vegetables.

Heat 2 tsp of oil on Sauté, then add the onion and cook until soft for 3 minutes. Add the garlic, chili., chopped vegetables, leaves, stock, salt, and pepper; then lock the lid

Cook on High pressure for 10 minutes. Once ready, release the pressure quickly and blend the ingredients. Add spirulina and zoodles, and cook for 5 more minutes, on Sauté. Garnish with parsley and serve.

Nutrition facts per serving: Calories 110, Protein 4g, Net Carbs 3.1g, Fat 4g

Coriander and Spinach Soup

Prep + Cook Time: 20 minutes | Servings: 4

INGREDIENTS:

1 cup baby Spinach
1 bunch Coriander, puree
2 cups Vegetable broth
1 cup Heavy Cream
½ cup Almond Milk

4-5 Garlic cloves, minced
½ tbsp Chili flakes
¼ tbsp Salt
2 tbsp Olive oil

DIRECTIONS:

Heat oil and add garlic cloves, cook for 1 minute on Sauté mode. Add broth, spinach, coriander, cream, chili flake, and salt, mix well. Seal the lid and cook on High pressure for 10 minutes. When ready, allow the pressure to release naturally for 10 minutes.

Open the lid, pour in milk and cook for 5 minutes on Sauté; lid off. Serve hot.

Nutrition facts per serving: Calories 187, Protein 2g, Net Carbs 3.1g, Fat 18.3g

Shrimp Soup

Prep + Cook Time: 25 minutes | Servings: 4

INGREDIENTS:

2 oz. Shrimp
2 cups Chicken broth
¼ cup Apple Cider Vinegar
4-5 Garlic cloves, minced
½ tbsp black Pepper

¼ tbsp Salt
1 tbsp Olive oil
2 Tomatoes, sliced
4 dollops of sour Cream

DIRECTIONS:

Heat oil on Sauté mode, add garlic cloves and cook for 1 minute. Add shrimp and fry for 10 minutes. Season with salt and pepper. Add broth, tomatoes, vinegar and stir well.

Seal the lid and cook on High pressure for 10 minutes. When ready, allow the pressure to release naturally for 10 minutes. Ladle the soup into 4 bowls. Serve with sour cream .

Nutrition facts per serving: Calories 135, Protein 11g, Net Carbs 2.1g, Fat 5.4g

Sausage and Seafood Stew

Prep + Cook Time: 40 minutes | Servings: 4

INGREDIENTS:

1 lb Halibut, skinless and cut into 1-inch pieces
1 lb Shrimp, peeled and deveined
2 lb Mussels, debearded and scrubbed
2 (16 oz) Clam Juice
6 cups Water
2 (8 oz) Andouille Sausage, sliced
1 cup White Wine
Salt and Black Pepper to taste
4 tbsp Olive oil
4 cloves Garlic, minced
2 small Fennel Bulb, chopped
4 small Leeks, sliced
A small pinch Saffron
2 Bay Leaves
2 (28 oz) can Diced Tomatoes
4 tbsp chopped Parsley

DIRECTIONS:

Heat the oil on Sauté, and add the sausages, fennel, and leeks. Cook for 5 minutes, stirring occasionally. Top with garlic, saffron, and bay leaf. Stir constantly for 30 seconds.

Stir in the wine, and cook for 2 minutes. Add tomatoes, clam juice, and water. Stir once. Add mussels, fish, and shrimp. Use the spoon to cover them with the sauce but don't stir.

Seal the lid, select Meat/Stew and cook on High pressure for 15 minutes. Once the ready, do a quick pressure release. Remove the bay leaf. Add parsley, pepper and salt; and stir.

Serve immediately with a side of low carb garlic bread.

Nutrition facts per serving: Calories 156, Protein 16.5g, Net Carbs 2.8g, Fat 2.6g

Creamy Chicken Mushroom Stew

Prep + Cook Time: 55 minutes | Servings: 4

INGREDIENTS:

4 Chicken Breasts, diced
1 ¼ lb White Button Mushrooms, halved
3 tbsp Olive oil
1 large Onion, sliced
5 cloves Garlic, minced
Salt and Black Pepper to taste
1 ¼ tsp Arrowroot Starch
½ cup Spinach, chopped
1 Bay Leaf
1 ½ cup Chicken Stock
1 tsp Dijon Mustard
1 ½ cup Sour Cream
3 tbsp Chopped Parsley

DIRECTIONS:

Heat the oil and stir-fry the onion for 3 minutes, on Sauté. Stir in mushrooms, chicken, garlic, bay leaf, salt, pepper, Dijon mustard, and chicken broth.

Seal the lid, press Meat/Stew and cook on High pressure for 15 minutes. Once ready, do a natural pressure release for 5 minutes, then a quick pressure release.

On Sauté, stir the stew, remove the bay leaf, and scoop some of the liquid into a bowl. Add the arrowroot starch to the liquid and mix until completely lump-free. Pour the liquid into the sauce, stir, and let the sauce thicken.

Top with the sour cream, stir, and pree Keep Warm. After 4 minutes, dish the sauce into serving bowls and garnish with parsley. Serve with squash mash and steamed green peas.

Nutrition facts per serving: Calories 170, Protein 12.1g, Net Carbs 0g, Fat 6.3g

Pork Chunk Chili

Prep + Cook Time: 70 minutes | Servings: 4

INGREDIENTS:

1 ½ lb Pork Roast, cut into 1-inch cubes
1 lb Tomatillos, husks removed
2 tbsp Olive oil, divided into 2
1 bulb Garlic, tail sliced off
2 Green Chilies
½ cup Chicken Broth

1 Green Bell pepper, seeded, chopped
Salt and Pepper to taste
½ tsp Cumin Powder
1 tsp dried Oregano
1 Bay Leaf
1 bunch Cilantro, chopped into 2

DIRECTIONS:

Preheat an oven to 450 F. Put the garlic bulb on a baking tray and drizzle a little bit of olive oil over the garlic bulb. Place the green bell peppers, onion, green chilies, and tomatillos on the baking tray in a single layer. Tuck the tray in the oven and roast for 25 minutes.

After 25 minutes, remove from the oven and let cool. Peel the garlic using a knife and place in a blender. Add green bell pepper, tomatillos, onion, and green chilies to the blender.

Pulse for a few minutes not to be smooth but slightly chunky. Now, turn on the Instant Pot, open the lid, and select Sauté mode. Heat the remaining olive oil and season the pork to taste.

Add the pork to the oil and brown for 5 minutes. Stir in oregano, cumin, bay leaf, pour in the blended green sauce, and stir in the broth. Seal the lid, select Meat/Stew and cook on High pressure for 35 minutes. Once ready, let the pot sit closed for 10 minutes.

Do a natural pressure release for 5 minutes, and then a quick pressure release. Add in half of the cilantro, salt and pepper, and stir. Dish the chili into serving bowls and garnish with the remaining chopped cilantro. Serve with a side of low carb chips or crusted bread.

Nutrition facts per serving: Calories 192, Protein 24g, Net Carbs 0g, Fat 10g

Sweet and Sour Tomato Soup

Prep + Cook Time: 35 minutes | Servings: 3

INGREDIENTS:

1 cup Tomato sauce
½ cup Tomato Ketchup
2 cups Vegetable broth
¼ cup Water
3 tbsp Almond flour

2 tbsp Vinegar
2 Garlic cloves, minced
½ tbsp black Pepper
¼ tbsp Salt
1 tbsp Olive oil

DIRECTIONS:

Set the Instant Pot on Sauté mode. Heat the oil and add garlic cloves; cook for 1 minute.

Add tomato puree, tomato ketchup, and vinegar and cook for another 2 minutes. Stir in vegetable broth, and season with salt and pepper. Let simmer for 20-25 minutes on

Combine water with almond flour and mix well. Gradually add this mixture into the soup and stir continuously for 1-2 minutes. Pour into serving bowls and enjoy.

Nutrition facts per serving: Calories 176, Protein 5g, Net Carbs 4.3g, Fat 7.3g

Vegetable Soup

Prep + Cook Time: 40 minutes | Servings: 3

INGREDIENTS:

1 cup Broccoli florets
1 green Bell Pepper, sliced
1 red Bell Pepper, sliced
1 Carrot, sliced
1 Onion, sliced

2 cups Vegetable broth
1 tbsp Lemon juice
4-5 Garlic cloves, minced
Salt and Pepper, to taste
1 tbsp Olive oil

DIRECTIONS:

Heat oil on Sauté mode, add onion and garlic cloves, cook for 1 minute. Add all vegetables, stir-fry and cook for 5-10 minutes. Add broth, salt, and pepper and mix well.

Seal the lid and set to Meat/Stew mode. Cook on High pressure for 15 minutes. When ready, do a quick pressure release. Drizzle lemon juice and ladle into serving bowls.

Nutrition facts per serving: Calories 112, Protein 3g, Net Carbs 3.4g, Fat 5.5g

Pumpkin Soup

Prep + Cook Time: 16 minutes | Servings: 3

INGREDIENTS:

2 tbsp Olive oil
1 Onion, chopped
1 Carrot, chopped
2 cloves Garlic, minced

2 tsp Curry powder
4 cups Vegetable broth
2 tbsp Pumpkin seeds
Salt and Pepper, to taste

DIRECTIONS:

Heat oil on Sauté mode. Add the onion and garlic; cook for 3 minutes until tender. Add broth, pumpkin seeds, curry powder, garlic, and carrots. Season with salt and pepper.

Seal the lid and press the Manual button. Cook on High pressure for 10 minutes. When done, allow the pressure to release naturally for 10 minutes.

Nutrition facts per serving: Calories 356, Protein 27g, Net Carbs 5.1g, Fat 23g

Crème de la Broc

Prep + Cook Time: 25 minutes | Servings: 6

INGREDIENTS:

3 cups Heavy Cream
3 cups Chicken Broth
4 tbsp Butter
4 tbsp Almond flour
4 cups chopped Broccoli Florets, only the bushy tops
1 medium Red Onion, chopped

3 cloves Garlic, minced
1 tsp Italian Seasoning
Salt and Black Pepper to taste
1.5 oz Cream Cheese
1½ cups grated Cheddar Cheese + extra for topping

DIRECTIONS:

Melt butter on Sauté, add almond flour and use a spoon to stir until it clumps up. Gradually pour in heavy cream while stirring until white sauce forms. Fetch out the butter sauce into a bowl; set aside.

Add onions, garlic, broth, broccoli, Italian seasoning, and cream cheese. Use a wooden spoon to stir the mixture. Seal the lid, select Soup mode and cook on High pressure for 15 minutes. Once ready, do a quick pressure release. Leave the pot on Keep Warm mode.

Add the butter sauce and cheddar cheese, salt, and pepper. Stir with a spoon until the cheese melts. Dish the soup into serving bowls, top with extra cheese, and serve with low-carb bread.

Nutrition facts per serving: Calories 385, Protein 11g, Net Carbs 6.7g, Fat 25.5g

Garlic Chicken and Egg Soup

Prep + Cook Time: 35 minutes | Servings: 3

INGREDIENTS:

¼ lb Chicken, cut into small pieces
1 Onion, chopped
2 Eggs, whisked
2 cups Chicken broth
¼ cup Water

3 tbsp of Almond flour
4-5 Garlic cloves, minced
½ tbsp black Pepper
¼ tbsp Salt
1 tbsp Olive oil

DIRECTIONS:

Heat oil on Sauté mode, cook garlic and onion for 1 minute. Add the chicken and cook for another 10 minutes. Season with black pepper and salt.

Add the chicken broth, simmer for 15 minutes on Sauté mode.

In a bowl, combine water and almond flour; mix well. Gradually pour this mixture into soup and stir continuously for 2 minutes. Add the eggs gradually. Cook for another 2 minutes. Ladle into bowls and enjoy.

Nutrition facts per serving: Calories 215, Protein 17.3g, Net Carbs 4.1g, Fat 14.5g

Beef and Broccoli Stew

Prep + Cook Time: 35 Minutes | Servings: 4

INGREDIENTS

1 lb Beef stew meat
1 large quartered Onion
½ cup Beef or Bone broth
¼ cup Coconut aminos
2 tbsp Fish sauce

2 Garlic cloves, minced
1 tsp ground Ginger
½ tsp Salt
1 tbsp Coconut oil
¼ lb frozen Broccoli, chopped

DIRECTIONS

In the Instant Pot, place all ingredients except the broccoli. Lock the lid. Press the Meat/Stew and cook for 35 minutes on High. When ready, release the pressure quickly.

Add the broccoli to the inner pot. Place the lid loosely. Let the ingredients simmer for around 15 minutes, on Sauté. Serve hot.

Nutrition facts per serving: Calories 210, Protein 23g, Net Carbs 5.2g, Fat 8g

Spinach Soup

Prep + Cook Time: 40 minutes | Servings: 3

INGREDIENTS:

1 cup baby Spinach
2 cups Vegetable broth
½ cup Almond Milk
2 Garlic cloves, minced

½ tbsp Chili flakes
¼ cup sour Cream
2 tbsp Olive oil

DIRECTIONS:

In the pot, add all ingredients and seal the lid. Set on Meat/Stew mode, and cook for 25 minutes on High. When done, allow for a natural pressure release, for 10 minutes.

Transfer to a food processor and blend until creamy. Return the soup to the pot and cook for another 6 minutes on Sauté. Top with sour cream and serve.

Nutrition facts per serving: Calories 134, Protein 2g, Net Carbs 4.2g, Fat 13.4g

Delicious Full Chicken Soup

Prep + Cook Time: 30 minutes | Servings: 2

INGREDIENTS:

1 lb Chicken breast fillet, strips
1 tbsp Canola oil
1 tsp Oregano powder
2 red Bell Peppers, sliced
2 green Bell Peppers, sliced

2 Onions, sliced
4 slices Provolone cheese
4 cups Chicken broth
Salt and Pepper, to taste

DIRECTIONS:

Add canola oil and cook chicken fillets on Sauté mode. Stir in the oregano powder, salt and pepper, red bell pepper, green bell pepper and onion. Cook for 10 minutes.

Pour chicken broth, seal the lid and cook on High pressure for 4 minutes. When done, allow the pressure to release naturally for 10 minutes.

Nutrition facts per serving: Calories 456, Protein 53g, Net Carbs 7.6g, Fat 37.4g

Squash Soup

Prep + Cook Time: 15 minutes | Servings: 3

INGREDIENTS:

1 lb Squash
2 tbsp Butter
1 Onion, chopped
2 Garlic cloves, minced

3 cups Chicken broth
2 tbsp Nutmeg powder
½ cup Half and Half
1 lb Chicken breast, cubed

DIRECTIONS:

Heat oil in the on Sauté mode. Mix squash, broth, garlic, onion, nutmeg powder, chicken cubes and half and half. Seal the lid and set to Manual mode. Cook on High pressure for 10 minutes. When done, allow the pressure to release naturally for 10 minutes.

Nutrition facts per serving: Calories 325, Protein 35g, Net Carbs 6.7g, Fat 19g

Baby Spinach Soup

Prep + Cook Time: 19 minutes | Servings: 3

INGREDIENTS:

2 tbsp Ginger, minced
4 Garlic cloves, minced
1 tbsp Mustard seeds
1 tbsp Olive oil
1 cup Heavy cream

2 cups Vegetable broth
1 tbsp Coriander powder
1 tbsp Cumin powder
4 cups baby Spinach

DIRECTIONS:

Heat oil on Sauté mode. Stir in the mustard seeds, garlic, cumin powder, coriander powder and broth. Add spinach and heavy cream. Seal the lid and set to Manual mode. Cook on High pressure for 10 minutes. When done, release the pressure quickly.

Nutrition facts per serving: Calories 215, Protein 5g, Net Carbs 2.1g, Fat 12.5g

Butter Squash Soup

Prep + Cook Time: 25 Minutes | Servings: 6

INGREDIENTS

1 peeled and diced Butternut Squash.
1 peeled and diced Green Smith apple
1 tbsp Ginger powder or pureed Ginger
4 cups Chicken broth

1 cup Heavy cream
2 tbsp Coconut oil
Salt and Pepper, to taste

DIRECTIONS

Add the coconut oil and add some of the butternut squash cubes in. Brown lightly for 5 minutes on Sauté. Add the remaining squash and the rest of the ingredients.

Close and lock the Instant Pot and cook for 10 more minutes on High pressure. When the time is over, do a quick release. Puree the mixture in a blender. Serve and enjoy.

Nutrition facts per serving: Calories 235, Protein 7g, Net Carbs 6.2g, Fat 13g

Creamy Asparagus Soup

Prep + Cook Time: 20 Minutes | Servings: 4

INGREDIENTS

½ lb fresh Asparagus, cut into pieces
1 sliced yellow Onion
3 Garlic cloves, minced
3 tbsp Coconut oil

½ tsp dried Thyme
5 cups Bone broth
1 tbsp Lemon juice and zest
2 cups organic sour Cream

DIRECTIONS

Set to Sauté mode and add the coconut oil; then add the onions and the garlic. Cook for 2 minutes and stir occasionally; add the thyme and cook for 1 more minute.

Add the broth, asparagus, and lemon zest with the salt. Lock the lid and press Manual on high pressure. Set the timer to 5 minutes, and when the timer goes off, do a quick release, stir in the sour cream.

Nutrition facts per serving: Calories 350, Protein 11.6g, Net Carbs 7.3g, Fat 32.9g

Mushroom Soup

Prep + Cook Time: 16 minutes | Servings: 3

INGREDIENTS:

2 tbsp Butter
1 Onion, chopped
3 cups Mushrooms, chopped
2 Garlic cloves
2 cups Thyme, chopped

2 tbsp Almond flour
3 cups Chicken stock
2 cups Parmesan cheese, shredded
Salt and Pepper, to taste

DIRECTIONS:

Add butter and onion into the instant pot and cook for 2 minutes on Sauté mode. Stir in mushrooms, garlic cloves, thyme, chicken stock and flour. Season with salt and pepper.

Seal the lid, and cook on High pressure for 10 minutes. When done, allow the pressure to release naturally for 10 minutes. Top with shredded cheese and serve.

Nutrition facts per serving: Calories 321, Protein 25g, Net Carbs 3.4g, Fat 22.4g

KETO POULTRY RECIPES

Creamy Basil Chicken Breasts

Prep + Cook Time: 30 minutes | Servings: 4

INGREDIENTS

4 Chicken Breasts, skinless and boneless
½ cup Heavy Cream
⅓ cup Chicken Broth
⅓ tsp minced Garlic
Salt and Black Pepper to taste

⅓ tsp Italian Seasoning
¼ cup Roasted Red Peppers
1 tbsp Basil Pesto
1 tbsp Arrowroot Starch

DIRECTIONS

Place the chicken at the bottom of the Instant Pot. Pour in broth, and add Italian seasoning, garlic, salt, and pepper. Seal the lid, select Poultry and cook on High pressure for 15 minutes.

Once ready, do a natural pressure release for 5 minutes, then a quick pressure release to let the remaining steam out, and open the pot. Use a spoon to remove the chicken onto a plate; select Sauté mode. Scoop out any fat or unwanted chunks from the sauce.

In a bowl, add cream, arrowroot starch, red peppers, and pesto. Mix with a spoon. Pour the creamy mixture in the pot and whisk for 4 minutes until well-mixed and thickened.

Put the chicken back to the pot and let simmer for 3 minutes. Press Cancel and dish the sauce onto a serving platter. Serve with sauce over a bed of mixed spiralized zoodles.

Nutrition facts per serving: Calories 238, Protein 25g, Net Carbs 1g, Fat 12g

Lemon Chicken

Prep + Cook Time: 30 minutes | Servings: 4

INGREDIENTS

4 Chicken Thighs
1 ½ tbsp Olive oil
½ tsp Garlic Powder
Salt and Black Pepper to taste
½ tsp Red Pepper Flakes
½ tsp smoked Paprika
1 small Onion, chopped

2 cloves Garlic, sliced
¼ cup Chicken Broth
1 tsp Italian Seasoning
1 Lemon, zested and juiced
1 ½ tbsp Heavy Cream
Lemon slices and chopped Parsley to garnish

DIRECTIONS

Heat oil on Sauté, and brown the chicken thighs on each side for 3 minutes. Remove the browned chicken to a plate. Melt the butter, add the garlic, onions, and lemon juice. Stir with a spoon to deglaze the bottom of the pot and cook for 1 minute. Add the Italian seasoning, chicken broth, lemon zest, and the chicken. Seal the lid, select Poultry and cook on High pressure for 15 minutes. Once ready, do a quick pressure release.

Open the lid. Remove the chicken onto a plate and add in the heavy cream. Select Sauté and stir the cream into the sauce until it thickens. Press Cancel and add the chicken. Coat the chicken with sauce. Serve with steamed kale and spinach mix. Garnish with the lemons slices and parsley.

Nutrition facts per serving: Calories 358, Protein 28g, Net Carbs 0g, Fat 36g

Coq Au Vin

Prep + Cook Time: 50 minutes | Servings: 4

INGREDIENTS

3 Chicken Legs, cut into drumsticks and thighs
2 Bacon Slices, chopped in ¾-inch pieces
1 ½ cups Dry White Wine
Salt and Black Pepper to taste
½ bunch Thyme, divided
8 oz Shiitake Mushrooms, cut into 4 pieces

3 Shallots, peeled
3 tbsp Unsalted Butter, divided
3 skinny Carrots, cut into 4 crosswise pieces each
2 cloves Garlic, crushed
1 tbsp Almond flour
3 tbsp chopped Parsley for garnishing

DIRECTIONS

Season the chicken on both sides with salt and pepper.

In a plastic zipper bag, pour the wine. Add half of the thyme and chicken.

Zip the bag and shake to coat the chicken well with the wine. Place in the fridge. After 8 hours, turn on the Instant Pot on Sauté, and add the bacon to it. Fry until brown for 8 minutes; then remove to a plate. Pour in the mushrooms, season with salt and cook for 5 minutes. Remove to the side of the bacon.

Remove the chicken from the fridge. Discard the thyme but reserve the marinade. Pat the chicken dry with paper towels. In the the pot, melt half of the butter, and place in the chicken. Cook until dark golden brown color on each side for 12 minutes. Add the bacon, mushrooms, shallots, garlic, and carrots. Cook for 4 minutes and top with the wine and remaining thyme. Seal the lid, select Poultry and cook on High pressure for 15 minutes.

Add almond flour and the remaining butter in a bowl and smash together with a fork; set aside. Once ready, do a natural pressure release for 10 minutes and open the pot. Plate the chicken and vegetables with a slotted spoon and set the Instant Pot on Sauté mode. Discard the thyme.

Add the almond flour mixture to the sauce in the pot, stir until is well incorporated. Cook for 4 minutes. Spoon the sauce over the chicken. Garnish with parsley and serve with steamed asparagus.

Nutrition facts per serving: Calories 268, Protein 32g, Net Carbs 2g, Fat 12g

Coconut Chicken Curry

Prep + Cook Time: 32 minutes | Servings: 4

INGREDIENTS

4 Chicken Breasts
4 tbsp Red Curry Paste
2 cups Coconut Milk
4 tbsp Swerve Sugar
Salt and Black Pepper to taste

2 Red Bell pepper, seeded and cut in 2-inch sliced
2 Yellow Bell pepper, seeded and cut in 2-inch slices
2 cup Green Beans, cut in Half
2 tbsp Lime Juice

DIRECTIONS

Add the chicken, red curry paste, salt, pepper, coconut milk, and swerve. Seal the lid, select Poultry and cook on High pressure for 15 minutes. Once ready, do a quick pressure release. Remove to a cutting board and select Sauté on the pot. Add bell peppers, green beans, and lime juice. Stir the sauce with a spoon and let simmer for 4 minutes.

Slice the chicken with a knife and add back to the pot. Stir and simmer for 1 minute. Dish the chicken with sauce and vegetable into a serving bowl and serve with coconut flatbread.

Nutrition facts per serving: Calories 368, Protein 32g, Net Carbs 0g, Fat 24g

Chicken Taco Bowls

Prep + Cook Time: 25 minutes | Servings: 4

INGREDIENTS

4 Chicken Breasts
1 cup Chicken Broth
2 ¼ packets Taco Seasoning
2 cups Cauli Rice

To serve:

Grated Cheese, of your choice
Chopped Cilantro

2 Green Bell peppers, seeded and diced
2 Red Bell peppers, seeded and diced
2 cups Salsa
Salt and Black Pepper to taste

Sour Cream
Avocado Slices

DIRECTIONS

Pour the chicken broth in the pot, add the chicken, and pour the taco seasoning over. Add the salsa and stir lightly with a spoon.

Seal the lid, select Poultry and cook on High for 15 minutes. Once ready, do a quick pressure release. Add the cauli rice and bell peppers, and use a spoon to push them into the sauce.

Seal the lid, select Steam and cook on High pressure for 4 minutes. Once ready, do a quick pressure release. Gently stir the mixture, adjust the taste with salt and pepper and spoon the chicken dish into serving bowls. Top with sour cream, avocado slices, cilantro and cheese.

Nutrition facts per serving: Calories 240, Protein 34g, Net Carbs 0g, Fat 22g

Sweet Spicy Shredded Chicken

Prep + Cook Time: 35 minutes | Servings: 4

INGREDIENTS

4 Chicken Breasts, skinless
¼ cup Sriracha Sauce
2 tbsp unsalted Butter
1 tsp grated Ginger
2 cloves Garlic, minced
½ tsp Cayenne Pepper

½ tsp Red Chili Flakes
½ cup Monk Fruit Syrup
⅓ cup Chicken Broth
Salt and Black Pepper to taste
Chopped Scallion to garnish

DIRECTIONS

In a bowl, pour the broth. Add the monk fruit syrup, ginger, Sriracha sauce, red pepper flakes, cayenne pepper, and garlic. Use a spoon to mix them well and set aside.

Put the chicken on a plate and season with salt and pepper. Set aside too. Melt the butter on Sauté, and add the chicken in 2 batches; cook to brown on both sides for 3 minutes.

Add all the chicken back to the pot and pour the pepper sauce over. Seal the lid, select Poultry and cook on High pressure for 20 minutes. Once ready, do a natural pressure release for 5 minutes, then a quick pressure release to let the remaining steam out.

Remove the chicken on a cutting board and shred with two forks. Transfer to a serving bowl, pour the sauce over and garnish with the scallions. Serve with a side of zoodles.

Nutrition facts per serving: Calories 160, Protein 37g, Net Carbs 0g, Fat 16g

Chicken in Tomato Sauce

Prep + Cook Time: 30 minutes | Servings: 4

INGREDIENTS

4 Chicken Thighs, skinless but with Bone
4 tbsp Olive oil
1 cup Crushed Tomatoes
1 large Red Bell pepper, seeded and diced
1 large Green Bell pepper, seeded and diced
1 Red Onion, diced
Salt and Black Pepper to taste
1 tbsp chopped Basil
1 Bay Leaf
½ tsp dried Oregano

DIRECTIONS

Place the chicken on a clean flat surface and season with salt and pepper. Heat oil on Sauté, and brown the chicken on both sides for 6 minutes. Then, add the onions and bell peppers.

Cook to soften them for 5 minutes. Add the tomatoes, bay leaf, salt, pepper, and oregano. Stir using a spoon. Seal the lid, select Poultry and cook on High pressure for 20 minutes.

Once ready, do a natural pressure release for 5 minutes, then a quick pressure release to let the remaining steam out. Discard the bay leaf. Dish the chicken with the sauce into a serving bowl and garnish with basil. Serve over a bed of steamed squash spaghetti.

Nutrition facts per serving: Calories 133, Protein 14g, Net Carbs 6.5g, Fat 3g

Spinach Feta Stuffed Chicken

Prep + Cook Time: 30 minutes | Servings: 4

INGREDIENTS

4 Chicken Breasts, skinless
Salt and Black Pepper to taste
1 cup Baby Spinach, frozen
½ cup crumbled Feta Cheese
½ tsp dried Oregano
½ tsp Garlic Powder
2 tbsp Coconut Oil
1.2 tsp dried Parsley
1 cup Water

DIRECTIONS

Cover the chicken in plastic wrap and put them on a cutting board. Use a rolling pin to pound them flat to a quarter inch thickness. Then, remove the plastic wrap. In a bowl, add spinach, salt, and feta cheese. Use a spoon to mix well and scoop the mixture onto the chicken breasts.

Wrap the chicken to secure the spinach filling in it. Use toothpicks to secure the wrap firmly from opening. Season the chicken pieces with the oregano, parsley, garlic powder, and pepper. Turn on the Instant Pot, open the lid, and select Sauté mode. Add the coconut oil and chicken, and sear to golden brown on each side. Work in 2 batches. After, remove the chicken onto a plate and set aside.

Pour the water into the pot and use a spoon to scrape the bottom of the pot to let loose any chicken pieces or seasoning that is stuck to the bottom of the pot.

Then, fit the steamer rack into the pot with care as the pot will still be hot. Use a pair of tongs to transfer the chicken onto the steamer rack. Close the lid, secure the pressure valve, and select Poultry mode on High pressure for 15 minutes.

Once ready, do a quick pressure release. Plate the chicken and serve with side of sautéed broccoli, asparagus, and some slices of tomatoes.

Nutrition facts per serving: Calories 225, Protein 33g, Net Carbs 2g, Fat 17g

Meatballs Primavera

Prep + Cook Time: 30 minutes | Servings: 4

INGREDIENTS

1 lb Ground Chicken
1 Egg, cracked into a bowl
6 tsp Coconut Flour
Salt and Black Pepper to taste
2 tbsp chopped Basil + Extra to garnish
1 tbsp Avocado Oil + ½ tbsp Avocado Oil

1 ½ tsp Italian Seasoning
1 Red Bell pepper, seeded and sliced
2 cups chopped Green Beans
½ lb chopped Asparagus
1 cup chopped Tomatoes
1 cup Chicken Broth

DIRECTIONS

In a mixing bowl, add the chicken, egg, coconut flour, salt, pepper, 2 tbsp of basil, 1 tbsp of avocado oil, and Italian seasoning. Use your hands to mix well and make 16 large balls.

Set the meatballs aside. Select Sauté mode on the pot. Heat ½ a tsp of avocado oil and add bell pepper, green beans, and asparagus. Cook them for 3 minutes while stirring frequently.

After 3 minutes, use a spoon to remove the veggies to a plate; set aside. Heat the remaining oil and fry the meatballs in batches. Cook for 2 minutes on each side to brown lightly.

Put all the meatballs back into the pot as well as the vegetables. Pour the chicken broth over. Seal the lid, select Poultry and cook on High pressure for 15 minutes. Once ready, do a quick pressure release. Dish the meatballs with sauce into bowls and garnish with basil.

Nutrition facts per serving: Calories 135, Protein 16g, Net Carbs 0g, Fat 16.4g

Buffalo Chicken Soup

Prep + Cook Time: 37 minutes | Servings: 4

INGREDIENTS

4 Chicken Breasts, Boneless and skinless
½ cup Hot Sauce
2 large White Onion, finely chopped
2 cups finely chopped Celery
1 tbsp Olive oil
1 tsp dried Thyme

3 cups Chicken Broth
1 tsp Garlic Powder
½ cup crumbled Blue Cheese + extra for serving
4 oz Cream Cheese, cubed in small pieces
Salt and Pepper to taste

DIRECTIONS

Put the chicken on a clean flat surface and season with pepper and salt; set aside. Heat oil on Sauté, and add onion and celery. Cook, constantly stirring, until soft for 5 minutes.

Stir in garlic and thyme. Cook for about a minute, and add the chicken, hot sauce, and broth. Season with salt and pepper. Seal the lid, select Poultry and cook on High for 20 minutes.

Meanwhile, put the blue cheese and cream cheese in a bowl, and use a fork to smash them together. Set the resulting mixture aside. Once ready, do a quick pressure release.

Shred the chicken inside the pot and select Sauté mode. Mix in the cheese; press Cancel. Dish the soup into bowls. Sprinkle the remaining cheese and serve with low-carb baguette.

Nutrition facts per serving: Calories 114, Protein 4.1g, Net Carbs 0g, Fat 4.3g

Balsamic Chicken

Prep + Cook Time: 50 minutes | Servings: 4

INGREDIENTS

2 lb Chicken Thighs, Bone in and skin on
2 tbsp Olive oil
Salt and Pepper to taste
1 ½ cups diced Tomatoes
¾ cup Yellow Onion
2 tsp minced Garlic
½ cup Balsamic Vinegar
3 tsp chopped fresh Thyme
1 cup Chicken Broth
2 tbsp chopped Parsley

DIRECTIONS

Put the chicken thighs on a cutting board and use paper towels to pat dry. Season with salt and pepper. Heat oil on Sauté, and put the chicken with skin side down.

Cook until golden brown on each side for 9 minutes. Remove on a clean plate. Add the onions and tomatoes, and sauté for 3 minutes stirring occasionally. Top the onions with the garlic too and cook for 30 seconds, then, stir in the broth, salt, thyme, and balsamic vinegar.

Add the chicken back to the pot. Seal the lid, select Poultry and cook on High pressure for 20 minutes. Meanwhile, preheat an oven to 350 F.

Once ready, do a quick pressure release. Select Sauté mode. Remove the chicken onto a baking tray using tongs and leave the sauce in the pot to thicken for about 10 minutes.

Tuck the baking tray in the oven and let the chicken broil on each side to golden brown for about 5 minutes. Remove and set aside to cool slightly. Adjust the salt and pepper and when cooked to your desired thickness, press Cancel.

Place the chicken in a serving bowl and spoon the sauce all over it. Garnish with parsley and serve with thyme roasted tomatoes, carrots, and radishes.

Nutrition facts per serving: Calories 277, Protein 34g, Net Carbs 2g, Fat 10g

Tuscan Chicken

Prep + Cook Time: 30 minutes | Servings: 4

INGREDIENTS

4 Chicken Thighs, cut into 1-inch pieces
1 tbsp Olive oil
1 ½ cups Chicken Broth
Salt to taste
1 cup chopped Sun-Dried Tomatoes with Herbs
2 tbsp Italian Seasoning
2 cups Baby Spinach
¼ tsp Red Pepper Flakes
10 oz softened Cream Cheese, cut into small cubes
1 cup shredded Pecorino

DIRECTIONS

Pour in chicken broth and add the Italian seasoning, chicken, tomatoes, salt, and red pepper flakes. Stir them with a spoon. Seal the lid, select Poultry and cook on High for 15 minutes.

Once ready, do a quick pressure release. Add and stir in the spinach, parmesan cheese, and cream cheese until the cheese melts and is fully incorporated. Let in the warm for 5 minutes. Dish the Tuscan chicken over a bed of zoodles or a side of steamed asparagus and serve.

Nutrition facts per serving: Calories 385, Protein 45g, Net Carbs 2g, Fat 24g

Barbecue Chicken

Prep + Cook Time: 30 minutes | Servings: 4

INGREDIENTS

2 lb Chicken Drumsticks, Bone in and skin in
½ cup Chicken Broth
¼ tbsp Monk Fruit Powder
½ tsp Dry Mustard
½ tsp sweet Paprika
½ tbsp. Cumin Powder

½ tsp Onion Powder
¼ tsp Cayenne Powder
Salt and Pepper to taste
1 stick Butter, sliced in 5 to 7 pieces
Low Carb BBQ Sauce, to taste
Cooking Spray

DIRECTIONS

Pour the chicken broth in and fit the steamer rack at the bottom of the pot. In the zipper bag, pour in the monk fruit powder, dry mustard, cumin powder, onion powder, cayenne powder, salt, and pepper. Add the chicken, then zip, close the bag and shake to coat the chicken well.

Remove the chicken from the bag and lay on the steamer rack and place the butter slices on the drumsticks. Seal the lid, select Poultry and cook on High pressure for 20 minutes.

Meanwhile, preheat an oven to 350 F. Once ready, do a quick pressure release. Remove chicken onto a clean flat surface and brush with Barbecue sauce. Grease a baking tray with cooking spray and arrange the chicken pieces on it. Tuck the tray into the oven and broil the chicken for 4 minutes while paying close attention to prevent burning. Serve warm.

Nutrition facts per serving: Calories 234, Protein 28.4g, Net Carbs 2.6g, Fat 11.3g

Quick Chicken Fajitas

Prep + Cook Time: 30 minutes | Servings: 4

INGREDIENTS

2 lb Chicken Breasts, skinless and cut in 1-inch slices
¼ cup Chicken Broth
1 Yellow Onion, sliced
1 Green Bell peppers, seeded and sliced
1 Yellow Bell pepper, seeded and sliced
1 Red Bell pepper, seeded and sliced

Assembling:
Low Carb Tacos
Guacamole
Sour Cream

2 tbsp Cumin Powder
2 tbsp Chili Powder
Salt to taste
Half a Lime
Cooking Spray
Fresh cilantro, to garnish

Salsa
Cheese

DIRECTIONS

Grease the pot with cooking spray and line the bottom with the bell peppers and onion. Lay the chicken on the bed of peppers and sprinkle with salt, chili powder, and cumin powder.

Squeeze some lime juice and pour in the broth. Seal the lid, select Poultry and cook on High pressure for 20 minutes. Once ready, do a quick pressure release. Dish the chicken with the vegetables and juice onto a large serving platter. Add the sour cream, cheese, guacamole, salsa, and tacos in one layer on the side of the chicken.

Nutrition facts per serving: Calories 352, Protein 19.7g, Net Carbs 0g, Fat 12.1g

Stuffed Full Chicken

Prep + Cook Time: 51 minutes | Servings: 6

INGREDIENTS

4 lb Whole Chicken
1 tbsp Herbes de Provence Seasoning
1 tbsp Olive oil
Salt and Black Pepper to season
2 cloves Garlic, peeled

1 tsp Garlic Powder
1 Yellow Onion, peeled and quartered
1 Lemon, quartered
1 ¼ cup Chicken Broth

DIRECTIONS

Put the chicken on a clean flat surface and pat dry using paper towels. Sprinkle the top and cavity of the chicken with salt, black pepper, Herbes de Provence, and garlic powder. Stuff the onion, lemon quarters, and garlic cloves into the cavity of the chicken.

Open the Instant Pot and fit the steamer rack in it. Pour the chicken broth in and put the chicken on the rack. Seal the lid, select Poultry and cook on High pressure for 30 minutes.

Meanwhile, get a baking pan ready. Once ready, do a natural pressure release for 12 minutes, then a quick pressure release to let the remaining steam out, and press Cancel.

Open the pot and use two tongs to remove the chicken onto a prepared baking pan. Preheat an oven to 350 F and place the baking pan with the chicken in when it is ready.

Broil the chicken for 5 minutes to ensure that it attains a golden brown color on each side.

Dish the chicken on a bed of steamed mixed veggies for dinner. Right here, the choice is yours to whip up some good keto veggies together as your appetite instructs you.

Nutrition facts per serving: Calories 370, Protein 43g, Net Carbs 2g, Fat 14g

Chicken Wings

Prep + Cook Time: 35 minutes | Servings: 5

INGREDIENTS

3 Chicken breasts, cubed
1 tsp Garlic powder
1 cup Almond flour
2 tbsp Coriander, chopped
½ tsp Salt

½ tsp Chili Pepper
½ tsp Cinnamon powder
1 cup Olive oil
¼ cup Water

DIRECTIONS

In a bowl, mix flour, salt, chili powder, cumin powder, coriander and toss well. Add water and make a thick paste. Heat oil on Sauté mode.

Dip each chicken piece into the flour mixture and then put into the oil. Fry until golden and place on a paper towel to drain. Transfer to a dish and serve with mint sauce.

Nutrition facts per serving: Calories 456, Protein 31g, Net Carbs 0.9g, Fat 34g

Whole Chicken

Prep + Cook Time: 70 minutes | Servings: 6

INGREDIENTS

1 white Chicken
1 tsp Garlic paste
1 tsp Ginger paste
1 tsp salt
1 tsp Cayenne Pepper
¼ tsp Chili powder
½ tsp black Pepper

½ tsp Cinnamon powder
½ tsp Cumin powder
3 tbsp Lemon juice
2 tbsp Apple Cider Vinegar
2 tbsp Soya sauce
3 tbsp Olive oil

DIRECTIONS

In a bowl, combine vinegar, cayenne, lemon juice, ginger garlic paste, salt, pepper, chili, olive oil, cumin powder and cinnamon powder; mix well.

Pour over the chicken and rub with hands. Place the chicken in your greased Instant Pot and seal the lid. Set on Poultry for 45 minutes on High pressure. Do a quick release.

Nutrition facts per serving: Calories 245, Protein 33g, Net Carbs 1.2g, Fat 13g

Broccoli Chicken

Prep + Cook Time: 45 minutes | Servings: 3

INGREDIENTS

¼ lb Chicken, Boneless, cut into small pieces
1 cup Broccoli florets
2 Garlic cloves, minced
1 tsp salt

½ tsp black Pepper
3 tbsp Butter
1 cup Chicken broth
2 cup Cream

DIRECTIONS

Melt butter on Sauté and fry garlic for 1 minute. Add the chicken and stir-fry until golden.

Season with salt and pepper. Add broccoli and cream and pour in chicken broth. Seal the lid, and cook for 10 minutes on High pressure. Once ready, quick release the pressure.

Nutrition facts per serving: Calories 432, Protein 13g, Net Carbs 5.5g, Fat 42g

Simple Chicken Wings

Prep + Cook Time: 20 minutes | Servings: 4

INGREDIENTS

2 lb Chicken wings

1 cup BBQ sauce

DIRECTIONS

Put the chicken wings in the Instant pot and cover them with the BBQ sauce. Seal the lid and cook on High pressure for 20 minutes. When ready, do a quick release.

Nutrition facts per serving: Calories 305, Protein 51g, Net Carbs 3.3g, Fat 9g

Asian-Style Chicken Thighs

Prep + Cook Time: 20 minutes | Servings: 4

INGREDIENTS

1 tsp Olive oil
1 lb Chicken thighs
1 Onion, chopped
2 tsp Ginger, minced

2 tsp Garlic, minced
2 ½ cups Chicken broth
½ cup sugar-free Ketchup
2 tsp Wine Vinegar

DIRECTIONS

Heat oil on Sauté. Cook ginger and garlic for 1 minute. Add the chicken thighs and cook for 10 minutes. Add onion and chicken broth, seal the lid and press Manual.

Cook for 10 minutes on High pressure. Meanwhile, mix ketchup, mirin and wine vinegar in a bowl. When the pot beeps, quick-release the pressure. Serve hot with the sauce.

Nutrition facts per serving: Calories 276, Protein 19g, Net Carbs 2.6g, Fat 21g

Chicken with Sesame oil

Prep + Cook Time: 20 minutes | Servings: 3

INGREDIENTS

1 tsp flaxseed meal
2 egg whites
1 lb Chicken, sliced
½ cup Water
1 tsp soy sauce

1 tsp sesame oil
1 tsp Wine Vinegar
1 tsp Ginger, grated
2 tsp Garlic cloves, minced
Salt and Pepper, to taste

DIRECTIONS

Mix flaxseed meal and egg whites, in a bowl. Add the mixture into the instant pot. Stir in the chicken, soy sauce, sesame oil, vinegar, ginger, garlic, water, salt and pepper.

Seal the lid, press Manual and cook for 20 minutes on High. When ready, release the pressure quickly.

Nutrition facts per serving: Calories 214, Protein 33g, Net Carbs 2.5g, Fat 7.4g

Hot Garlic Chicken Breasts

Prep + Cook Time: 35 minutes | Servings: 4

INGREDIENTS

2 Chicken breasts
2 tbsp Apple Cider Vinegar
1 cup Tomato Ketchup
1 tsp Garlic powder

¼ tsp salt
½ tsp Chili powder
3 tbsp Olive oil

DIRECTIONS

Combine vinegar, ketchup, chili powder, salt, and garlic powder, in a bowl. Drizzle over the chicken and toss well. Set the Instant Pot on Sauté mode and heat the oil.

Transfer the chicken breasts to the pot. Cook for 25 minutes, turning multiple times until well cooked.

Nutrition facts per serving: Calories 254, Protein 23g, Net Carbs 1.2g, Fat 19g

Chicken Tenders with Garlic

Prep + Cook Time: 15 minutes | Servings: 2

INGREDIENTS

1 lb Chicken tenders
2 Garlic cloves, minced
2 tsp Paprika
2 tsp Oregano powder
2 tsp Olive oil
1 Onion, chopped
2 cups green Beans, frozen
1 cup Almond flour
1 cup Chicken stock
1 Egg, raw
Salt and Pepper, to taste

DIRECTIONS

Mix chicken tenders, garlic, paprika, oregano, onion, green beans, flour and chicken stock, in a bowl. Add egg, and stir well. Season with salt and pepper.

Seal the lid, press the Manual and cook for 10 minutes on High pressure. When ready, release the pressure quickly and serve hot.

Nutrition facts per serving: Calories 436, Protein 53g, Net Carbs 9.1g, Fat 18g

Tropic Shredded Chicken

Prep + Cook Time: 30 minutes | Servings: 4

INGREDIENTS

3 Chicken breasts, shredded, boiled
½ tsp Garlic paste
½ tsp salt
½ tsp soy sauce
2 tbsp Barbecue sauce
½ tsp Chili powder
2 tbsp Olive oil

DIRECTIONS

Heat oil on Sauté mode and fry garlic for a minute. Add chicken breasts and brown until lightly golden. Add soy sauce, barbecue sauce, salt, and chili powder and fry well. Serve with mashed cauliflower and green salad.

Nutrition facts per serving: Calories 487, Protein 53g, Net Carbs 4.5g, Fat 28g

Hot Butter Chicken

Prep + Cook Time: 40 minutes | Servings: 4

INGREDIENTS

¼ lb Chicken, Boneless, pieces
1 cup Tomato puree
1-inch Ginger slice
1-2 red Chilies, diced
½ tsp Garlic paste
1 tsp salt
¼ tsp black Pepper
4 tbsp Butter

DIRECTIONS

In a blender, add tomato puree, chilies, ginger, garlic, salt, and pepper and blend well. Melt butter on Sauté mode and fry the chicken for 5-10 minute. Transfer the tomato mixture and combine. Simmer for 10-15 minutes until the chicken tenders.

Nutrition facts per serving: Calories 154, Protein 10g, Net Carbs 4.3g, Fat 9.4g

Egg and Carrot Spread

Prep + Cook Time: 25 minutes | Servings: 3

INGREDIENTS
4 Eggs, whisked
3 Carrots, shredded, boiled
¼ tsp salt
½ tsp black Pepper
3 tbsp Butter

DIRECTIONS
In a blender, blend the carrots to a puree. Add them to the Instant Pot and let simmer for 2 minutes on Sauté. Add eggs, butter, salt, and pepper. Stir continually for 15 minutes. Serve chilled.

Nutrition facts per serving: Calories 129, Protein 6.2g, Net Carbs 2.1g, Fat 10g

Roasted Eggs Gravy

Prep + Cook Time: 30 minutes | Servings: 4

INGREDIENTS
4 Eggs
1 Onion, chopped
2 Tomatoes, chopped
A pinch of Salt
½ tsp Chili powder
¼ tsp Turmeric powder
⅓ tsp Cumin powder
2 Garlic cloves, minced
2 tbsp Olive oil

DIRECTIONS
Heat oil on Sauté mode and fry the eggs until lightly golden; set aside. In the same oil, cook onion until lightly golden. Add in tomatoes, garlic, salt, chili, and turmeric.

Stir-fry until the tomatoes soften. Transfer to a blender and puree until smooth. Return the mixture to the pot, add a few splashes of water and cook for another 2 minutes. Stir in the roasted eggs and toss around.

Nutrition facts per serving: Calories 149, Protein 6.6g, Net Carbs 4.5g, Fat 11.4g

Squash with Eggs

Prep + Cook Time: 30 minutes | Servings: 4

INGREDIENTS
4 Eggs
1 Squash, cut into 1-inch thick rings
A pinch Salt
A pinch Chili powder
2 tbsp Olive oil

DIRECTIONS
Grease the basket with oil. Pour half cup of water, add the basket, and place the squash rings inside. Crack an egg into each ring. Season to taste. Seal the lid and cook for 25 minutes on High pressure. When done, do a quick pressure release and serve hot.

Nutrition facts per serving: Calories 130, Protein 6.1g, Net Carbs 1.4g, Fat 11g

Tomato Eggs

Prep + Cook Time: 10 minutes | Servings: 2

INGREDIENTS

2 Eggs, whisked
2 Tomatoes, sliced
1 tsp Garlic powder

¼ tsp salt
½ tsp Chili powder
3 tbsp Butter

DIRECTIONS

Melt butter on Sauté. Add the eggs and spread all over. Cook for 2 minutes; then flip. Cook for 2 more minutes. Place the tomato slices and in the Instant Pot and seal the lid.

Cook on high pressure on Manual mode for 10 minutes. Season with salt and chili powder.

Nutrition facts per serving: Calories 180, Protein 6.7g, Net Carbs 1.7g, Fat 15.9g

Zucchini Eggs

Prep + Cook Time: 15 minutes | Servings: 2

INGREDIENTS

2 Eggs, whisked
1 large Zucchini, sliced
1 tsp Garlic powder

¼ tsp salt
¼ tsp black Pepper
3 tbsp Butter

DIRECTIONS

Melt butter on Sauté. Add zucchini and cook for 3-4 minutes. Pour the eggs mixture and spread evenly. Cook for 2-3 minutes; then flip and cook for 3 more. Season with salt and pepper, and serve immediately.

Nutrition facts per serving: Calories 177, Protein 7.1g, Net Carbs 1.5g, Fat 15.8g

Tomato and Coconut Chicken

Prep + Cook Time: 30 minutes | Servings: 4

INGREDIENTS

1 Onion, diced
1 pound Chicken Breasts, cubed
1 cup Coconut Cream
1 tsp minced Garlic

3 tbsp Butter
1 (14-ounce) can diced Tomatoes, undrained
¼ cup Chicken Broth
Salt and Pepper, to taste

DIRECTIONS

Melt the butter on Sauté. Add the onions and cook for 3-4 minutes. When softened, stir in the garlic and cook for 1 minute. Stir in the chicken and tomatoes and season to taste.

Pour in the broth and seal the lid. Cook on SOUP/BROTH on High pressure for 15 minutes. When the timer goes off, release the pressure quickly. Open the lid and stir in the coconut cream. Taste and season with some more salt and pepper if needed. Serve immediately.

Nutrition facts per serving: Calories 410, Protein 38g, Net Carbs 5g, Fat 40g

Pepperoni Pizza Egg

Prep + Cook Time: 15 minutes | Servings: 2

INGREDIENTS

2 Eggs, whisked
1 tsp Garlic powder
¼ tsp salt
½ tsp black Pepper
1 Onion, chopped
4 Pepperoni slices
3 tbsp Butter

DIRECTIONS

In a bowl, whisk eggs, and add in onion, pepperoni, season with salt, garlic and pepper. Melt butter in the Instant Pot on Sauté mode. Pour the eggs mixture, cook for 5 minutes, stirring continuously. Transfer to a serving platter and serve immediately.

Nutrition facts per serving: Calories 219, Protein 8.1g, Net Carbs 4.5g, Fat 17.4g

Poached Eggs

Prep + Cook Time: 10 minutes | Servings: 3

INGREDIENTS

3 Eggs
3 cups Water
2 tbsp Vinegar
1 pinch Salt

DIRECTIONS

Set the Instant Pot on Sauté mode. Add water and boil. Crack 1 egg into a bowl and pour it in the boiled water. Repeat for all eggs. Seal the lid and cook for 5 minutes on High pressure. Ladle to cold water, peel and serve.

Nutrition facts per serving: Calories 65, Protein 5.6g, Net Carbs 0.4g, Fat 4.2g

Asian Style Steamed Eggs

Prep + Cook Time: 10 Minutes | Servings: 2

INGREDIENTS

2 large Eggs
⅓ cup cold Water
2 stem of Scallions, chopped
1 pinch Sesame seeds
1 pinch fine Garlic powder
Salt and black Pepper, to taste
2 Avocados, sliced
1 tsp Ginger
1 tsp Flaxseed powder
1 tsp of Coconut oil

DIRECTIONS

Start by placing the eggs in water, in a bowl. Strain the eggs mixture above a mesh strainer above a heatproof bowl. Add what is left of the ingredients, except the avocados.

Mix well and set aside. Pour water in the inner pot of the Instant Pot and place the trivet. Place the bowl on top, seal the lid and cook on High pressure for 5 minutes.

When ready, do a quick pressure release and serve with avocado.

Nutrition facts per serving: Calories 419, Protein 8.1g, Net Carbs 5.3g, Fat 38.4g

Jalapeno and Cheddar Chicken

Prep + Cook Time: 22 minutes | Servings: 4

INGREDIENTS

1 pound Chicken Breasts
8 ounces Cream Cheese
8 ounces shredded Cheddar Cheese
3 Jalapenos, seeded and diced

½ cup Water
7 ounces Sour Cream
Salt and Pepper, to taste

DIRECTIONS

Add water, cream cheese, and sour cream, to the Instant Pot. Whisk until well-combined. Stir in the jalapenos and cheddar. Add in the chicken and seal the lid.

Set the cooking time to 12 minutes and cook on HIGH pressure. When the timer goes off, do a quick pressure release. Shred the chicken with forks and stir. Serve hot.

Nutrition facts per serving: Calories 305, Protein 23g, Net Carbs 4g, Fat 25g

Cream Cheese Chicken with Tomatoes and Zucchini

Prep + Cook Time: 35 minutes | Servings: 4

INGREDIENTS

1 cup Cream Cheese
1 cup Tomato Sauce
2 Tomatoes, peeled and diced
1 cup shredded Zucchini

1 ½ cups Chicken Broth
½ tsp Garlic Powder
1 lb Chicken Breasts, cut into 4 fillets
Salt and Pepper, to taste

DIRECTIONS

Pour in chicken broth and add the chicken. Seal the lid, and cook on HIGH pressure for 20 minutes. When you hear the beep, do a quick pressure release and open the lid carefully.

Stir in all remaining ingredients. Seal the lid again and cook for 5 minutes on HIGH pressure. Do a quick pressure release. Serve with tomato sauce.

Nutrition facts per serving: Calories 260, Protein 28g, Net Carbs 4.5g, Fat 19g

Sour Cream Chicken with Cauliflower

Prep + Cook Time: 25 minutes | Servings: 4

INGREDIENTS

4 Chicken Breasts, chopped
4 tbsp Butter
1 cup Chicken Broth

1 cup Sour Cream
½ Cauliflower Head, broken into florets
1 tsp minced Garlic

DIRECTIONS

Melt the butter on Sauté. When melted, whisk in the broth and sour cream. Stir in the remaining ingredients and seal the lid on. Cook on HIGH pressure for 15 minutes.

When it goes off, release the pressure quickly. Open the lid, stir well and serve immediately.

Nutrition facts per serving: Calories 465, Protein 35g, Net Carbs 3.5g, Fat 35g

Hot Chicken Chili

Prep + Cook Time: 25 minutes | Servings: 3

INGREDIENTS

2 Chicken breasts
1 cup Chili Garlic sauce
¼ cup Tomato Ketchup
4 tbsp Stevia
2 tbsp Soy sauce

2 Tomatoes, chopped
¼ tsp salt
¼ tsp Cayenne Pepper
3 tbsp Olive oil

DIRECTIONS

Combine the chili garlic sauce, tomato ketchup, soya sauce, stevia, salt, and pepper and mix. Pour the sauce over the chicken and toss well.

Heat oil in the Instant Pot on Sauté mode and add in the chicken breasts. Seal the lid and cook on pressure cook mode for 20 minutes. Transfer to a serving dish and serve.

Nutrition facts per serving: Calories 423, Protein 41g, Net Carbs 7.1g, Fat 32g

Chicken Breast with Green Onions

Prep + Cook Time: 25 minutes | Servings: 4

INGREDIENTS

4 Chicken breast, diced
½ tsp soy sauce
2 cups Water
½ tsp stevia
2 tsp Wine Vinegar

1 tsp sesame oil
2 tsp Chili Garlic sauce
1 tsp Flaxseed meal
2 green Onions, chopped
½ tsp red Pepper flakes

DIRECTIONS

Add water, soy sauce and wine vinegar into the Instant pot. Cook for 10 minutes on Sauté. Add the chicken pieces; mix well. Add sesame oil, chili garlic sauce, green onions, red pepper flakes and flaxseed meal.

Seal the lid, press Manual and cook for 10 minutes on High pressure. Meanwhile, mix ketchup, mirin and wine vinegar in a bowl. When the pressure cooker beeps, quick-release the pressure. Serve with the sauce and enjoy.

Nutrition facts per serving: Calories 331, Protein 38g, Net Carbs 2.5g, Fat 18g

Chicken with Sweet Potatoes

Prep + Cook Time: 30 minutes | Servings: 4

INGREDIENTS

2 cups cubed and peeled sweet potatoes
2 tsp Coconut oil
1 lb of skinless and boneless cubed Chicken breasts
3 Garlic cloves, minced
6 tsp Tamari Soy sauce
1 cup Water
3 tsp Stevia

3 tsp Hot sauce
1 peeled and diced Mango
¼ tsp smashed red Pepper flakes
1 tsp Flaxseed meal
1 tsp Ginger
1 cup warm Water

DIRECTIONS

Place the sweet potatoes in the Instant Pot and pour enough water to cover. Seal the lid, press Manual and set the timer to 10 minutes on High pressure.

When ready, quickly release the pressure and drain the potatoes. Place 2 tbsp of coconut oil in the Instant Pot and cook the chicken for 5 minutes on Sauté.

Sprinkle ginger and garlic; cook for 5 more minutes. Add tamari, a cup of warm water, stevia and hot sauce. Add the flaxseed meal to the mixture and set on Sauté for 10 minutes; stirring occassionally. Serve warm.

Nutrition facts per serving: Calories 214, Protein 29g, Net Carbs 3.5, Fat 8.2g

Bell Pepper and Egg Tortilla

Prep + Cook Time: 25 minutes | Servings: 3

INGREDIENTS

4 Eggs, whisked
1 red Bell Pepper, chopped
1 Onion, chopped
¼ tsp salt
½ tsp black Pepper
3 tbsp Butter

DIRECTIONS

In a bowl, add eggs, onion, bell peppers, salt, and pepper, mix well. Melt butter on Sauté mode. Pour the eggs mixture and spread all over and seal the lid. Cook for 15 minutes, flipping once halfway through cooking. Serve hot and enjoy.

Nutrition facts per serving: Calories 133, Protein 6.5g, Net Carbs 3.2g, Fat 10g

Chicken with Avocado Cream

Prep + Cook Time: 35 minutes | Servings: 6

INGREDIENTS

4 lb organic Chicken breasts
1 tsp Coconut oil
1 tsp Paprika
1 ½ cups Pacific Chicken Bone Broth
1 tsp dried Thyme
¼ tsp freshly ground black Pepper
1 tsp Ginger
2 tsp Lemon juice
½ tsp sea Salt
6 cloves peeled Garlic
1 Avocado

DIRECTIONS

In a bowl, mix paprika, thyme, salt, dried ginger, and pepper. Then rub the seasoning onto chicken. Heat oil on Sauté mode. Add the breasts side down and cook for 6 minutes.

Flip the chicken and pour in broth, lemon juice, and garlic cloves. Lock the lid and set the timer to 30 minutes on High pressure on Manual mode.

Prepare the avocado cream by whisking the contents of the avocado with 2 tsp of coconut oil and ½ tsp. of salt. Once the timer beeps, quickly release the pressure.

Remove the chicken from the pot and pour the sauce over, to serve.

Nutrition facts per serving: Calories 455, Protein 61g, Net Carbs 1.5g, Fat 21.5g

Chicken and Turnip Stew

Prep + Cook Time: 45 minutes | Servings: 7

INGREDIENTS

- 1 Onion, chopped
- 2 Tomatoes, chopped
- 1 cup Chicken pieces
- 2-3 Turnips, peeled, diced
- 2 cups Chicken broth
- 1 Carrot, sliced
- 1 tbsp Coriander, chopped
- ½ tsp Garlic paste
- ½ tsp Ginger paste
- ½ tsp Cumin powder
- ½ tsp Cinnamon powder
- ½ tsp Chili powder
- ¼ tsp salt
- ¼ tsp Turmeric powder
- 3 tbsp Olive oil
- 2 green Chilies, whole

DIRECTIONS

Heat oil on Sauté and stir-fry onion for 1 minute. Stir in tomatoes, ginger garlic paste, salt, chili powder, and turmeric powder and fry for 1 minute. Add the chicken pieces and cook until lightly golden. Add the turnips and fry until tender.

Add the chicken broth, coriander, carrots, and green chili, seal the lid and cook on Low Pressure for 25 minutes. When ready, do a quick pressure release and serve hot.

Nutrition facts per serving: Calories 218, Protein 29g, Net Carbs 2.3g, Fat 11g

Chicken Mushroom Mix

Prep + Cook Time: 14 minutes | Servings: 4

INGREDIENTS

- 3 cups Chicken, shredded
- 1 tsp Olive oil
- 1 Onion, chopped
- 6 small Mushrooms, chopped
- 2 minced Garlic cloves
- 1 cup Spinach
- ½ cup Parsley, chopped
- 2 cups Almond Milk
- Salt and Pepper, to taste
- Almonds for seasoning

DIRECTIONS

Place chicken in a bowl. In a separate bowl, mix onion, mushrooms, garlic, spinach and parsley. Add milk, salt, and pepper. Get a round baking tray and grease it with oil.

Add chicken and the mixture. Place the trivet inside the pot, add 1 cup of water to the bottom and place the baking tray inside. Seal the lid and cook for 10 minutes on High pressure. When ready, do a quick pressure release and serve with almond seasoning.

Nutrition facts per serving: Calories 295, Protein 41g, Net Carbs 6.3g, Fat 9g

Chicken Meatballs with Parmesan

Prep + Cook Time: 25 minutes | Servings: 4

INGREDIENTS

- 1 pound ground Chicken
- ½ Onion, grated
- ½ cup Almond flour
- ¼ cup grated Parmesan Cheese
- ¼ cup Salsa or Tomato Sauce
- 1 Egg
- Salt and Pepper, to taste

DIRECTIONS

Pour the water in the Pot and lower the trivet. Place all ingredients in a large bowl and mix with hands until well combined. Shape into meatballs, and arrange on a previously greased baking dish that can fit inside the Instant Pot.

Place the dish on top of the trivet and seal the lid, Cook on HIGH pressure for 15 minutes. After the beep, do a quick pressure release and open the lid carefully. Serve immediately.

Nutrition facts per serving: Calories 223, Protein 22g, Net Carbs 2g, Fat 12g

Tasrty Fried Chicken

Prep + Cook Time: 35 minutes | Servings: 4

INGREDIENTS

1 cup ground Chicken
1 Onion, chopped
2 Garlic cloves, minced
¼ tsp Cumin powder
¼ tsp Cinnamon powder

2 Tomatoes, chopped
1 tsp salt
½ tsp black Pepper
2 tbsp Olive oil

DIRECTIONS

Heat oil on Sauté, and stir-fry garlic and onion for 1 minute. Add the ground chicken and stir fry until its color changes. Season with salt and pepper.

Stir in the tomatoes and sauté for 3-4 minutes. Cook for 5-8 minutes more, then press Cancel. Sprinkle cumin and cinnamon powder, and serve hot.

Nutrition facts per serving: Calories 452, Protein 41g, Net Carbs 4.1g, Fat 43g

Curried Chicken Patties

Prep + Cook Time: 23 minutes | Servings: 4

INGREDIENTS

1 Egg
¼ cup grated Parmesan Cheese
1 pound Ground Chicken
1 tbsp chopped Parsley
¼ cup Cauliflower Rice

1 tsp Curry Powder
Salt and Pepper, to taste
2 tbsp Olive oil
1 ½ cups Water

DIRECTIONS

Pour in water t and lower the trivet. Grease a baking dish that fits in the pot with cooking spray.Place the chicken, egg, curry powder, parsley, cauliflower, and parmesan in a large bowl.

Season with salt and pepper, and mix the mixture with hands. Shape the mixture into 4 patties and arrange them in the baking dish. Place the dish on top of the trivet and seal the lid.

Cook for 10 minutes on HIGH pressure. When ready, do a quick pressure release. Set the baking dish aside an discard the water. Wipe the pot clean.

Set on Sauté and heat half of the oil. Place 2 patties inside and cook for 2 minutes per side, until golden. Repeat with the remaining oil and patties. Serve with tomato or yogurt dip.

Nutrition facts per serving: Calories 223, Protein 25g, Net Carbs 2g, Fat 19g

Turkey Stew with Veggies

Prep + Cook Time: 25 minutes | Servings: 4

INGREDIENTS

2 Turkey Breasts, chopped finely
1 cup Broccoli Florets
1 cup chopped Celery
1 cup chopped Snow Peas
1 cup Spinach

1 cup diced Tomatoes
3 cups Chicken Broth
Salt and Pepper, to taste
2 tbsp Butter
Salt and Pepper, to taste

DIRECTIONS

Melt butter on Sauté. Season the turkey with salt and peppers, and add in the pot. Cook for 5 minutes, or until golden and cooked through. Stir in tomatoes and celery; cook for 2 minutes.

Stir in the remaining ingredients and season with salt and pepper. Seal the lid, select Manual and set the cooking time to 8 minutes. Cook on HIGH pressure. When it goes off, do a natural pressure release by allowing the pressure valve to drop on its own.

Nutrition facts per serving: Calories 316, Protein 22g, Net Carbs 8.9g, Fat 12g

Turkey Breasts in Italian Sauce

Prep + Cook Time: 30 minutes | Servings: 6

INGREDIENTS

1 cup Tomato Sauce
½ cup Sour Cream
1 tsp Italian Seasoning
⅓ cup chopped Sun-Dried Tomatoes
1 pound Turkey Breasts, chopped

1 tbsp Olive oil
1 tbsp chopped Basil
2 Garlic Cloves, minced
2 tbsp grated Parmesan Cheese

DIRECTIONS

Heat the olive oil on Sauté. When hot and sizzling, add the garlic and cook for 40 seconds. Add the breasts, season with salt and pepper, and cook until golden.

Stir in tomato sauce, sour cream, tomatoes, and Italian seasoning. Seal the lid, select Manual and set the cooking time to 10 minutes. Cook on HIGH pressure.

When ready, do a quick pressure release. Stir in the basil and sprinkle with Parmesan cheese.

Nutrition facts per serving: Calories 346, Protein 31g, Net Carbs 6.1g, Fat 22g

Simple Chicken Soup

Preparation Time: 46 minutes | Servings: 2

INGREDIENTS

2 tbsp Olive oil
1 large Carrot, chopped
1 large Celery Stalk, chopped
1 large White Onion, chopped
6 cloves Garlic, minced
1 Green Chili Pepper, sliced
Salt to taste

Black Pepper to taste
1 inch Ginger, grated
2 cups Chicken Broth
1 cup Water
2 tbsp Palin Vinegar
1 lb Chicken Breasts

DIRECTIONS

Heat oil on Sauté, and add all vegetables. Stir and cook for 3 minutes. Stir in broth, chicken, vinegar and water. Seal the lid and cook on Soup for 10 minutes on High.

Once ready, release pressure naturally for 10 minutes, then quickly release the pressure. Remove the chicken, shred and return to the pot. Select Sauté and cook for 3 minutes.

Nutrition facts per serving: Calories 146, Protein 14g, Net Carbs 4g, Fat 4g

Worcestershire Turkey Cubes

Prep + Cook Time: 24 minutes | Servings: 4

INGREDIENTS

1 pound Turkey Breast
1 ½ cups Chicken Broth
1 tbsp Worcestershire Sauce
1 cup Sour Cream
¼ cup grated Parmesan Cheese
1 tsp Dijon Mustard
¼ tsp Garlic Powder
Salt and Pepper, to taste

DIRECTIONS

Add the turkey and broth in the Instant Pot and seal the lid. Select Manual and cook on HIGH pressure for 10 minutes. When the timer goes off, do a quick pressure release.

Transfer the turkey to a cutting board and cut into cubes. Discard broth and wipe the pot clean. Whisk together the remaining ingredients and place the cubes inside. Cook on Sauté for 2 minutes.

Nutrition facts per serving: Calories 283, Protein 27g, Net Carbs 3.5g, Fat 21g

Chicken Enchilada Soup

Preparation Time: 35 minutes | Servings: 5

INGREDIENTS

2 tbsp Olive oil
2 ½ cups Carrots, chopped
2 ½ cups Celery, chopped
1 cup Yellow Onions, chopped
3 cloves Garlic, minced
3 tbsp Taco Seasoning
Salt to taste
Pepper to taste
1 ½ cups Diced Tomatoes
2 ½ cups Chopped Butternut Squash
5 ½ cups Chicken Broth
2 lb Chicken Breast, skinless
3 tsp Lime Juice
Lime Wedges to garnish
Chopped Cilantro to garnish

DIRECTIONS

Heat oil on Sauté, add celery, onion, carrots, garlic, taco seasoning, pepper, and salt. Keep stirring for 5 minutes. Stir in the remaining ingredients, seal the lid and cook on Soup mode for 10 minutes. Once ready, press Cancel and do a quick release.

Remove the chicken on a plate and shred. Stir the chicken back to the pot. Serve the soup, garnish with cilantro and lemon wedges.

Nutrition facts per serving: Calories 213, Protein 10g, Net Carbs 3g, Fat 13g

Perfected Butter Chicken

Preparation Time: 20 minutes | Servings: 3

INGREDIENTS

4 Chicken Breasts, skinless and cubed
1 tbsp Olive oil
1 Onion, chopped
Salt to taste
1 tsp Garlic Powder
1 tsp Ginger Powder
1 tsp Turmeric
1 tsp Paprika
1 tsp Cayenne Powder
2 cups Diced Tomato
2 tbsp Tomato Puree
1 cup Coconut Milk Whey
1 cup Coconut Cream
¼ cup Almonds, sliced
¼ cup Chopped Cilantro

DIRECTIONS

Heat oil on Sauté, and cook the onions and salt for 3 minutes. Add the remaining listed spices and pepper. Stir and cook for 2 minutes. Add the tomatoes and coconut milk whey, and stir.

Add chicken, stir well, and seal the lid. Cook on High Pressure for 10 minutes. Once ready, quickly release the pressure. Add the tomato puree, coconut milk and cilantro. Stir and adjust salt seasoning. Serve stew with almond garnishing.

Nutrition facts per serving: Calories 243, Protein 24g, Net Carbs 4g, Fat 13g

Sweet and Chili Goose Breasts

Prep + Cook Time: 30 minutes | Servings: 6

INGREDIENTS

1 pound Goose Breasts
1 cup Chicken Broth
3 tbsp Tamari Sauce
1 tbsp Sweetener
3 tbsp Low-Carb Chili Sauce
Salt and Pepper, to taste
½ cup water

DIRECTIONS

Season the goose breasts with salt and pepper and place them in the Instant Pot. In a bowl, whisk together all remaining ingredients and pour mixture over the goose. Seal the lid, select Manual and set the cooking time to 15 minutes. Cook on HIGH pressure.

When ready, press Cancel, do a quick pressure release. Serve topped with the sauce.

Nutrition facts per serving: Calories 312, Protein 28g, Net Carbs 5.5g, Fat 19g

Chicken Zoodle Soup

Preparation Time: 36 minutes | Servings: 2

INGREDIENTS

1 tbsp Olive Oil
1 small Onion, chopped
2 Carrots, sliced
2 Celery Ribs, diced
1 small Banana Pepper, minced
1 clove Garlic, minced
Salt and Black Pepper to taste
1 small Bay Leaf
2 Chicken Breasts, skinless
3 cups Chicken Broth
1 tbsp Plain Vinegar
3 small Zucchinis, spiralized

DIRECTIONS

Heat oil on Sauté, stir in onion, celery, carrots, garlic, pepper, salt and black pepper and cook for 4 minutes. Add bay leaf and place the chicken on the veggies. Pour in broth and vinegar.

Seal the lid and cook on High Pressure for 15 minutes. Once ready, quickly release the pressure. Remove the chicken, shred and return to the soup. Add the zucchinis, select Sauté and cook for 2 minutes. Dish into soup bowls and serve.

Nutrition facts per serving: Calories 164, Protein 19g, Net Carbs 3g, Fat 5g

Crack Chicken

Preparation Time: 23 minutes | Servings: 3 to 5

INGREDIENTS

10 Bacon Slices, chopped
2 lb Chicken Breast, Boneless
1 packet Ranch Seasoning

10 oz Cream Cheese
½ cup Water
1 ½ cups Cheddar Cheese

DIRECTIONS

Add cream cheese and chicken to the Instant Pot. Sprinkle the seasoning over and pour the water. Seal the lid, and cook on High Pressure for 15 minutes. Do a quick pressure release.

Remove the chicken, shred and return to the pot. On Sauté, add the bacon and cream cheese. Cook until fully melted. Serve as a dip, sauce or appetizer.

Nutrition facts per serving: Calories 466, Protein 41g, Net Carbs 2g, Fat 34g

Creamy Garlic Tuscan Chicken Thighs

Preparation Time: 41 minutes | Servings: 4

INGREDIENTS

6 Chicken Thighs, fat removed
6 oz Cream Cheese
3 cups Spinach
½ cup Sundried Tomatoes
2 tbsp Chicken Stock Seasoning
½ cup Parmesan Cheese, grated
4 cloves Garlic, minced
2 tsp Olive oil

2 cups Chicken Broth
1 ½ cups Unsweetened Almond Milk
3 tbsp Heavy Cream
3 tsp Italian Seasoning
2 tsp Water
Salt and Black Pepper to taste
Chopped Parsley to garnish

DIRECTIONS

Season chicken with pepper, salt, and Italian seasoning. Heat oil on Sauté, and brown the chicken for 6 minutes in total. Add milk, broth, stock seasoning and Italian seasoning.

Seal the Instant Pot, and cook on High Pressure for 15 minutes. Once ready, quickly release the pressure. Remove the chicken on a plate.

To the pot, add tomatoes, heavy cream, cheese cream, Parmesan, spinach and garlic. Select Sauté and cook for 5 minutes. Add the chicken to the sauce, and coat well. Top with parsley.

Nutrition facts per serving: Calories 211, Protein 17g, Net Carbs 6g, Fat 9g

Creamy Duck with Spinach

Prep + Cook Time: 23 minutes | Servings: 4

INGREDIENTS

1 pound Duck Breasts
2 cups Spinach
¼ cup grated Parmesan Cheese
1 cup Heavy Cream
8 ounces Cream Cheese
¼ cup Chicken Broth
1 tbsp Olive oil
1 tsp minced Garlic
Salt and Pepper, to taste

DIRECTIONS

Set on Sauté and add the olive oil to it. When hot, add the garlic and cook 1 minute. Add the duck and cook for about 3-4 minutes per side, until golden. Transfer to a plate and slice thinly.

Whisk together the remaining ingredients in the Instant Pot and add the duck inside. Seal the lid, select Manual and set the cooking time to 5 minutes. Cook on HIGH pressure.

When it goes off, press Cancel, do a quick pressure release and serve immediately.

Nutrition facts per serving: Calories 355, Protein 30g, Net Carbs 4g, Fat 18g

Creamy Chicken with Broccoli

Preparation Time: 40 minutes | Servings: 4

INGREDIENTS

2 tbsp Olive oil
2 tbsp Butter
3 Chicken Breasts, cut in 1 inch pieces
2 Onions, chopped
2 cups Chicken Broth
Salt and Black Pepper to taste
¼ tsp Red Chili Flakes
2 tbsp Dried Parsley
6 oz Cream Cheese, cubed in 2 inch pieces
1 ¼ cup Cheddar Cheese
4 cups Broccoli florets, steamed

DIRECTIONS

Season the chicken breasts with pepper and salt. Heat oil and butter on Sauté, and brown the chicken on each side for 4 minutes. Set aside. Add onion, stir and cook for 5 minutes.

Add the broth, pepper, salt, red pepper flakes, chicken, and parsley. Seal the lid, and cook on High Pressure for 4 minutes. Once ready, quickly release the pressure.

Press Sauté, add the cream and cheddar cheeses. Cook until the cheese is fully melted. Add the broccoli, and cook until heated through. Turn off Instant Pot and serve immediately.

Nutrition facts per serving: Calories 195, Protein 18g, Net Carbs 2g, Fat 11.5g

Chicken Taco Filling

Preparation Time: 40 minutes | Servings: 6

INGREDIENTS

2 Onion, chopped
4 tbsp Olive oil
8 Chicken Breast, Boneless
1 ½ cups Chopped Tomatoes
2 tbsp Chili Powder
Salt to taste
Pepper to taste

DIRECTIONS

Heat oil on Sauté, and cook the onion for 5 minutes. Add the remaining ingredients. Seal the lid and cook on High Pressure for 15 minutes. Once ready, quickly release the pressure.

Remove the chicken onto a plate and shred with a fork. Return the chicken to the pot and stir in the tomato sauce. Select Sauté mode and cook until liquid evaporates.

Nutrition facts per serving: Calories 215, Protein 33g, Net Carbs 0g, Fat 6g

No Cream Chicken and Broccoli

Preparation Time: 23 minutes | Servings: 3

INGREDIENTS

4 Chicken Breasts, Boneless and skinless
1 cup Chicken Broth
1 cup Coconut Aminos
3 tbsp Olive oil
½ tsp Fish Sauce
1 inch Ginger, grated
1 clove Garlic, minced

Salt and Black Pepper to taste
¼ tsp Plain Vinegar
4 cup Broccoli Florets
Sesame seeds, for garnish
2 tbsp Arrowroot Flour
2 tbsp Water

DIRECTIONS

Add chicken, broth, olive oil, garlic, ginger, coconut aminos, pepper, and salt. Seal the lid, and cook on High Pressure for 8 minutes. Once ready, quickly release the pressure.

In a bowl, mix the arrowroot and water, and add to the pot. Select Sauté, add the broccoli, stir and cook for 5 minutes. Add the vinegar, stir and serve sauce. Garnish with sesame seeds.

Nutrition facts per serving: Calories 213, Protein 18g, Net Carbs 2g, Fat 15g

Buffalo Chicken Meatballs

Preparation Time: 52 minutes | Servings: 3

INGREDIENTS

1 lb Ground Chicken
¼ cup Almond Meal
Salt to taste
1 clove Garlic, minced
1 Scallion, sliced thinly

2 tbsp Olive oil
3 tbsp Hot Sauce
2 tbsp Butter
Chopped Scallions to garnish

DIRECTIONS

In a bowl, add almond meal, chicken, garlic, salt and scallions. Mix everything with hands to coat the meat. Oil your hands and make meatballs out of the mixture.

Heat oil on Sauté, and fry the meatballs until brown for about 25 minutes; cook in batches if needed. Meanwhile, add the butter and hot sauce to a bowl, and heat them in a microwave.

Stir and set aside. Place all meat balls back to the pot and pour the hot sauce over. Seal the lid, and cook on High Pressure for 15 minutes. Once ready, quickly release the pressure.

Nutrition facts per serving: Calories 165, Protein 20g, Net Carbs 1g, Fat 12g

Ranch and Lemon Whole Chicken

Prep + Cook Time: 40 minutes | Servings: 6

INGREDIENTS

1 Chicken (medium size)
1 ½ cups Chicken Broth
1 Onion, quartered
1 ½ tsp Ranch Seasoning
½ tsp Lemon Pepper

1 Lemon, halved
1 Thyme Sprig
1 Rosemary Sprig
2 Garlic Cloves
1 tbsp Butter

DIRECTIONS

In a bowl combine the Ranch seasoning and lemon pepper, and rub the seasoning onto the chicken. Melt butter on Sauté. add the chicken and sear on all sides, until golden. Set aside.

Stuff the chicken's cavity with lemon, onion, garlic, thyme, and rosemary. Place the chicken back in the Instant Pot and pour the broth in. Seal the lid and cook on POULTRY for 30 minutes on High pressure.

When ready, do a quick pressure release. Let chicken sit for 10 minutes before serving.

Nutrition facts per serving: Calories 243, Protein 25g, Net Carbs 2.5g, Fat 28g

Chicken Thighs with Bacon and Cheese

Prep + Cook Time: 30 minutes | Servings: 4

INGREDIENTS

4 Chicken Thighs
8 ounces Cream Cheese
½ cup shredded Cheddar Cheese
5 Bacon Slices, cooked and crumbled
¼ tsp Garlic Powder

¼ tsp Italian Seasoning
Salt and Pepper, to taste
1 cup Chicken Broth
2 tbsp Arrowroot

DIRECTIONS

Whisk together the chicken broth, cream cheese, and all seasonings. Place the chicken thighs inside and seal the lid. Cook on HIGH pressure for 18 minutes.

When ready, do a quick pressure release. Remove the thighs to a plate and set to Sauté. Whisk in the arrowroot and cook for 2 minutes, or until the sauce thickens. Serve hot.

Nutrition facts per serving: Calories 419, Protein 40g, Net Carbs 4.5g, Fat 45g

Hot Chicken Stew

Prep + Cook Time: 25 minutes | Servings: 4

INGREDIENTS

1 ½ cups Chicken Broth
⅓ cup Hot Sauce
½ Onion, diced
2 Garlic Cloves, minced
1 Jalapeno, seeded and diced
1 cup Heavy Cream

2 cups shredded Cheddar Cheese
2 Chicken Breasts
2 tbsp Butter
1 Celery Stalk, diced
½ cup chopped Cauliflower Florets
Salt and Pepper, to taste

DIRECTIONS

Place everything, except the cream and cheese, inside your Instant Pot. Give it a good stir to combine and seal the lid on. Turn the lid clockwise to seal the pot properly.

Cook on HIGH pressure for 15 minutes. When it goes off, do a quick pressure release. Stir in the heavy cream and the cheese, and ladle into 4 bowls to serve.

Nutrition facts per serving: Calories 476, Protein 42g, Net Carbs 3.7g, Fat 35g

Chicken Breasts with Button Mushrooms and Coconut

Prep + Cook Time: 25 minutes | Servings: 4

INGREDIENTS

4 Chicken Breasts, boneless and skinless
⅔ cup Chicken Broth
1 can Coconut Cream
1 pound Button Mushrooms, sliced

2 tbsp Arrowroot
2 tbsp Water
Salt and Pepper, to taste
¼ tsp Garlic Powder

DIRECTIONS

Combine the broth and coconut cream in your Instant Pot. Stir in the garlic powder and season with salt and pepper. Season the breasts with salt and pepper, and place them inside the Pot.

Stir in the mushrooms. Seal the lid, select MANUAL and cook for 10 minutes on HIGH pressure. When it goes off, release the pressure quickly. Transfer the chicken to a plate.

Whisk the water and arrowroot together and stir the mixture into the sauce. Set the Instant Pot to Sauté and cook for 2 minutes until it thickens. Return the chicken to the pot and cook for 1 minute. Serve immediately!

Nutrition facts per serving: Calories 370, Protein 35g, Net Carbs 6g, Fat 29g

Chicken Soup with Veggies

Prep + Cook Time: 30 minutes | Servings: 6

INGREDIENTS

½ pound Chicken Breast, whole
1 cup Broccoli Florets
1 cup Cauliflower Florets
½ cup chopped Celery Stalk
1 Tomato, diced
1 cup chopped Zucchini

6 cups Chicken Broth
½ cup Sour Cream
½ tsp Garlic Powder
½ tsp Onion Powder
1 tbsp chopped Parsley
Salt and Pepper, to taste

DIRECTIONS

Add chicken and broth to the Instant Pot. Seal the lid, select Manual and ook on HIGH pressure for 15 minutes. When the timer goes off, do a quick pressure release.

Transfer the chicken to a cutting board and shred with two forks. Stir in the remaining ingredients, except the sour cream. Seal the lid and cook on HIGH pressure for 5 minutes.

Do a quick pressure release. Stir in the chicken and sour cream and serve immediately.

Nutrition facts per serving: Calories 255, Protein 22g, Net Carbs 6.2g, Fat 18g

Greek Chicken Casserole

Prep + Cook Time: 25 minutes | Servings: 4

INGREDIENTS

1 pound Chicken Breasts, chopped
½ cup sliced Kalamata Olives
1 cup halved Cherry Tomatoes
1 cup Cauliflower Rice
1 tbsp chopped Basil

1 tsp chopped Oregano
1 cup Chicken Broth
1 cup Sour Cream or Cream Cheese
Salt and Pepper, to taste

DIRECTIONS

Dump all ingredients in your Instant Pot. Give the mixture a good stir until fully incorporated. Seal the lid and cook on HIGH pressure for 15 minutes. When you hear the beep, release the pressure quickly. Careful open the lid and stir once again before serving.

Nutrition facts per serving: Calories 382, Protein 35g, Net Carbs 4.5g, Fat 35g

Easy and Cheesy Chicken and Cauliflower

Prep + Cook Time: 10 minutes | Servings: 4

INGREDIENTS

2 ½ cups cooked and shredded Chicken
½ cup Half and Half
2 cups chopped Cauliflower
½ cup shredded Mozzarella Cheese

½ cup Chicken Broth
¼ tsp Garlic Powder
A pinch of Onion Powder
Salt and Pepper, to taste

DIRECTIONS

Place all ingredients in your Instant Pot. Stir well to combine and seal the lid. Turn it clockwise for proper sealing. Select MANUAL and cook on HIGH pressure for 2 minutes.

When it goes off, do a quick pressure release and open the lid. Set to Sauté. Cook for 3 lid off.

Nutrition facts per serving: Calories 344, Protein 30g, Net Carbs 2.5g, Fat 25g

Mexican Chicken

Prep + Cook Time: 25 minutes | Servings: 4

INGREDIENTS

1 pound Chicken Breasts, boneless and skinless
¾ tsp Cumin
1 Jalapeno, seeded and diced
1 cup mild Salsa or Tomato Sauce
½ tsp Onion Powder

¼ tsp Garlic Powder
1 cup Sour Cream
A pinch of Smoked Paprika
Salt and Pepper, to taste

DIRECTIONS

Whisk together the salsa and sour cream inside the Instant Pot. Stir in the jalapeno and all the spices. Place the chicken inside and seal the lid. Cook on HIGH pressure for 15 minutes.

When the timer goes off, do a quick pressure release. Shred the chicken inside the pot, stir and serve.

Nutrition facts per serving: Calories 251, Protein 29g, Net Carbs 5g, Fat 21g

Chicken Carnitas

Preparation Time: 59 minutes | Servings: 3

INGREDIENTS

1 lb Chicken Breast, skinless
1 tbsp Olive oil + more
½ tbsp Cumin Powder
½ tsp dried Oregano
1 tsp Chili Powder
Salt and Black Pepper to taste
1 Lemon, zested and juiced
3 tbsp Lime Juice

¼ cup Chicken Broth
3 cloves Garlic, minced
1 medium White Onion, chopped
1 Chipotle Pepper
1 tbsp Adobo Sauce
1 bay Leaf
¼ cup Cilantro, chopped

Sauce:

¼ cup Mayonnaise
2 tsp Milk
1 Chipotle Pepper

1 tbsp Adobo Sauce
A pinch Salt
A pinch Garlic Powder

DIRECTIONS

In a bowl, mix oregano, salt, pepper, and chili powder. Season the chicken with the pepper mixture. Set the pot on Sauté, add 1 tbsp of oil, and sear the chicken on both sides. Remove to a plate.

Add in garlic and onion, stir and cook for 2 minutes. Add the chicken with the lemon zest, lemon juice, chipotle pepper, bay leaf, adobo sauce, chicken broth and cilantro. Seal the lid and cook on High Pressure for 10 minutes. Once ready, do a quick pressure release.

Preheat oven to 350 F. Transfer the chicken to a bowl and shred it with 2 forks. Drizzle 6 tablespoons of the cooking liquid over it and stir. Coat a baking tray with olive oil, add the chicken and level it. Drizzle another tablespoon of oil on top of the chicken.

Place the tray in the oven and broil for 12 minutes. Toss the chicken and drizzle some more cooking liquid on 6 minutes into broiling. To make the sauce, place all sauce ingredients in a blender and process until smooth. Serve chicken with sauce.

Nutrition facts per serving: Calories 192, Protein 26.4g, Net Carbs 1g, Fat 6.8g

Cajun Drumsticks

Prep + Cook Time: 30 minutes | Servings: 5

INGREDIENTS

1 tbsp Butter
½ Onion, diced
2 tsp Cajun Seasoning
2 Garlic Cloves, minced

1 ½ cups Chicken Broth
2 tbsp Tomato Paste
5 Chicken drumsticks
Salt and Pepper, to taste

DIRECTIONS

Set on Sauté and melt the butter. Add the onions and cook for 3-4 minutes. Stir in the garlic cloves and cook for 1 minute. When fragrant, pour in broth and whisk in the tomato sauce.

Season the drumsticks with the Cajun seasoning, salt, and pepper, and place them inside the tomato-flavored broth. Seal the lid, select Manual and cook for 15 minutes on HIGH pressure.

When ready, allow for a natural pressure release, for 10 minutes. Serve with cauli rice.

Nutrition facts per serving: Calories 453, Protein 42g, Net Carbs 1g, Fat 35g

Chicken Daikon and Cabbage Soup

Preparation Time: 50 minutes | Servings: 4

INGREDIENTS

2 lb assorted Chicken Pieces, Bone in
1 White Onion, quartered
½ inch Ginger, grated
2 tsp Coriander Seeds
½ tsp Green Cardamom Pods
1 Black Cardamom Pods
½ inch Cinnamon Stick
4 Cloves

Garnishing:
Lime Wedges
1 Jalapeno, sliced thinly

4 cups Chicken Broth
½ Lemongrass Stalk, cut in long chops
3 tbsp Fish Sauce
½ cup Cilantro, chopped
1 small head Green Cabbage
1 Daikon, spiralized
Salt to taste

1 small White Onion, sliced thinly
3 Basil Leaves

DIRECTIONS

Place a pan over medium heat, add toast the coriander seeds until fragrant. Turn the heat off, and set aside. Place the chicken in the Instant Pot, add the cilantro, fish sauce, chicken broth, lemongrass, onion, coriander seeds and all other listed dry spices.

Seal the lid, secure the pressure valve and cook on High Pressure for 10 minutes. Once ready, quickly release the pressure. Shred the chicken in the pot, and strain the content afterwards. Return the broth to the pot, season with salt. Select Sauté and simmer for 3 minutes. Add the vegetables and cook for 6 minutes. Serve the soup wth garnishing ingredients.

Nutrition facts per serving: Calories 130, Protein 16g, Net Carbs 2.1g, Fat 3g

Mexican Risotto with Turkey

Prep + Cook Time: 33 minutes | Servings: 4

INGREDIENTS

4 cups Cauliflower Rice
2 Turley Breasts
1 ½ cup Chicken Broth
¼ tsp Cumin
¼ tsp Garlic Powder
¼ Red Onion, diced

1 Jalapeno, diced and seeded
½ cup mild Salsa
½ cup Tomato Sauce
Salt and Pepper, to taste
1 tbsp Olive oil

DIRECTIONS

Pour in the broth. Season the turkey with salt and pepper, and add it to the Instant Pot. Seal the lid, select Manual and set the cooking time to 15 minutes. Cook on HIGH pressure.

When ready, do a quick pressure release. Remove the turkey to a cutting board. Grab two forks and shred the meat. Discard broth and wipe the pot clean.

Set on Sauté, and add olive oil. When hot, add the onions and cook until soft. Stir in the remaining ingredients, including the turkey, and cook for 5 minutes. Serve immediately.

Nutrition facts per serving: Calories 346, Protein 18g, Net Carbs 5g, Fat 22g

Chicken Lazone

Preparation Time: 47 minutes | Servings: 6

INGREDIENTS

3 tsp Garlic Powder
2 tsp Onion Powder
2 tsp Paprika
2 tsp Cayenne Powder
Salt to taste
Pepper to taste

2 ½ Chicken Strips
3 tbsp Butter
3 tbsp Oil
⅓ cup Chicken Broth
2 ½ cups Heavy Cream
3 tbsp Chopped Parsley

DIRECTIONS

Add onion powder, salt, pepper, cayenne pepper, garlic powder and paprika to a large bowl, and mix. Rub the spices onto and add it to the pot. Heat oil and butter on Sauté, and brown the chicken pieces; cook in batches. About 10 minutes per batch. Remove to on a plate.

Return the chicken and broth back to the pot. Seal the lid and cook on High Pressure for 4 minutes. Once ready, quickly release the pressure. Select Sauté and stir in the heavy cream. Cook until the sauce thickens. Dish sauce in serving bowls and garnish with parsley.

Nutrition facts per serving: Calories 484, Protein 28g, Net Carbs 2.2g, Fat 29g

Butternut Squash with Turkey Chili

Preparation Time: 44 minutes | Servings: 5

INGREDIENTS

2 tbsp Olive oil
2 Onions, chopped
5 cloves Garlic, minced
3 tsp Turmeric
3 tsp Cumin Powder
2 tsp Cayenne Powder
2 tsp Cinnamon Powder
Salt to taste
Black Pepper to taste

1 ½ lb Minced Turkey
6 cups Chopped Butternut Squash
6 cups Vegetable Broth
2 cups Diced Tomatoes
2 cups light Coconut Milk
4 tbsp Tomato Puree
3 tbsp Plain Vinegar
3 cups Kale
Chopped Scallions and Cilantro for garnishing

DIRECTIONS

Heat oil on Sauté and cook garlic and onion for 5 minutes. Brown the turkey and stir to break up the lumps. Add the spices, stir and cook for 2 minutes. Stir in tomatoes, broth, squash, tomato paste, coconut milk and vinegar.

Seal the lid and cook on Soup mode for 20 minutes. Once ready, quickly release the pressure. Stir in the kale leaves, and allow the leaves wilt for a few minutes. Serve chili, garnish with scallions and cilantro.

Nutrition facts per serving: Calories 224, Protein 20g, Net Carbs 2g, Fat 8g

Lemon and Olive Ligurian

Preparation Time: 40 minutes | Servings: 4

INGREDIENTS

Marinade:

3 cloves Garlic, minced
4 sprigs Rosemary, chopped
3 sprigs Fresh Sage
¼ cup Parsley, not chopped
4 Lemons, juice

5 tbsp Olive oil
Salt to taste
Pepper to taste
2 cups Water

Other Ingredients

1 lb Chicken Thighs, skinless
¼ cup Dry White Wine
2 cups Black Olives, cured
3 tbsp Olive oil

2 Lemon Wedges for garnishing
1 sprig Rosemary for garnishing
Water

DIRECTIONS

In a bowl, mix all marinade ingredients and pour over the chicken. Marinate for 4 hours. Heat the oil on Sauté and brown the chicken on all sides; set aside.

Pour in wine to deglaze the bottom of the pot, and boil for 3 minutes. Add the chicken back to the pot, and pour the marinade and a little bit of water to about halfway up the chicken.

Seal the lid and cook on High Pressure mode for 10 minutes. Once ready, quickly release the pressure. Remove chicken on a serving a plate. Select Sauté and simmer the juices in the pot until boil down to a thicker consistency. Drizzle sauce over chicken, and serve.

Nutrition facts per serving: Calories 204, Protein 17.8g, Net Carbs 2.8g, Fat 12.2g

Tarragon and Mushroom Chicken

Prep + Cook Time: 25 minutes | Servings: 4

INGREDIENTS

1 tbsp chopped Tarragon
4 Chicken Thighs
1 tbsp Tomato Paste
¼ cup Butter

2 cups sliced Mushrooms
1 ¼ cups Chicken Broth
Salt and Pepper, to taste
1 tsp minced Garlic

DIRECTIONS

Set Sauté and melt the butter. Add the garlic and cook for 30 seconds. Season the chicken thighs with salt and pepper and place them inside the Pot. Cook for 3 minutes, or until golden.

Remove thighs to a plate. Add the mushrooms and tomato paste to the pot and cook for 2 minutes. Then, pour in broth and stir to combine the mixture.

Stir in tarragon and return the thighs. Seal the lid and cook on High pressure for 10 minutes. When ready, do a quick pressure release. Serve with steamed greens.

Nutrition facts per serving: Calories 262, Protein 19g, Net Carbs 2,2g, Fat 24g

Leftover Chicken in Spicy Tomato Sauce

Prep + Cook Time: 16 minutes | Servings: 4

INGREDIENTS

2 cups cooked and shredded Chicken Meat
14 ounces diced canned Tomatoes
¼ cup Chicken Broth
1 tsp Chili Powder
¼ tsp Garlic Powder

¼ tsp Pepper
¼ tsp salt
1 cup Cauliflower Rice
¼ cup Sour Cream

DIRECTIONS

Place all ingredients in the Instant Pot. Give it a good stir, until chicken is thoroughly coated with the sauce. Seal the lid, press Manual, and cook for 6 minutes on HIGH pressure.

When ready, press Cancel and do a quick pressure release. Serve hot with keto bread.

Nutrition facts per serving: Calories 311, Protein 19g, Net Carbs 6.2g, Fat 18g

Simple Alfredo Shredded Chicken

Prep + Cook Time: 35 minutes | Servings: 6

INGREDIENTS

1 ½ lb boneless and skinless Chicken Breast
½ cup Keto Alfredo Sauce
½ cup Heavy Cream

¼ cup Chicken Broth
¼ tsp Garlic Powder
Salt and Pepper, to taste

DIRECTIONS

Whisk together broth, heavy cream, and Alfredo sauce. Season the chicken and sauce, with salt and pepper, and sprinkle with garlic powder. Seal the lid and turn the lid clockwise.

Press Manual and set the cooking time to 25 minutes on HIGH pressure. When it goes off, do a quick pressure release. With two forks shred the chicken inside the pot and serve.

Nutrition facts per serving: Calories 280, Protein 24g, Net Carbs 3.2g, Fat 12g

Shredded Chicken Pizza Casserole

Prep + Cook Time: 30 minutes | Servings: 6

INGREDIENTS

1 pound Chicken Breast
1 ¾ cups Marinara Sauce
1 tbsp Butter
½ tsp Italian Seasoning

4 ounces Pepperoni, sliced
6 ounces shredded Mozzarella Cheese
¼ cup Chicken Broth
Salt and Pepper, to taste

DIRECTIONS

Combine everything, except the cheese, in your Instant Pot. Give it a good stir and seal the lid. Select Manual and set the cooking time to 15 minutes. Cook on HIGH pressure.

After the beep, release the pressure quickly. Grab two forks and shred the chicken inside. Stir in the mozzarella cheese and set to Sauté. Cook for 5 minutes, until the cheese melts.

Nutrition facts per serving: Calories 335, Protein 27g, Net Carbs 3g, Fat 11g

No Beans Chicken Chili

Preparation Time: 27 minutes | Servings: 4

INGREDIENTS

1 lb Chicken Breast
6 oz Cream Cheese
¼ tsp Cumin Powder
Salt to taste
White Pepper to taste

1 cup Chicken Broth
½ tsp Cayenne Powder
½ cup Diced Tomatoes
Shredded American Cheese for garnishing
Sour Cream for garnishing

DIRECTIONS

Add all ingredients, except the cheese and sour cream. Seal the lid and cook on High Pressure for 15 minutes. Once ready, do a natural pressure release for 10 minutes, then quickly release the pressure. Shred with 2 forks and dish into bowls. Top with sour cream and cheese.

Nutrition facts per serving: Calories 417, Protein 31g, Net Carbs 1g, Fat 21g

Lemon Garlic Chicken

Preparation Time: 30 minutes | Servings: 3 to 4

INGREDIENTS

1 lb Chicken Breasts
Salt to taste
1 medium Onion, diced
1 tbsp Olive oil
3 cloves Garlic

¼ cup Chicken Broth
1 tsp dried Parsley
½ tsp Paprika
2 Lemons, juiced
2 tsp Almond flour

DIRECTIONS

Heat oil on Sauté, add onions and cook for 5 minutes. Stir in the remaining listed ingredients except for the flour. Seal the lid and cook on High Pressure for 15 minutes.

Once ready, quickly release the pressure. Fetch out a quarter cup of the sauce, add the flour, stir to combine, and add back the remaining sauce evenly. Stir and serve.

Nutrition facts per serving: Calories 153, Protein 21g, Net Carbs 6g, Fat 4g

KETO RED MEAT RECIPES

Beef and Broccoli Sauce

Prep + Cook Time: 45 minutes | Servings: 3

INGREDIENTS

1 lb Beef Chuck Roast, Boneless and cut in strips
Salt and Pepper to taste
2 tsp Olive oil
1 Onion, chopped
3 cloves Garlic
½ cup Beef Broth
¼ cup Soy Sauce
¼ cup Swerve Sweetener
2 tbsp Sesame OIl
⅛ Red Pepper Flakes
½ lb Broccoli Florets
2 tbsp Water
2 tbsp Arrowroot Flour
Toasted Sesame Seeds to garnish

DIRECTIONS

On Sauté, heat the olive oil, season the beef with pepper and salt. and brown on all sides. Remove to a plate and set aside. Add onion to the pot. Stir and cook for 2 minutes.

Add the garlic and cook for 1 minute. Add the pepper flakes, soy sauce, broth, sesame oil and sweetener. Mix until fully incorporated. Stir in the beef and resulting juices.

Seal the lid, select Manual and cook on HIgh Pressure mode for 12 minutes. Meanwhile, place broccoli in a bowl with ¼ cup of water and steam in a microwave for 3 minutes. To the pot, do a quick release. Mix the arrowroot flour with 2 tbsp of water, and stir in the sauce. Stir in the broccoli and serve in bowls with sesame seeds garnishing.

Nutrition facts per serving: Calories 235, Protein 19g, Net Carbs 2g, Fat 17g

Homemade Beef Stew

Prep + Cook Time: 55 minutes | Servings: 5

INGREDIENTS

2 lb Beef Chuck Roast, cubed in 2-inch pieces
Salt and Black Pepper to taste
1 tbsp Olive oil
1 large Onion., diced
½ lb Cremini Mushrooms, cleaned and quartered
1 tbsp Tomato Paste
4 cloves Garlic, crushed
1 ½ tbsp Coconut Aminos
1 tsp Fish Sauce
1 tsp dried Thyme
1 Bay Leaf
¼ cup Parsley, chopped

DIRECTIONS

Season the beef with salt. Heat the oil on Sauté, add the mushrooms, onions, and a pinch of salt. Stir and cook for 5 minutes. Add the garlic and tomato paste; cook for 1 minute.

Add the beef, thyme, coconut aminos, bay leaf and thyme. Stir well. Seal the lid, secure the pressure valve, and select Meat/Stew mode until the timer goes off, for 35 minutes.

Once ready, quickly release the pressure. Remove the bay leaf and scoop off any extra oils. Serve garnished with parsley.

Nutrition facts per serving: Calories 241, Protein 13g, Net Carbs 0g, Fat 13g

Beef, Tomato & Cabbage Soup

Prep + Cook Time: 65 minutes | Servings: 5 to 7

INGREDIENTS

2 lb Ground beef
Salt to taste
1 cup Diced Onion
1 cup Diced Celery
1 cup Diced Carrot

2 cups Crushed Tomatoes
6 cups Chopped Cabbages
5 cups Beef Broth
3 Bay Leaves

DIRECTIONS

Heat oil on Sauté, add the beef and brown while stirring. Add onion, carrots and celery. Stir and cook for 5 minutes. Add the cabbages, bay leaves, tomatoes and beef stock.

Close the lid, secure the pressure valve, and select Manual mode on High Pressure mode for 20 minutes. Once done, quickly release the pressure. Remove the bay leaf and stir.

Nutrition facts per serving: Calories 181, Protein 15.5g, Net Carbs 6g, Fat 6g

Beef Stroganoff

Prep + Cook Time: 30 minutes | Servings: 6

INGREDIENTS

2 lb Sirloin Steak Tips, cut into small cubes
1 large Onion, diced
5 cloves Garlic, minced
12 oz Mushrooms, chopped
1 ½ cups Beef Broth
½ cup Soy Sauce
½ Red Wine Vinegar

1 tsp Onion Powder
1 tsp Garlic Powder
1 cup Coconut Cream
2 tbsp Arrowroot Flour + 1 tbsp Water, mixed
Salt and Pepper to taste
2 tbsp Olive oil

DIRECTIONS

Heat oil on Sauté and stir-fry the onion and garlic for 2 minutes. Season the beef with onion powder, salt, garlic powder and pepper. Add to the pot.

In a bowl, mix the soy sauce, vinegar and broth. Pour over the beef, and add the mushrooms. Seal the lid and cook on High Pressure for 15 minutes. Once done, do a quick release. Stir in the coconut cream and cook for 3 minutes on Sauté. Add the arrowroot flour mixture and stir.

Nutrition facts per serving: Calories 394, Protein 26g, Net Carbs 6.3g, Fat 25g

Swedish Meatballs with Mushroom Gravy

Prep + Cook Time: 45 minutes | Servings: 4

INGREDIENTS

1 ½ lb Ground Beef
1 ½ lb Ground Pork
½ cup Chopped Parsley
3 tbsp dried Minced Onion
2 tsp dried Sage
1 tsp Nutmeg Powder

Salt to taste
3 cups Cremini Mushrooms, sliced
2 Onions, chopped
1 cup Beef Broth
3 tbsp Coconut Aminos

DIRECTIONS

In a bowl, mix the meats, parsley, onion, sage and nutmeg, and make 1-inch sized meatballs. Place the remaining ingredients in the Instant Pot and add in the meatballs. Seal the lid, secure the pressure valve, and select Meat/Stew mode for 35 minutes on High.

Once done, quick release the pressure. Remove the meatballs to a plate and puree the sauce in the pot with a stick blender. Spoon sauce over meatballs, garnish with parsley and serve.

Nutrition facts per serving: Calories 393, Protein 31g, Net Carbs 3g, Fat 14g

Beef Stuffed Grape Leaves

Prep + Cook Time: 1 hour 30 minutes | Servings: 12

INGREDIENTS

2 cups Grape Leaves, rinsed and separated
1 small Cauliflower, riced
2 lb Ground beef
2 tbsp Chopped Mint Leaves
2 tbsp Chopped Parsley
2 cloves Garlic, minced
1 tsp Cinnamon

2 tsp dried Oregano
2 tsp Garlic Powder
2 tsp Onion Powder
Salt to season
½ cup Water
2 Lemons, juiced

DIRECTIONS

In a bowl, add the beef, cauli rice, spices and herbs. Combine evenly with hands. Arrange a few grape leaves at the bottom of the pot. Place leaves on a flat surface and spoon beef mixture onto each leave. The size of the leaf will determine the quantity of beef mixture for it.

Fold the sides of each leaf first and roll it tightly. Arrange half of the wraps in the pot in the same direction, and repeat the same method for the second batch but in opposite directions. Add the water and lemon juice to the pot. Seal the lid, and cook on High Pressure for 30 minutes. Once ready, quickly release the pressure.

Nutrition facts per serving: Calories 245, Protein 24g, Net Carbs 5g, Fat 10.4g

Beef Short Ribs

Prep + Cook Time: 50 minutes | Servings: 3

INGREDIENTS

1 lb Beef Short Ribs
1 small Onion, chopped
1 tbsp Curry Powder
3 Star Anise

½ cup Water
1 ½ tbsp Tamari Sauce
1 tbsp White Wine
Salt to taste

DIRECTIONS

Put all ingredients in the Instant Pot. Seal the lid, secure the pressure valve, and select Meat/Stew mode for 45 minutes on High pressure. Once ready, press Cancel and release the pressure quickly. Stir and serve immediately with BBQ or hot sauce.

Nutrition facts per serving: Calories 531, Protein 36g, Net Carbs 2g, Fat 41g

Beef and Zoodle Soup

Prep + Cook Time: 30 minutes | Servings: 3

INGREDIENTS

1 tbsp Olive oil
2 tbsp Grated Ginger
1 clove Garlic, minced
1 lb Sirloin Steak Tips, cut in 1 inch pieces
1 cup Broccoli Florets
4 oz Bella Mushrooms, chopped
3 cups Beef Broth
4 tbsp Plain Vinegar
4 tbsp Soy Sauce
4 tbsp Hot Sauce
1 Zucchini, spiralized
2 Scallions, chopped

DIRECTIONS

On Sauté, add oil, garlic, ginger and meat; cook until browned. Add the remaining ingredients, except the zucchini and scallions. Seal the lid and cook on High Pressure mode for 8 minutes.

Once done, quickly release the pressure. Stir in zucchini and scallions. Stir and serve.

Nutrition facts per serving: Calories 157, Protein 21g, Net Carbs 3g, Fat 6.5g

Texas Beef Chili

Prep + Cook Time: 60 minutes | Servings: 3

INGREDIENTS

2 lb Ground beef
2 Green Bell pepper, diced
2 Onions, diced
6 large Carrots, chopped
1 cup Chopped Tomatoes
Salt and Black Pepper to taste
2 tsp Onion Powder
2 tbsp Chopped Parsley
2 tbsp Worcestershire Sauce
7 tsp Chili Powder
2 tsp Paprika
½ tsp Cumin Powder

DIRECTIONS

Set on Sauté and brown the beef. Stir in the remaining ingredients, seal the lid, and cook on Meat/Stew mode for 35 minutes on High. Once over, quickly release the pressure. Serve hot.

Nutrition facts per serving: Calories 225, Protein 14g, Net Carbs 2g, Fat 16g

Beef Curry Stew

Prep + Cook Time: 50 minutes | Servings: 3

INGREDIENTS

1 lb Beef Stew Chunks
2 cups Broccoli Florets
2 Zucchinis, cut in 3 inch chunks
¼ cup Chicken Broth
1 tbsp Curry Powder
1 tbsp Garlic Powder
Salt to taste
1 cup Coconut Milk

DIRECTIONS

Mix all ingredients, except the coconut milk, in the pot, while keeping the beef at the bottom.

Seal the lid, select Manual and cook on High Pressure mode for 45 minutes. Once done, quickly release the pressure. Stir in the coconut milk, and serve.

Nutrition facts per serving: Calories 490, Protein 30g, Net Carbs 5g, Fat 30g

Mocha Rubbed Pot Roast

Prep + Cook Time: 65 minutes | Servings: 6

INGREDIENTS

Mocha Rub:

2 ½ tbsp Ground Coffee
2 ½ tbsp Smoked Paprika
1 ½ tsp Black Pepper
1 ½ tsp Cocoa Powder

1 ½ tsp Red Pepper Flakes
1 ½ tsp Chili Powder
1 ½ tsp Ginger Paste
1 ½ tsp Salt

Roast:

2 ½ lb Beef Chuck Roast, cut in 2 inch cubes
1 ½ cup Brewed Coffee
1 ½ cup Beef Broth
1 medium Onion, chopped

2 tbsp Monk Fruit Syrup
3 tbsp Plain Vinegar
Salt and Black Pepper to taste

DIRECTIONS

Mix the mocha rub and rub onto beef. Pour coffee, monk fruit syrup, vinegar, onion and broth in a blender, and pulse to smooth. Add the beef to the Instant Pot and pour in coffee mixture.

Seal the lid, select Meat/Stew and cook for 35 minutes on High. Once ready, do a natural release for 15 minutes. Transfer to a platter, shred with forks and spoon sauce over, to serve.

Nutrition facts per serving: Calories 438, Protein 43g, Net Carbs 8g, Fat 23g

Plain Beef Broth Stew

Prep + Cook Time: 30 minutes | Servings: 3

INGREDIENTS

Spice Mix:

½ tsp Cumin Seeds
½ tsp Coriander Seeds
¼ tsp Black Peppercorns
½ tsp Salt

½ inch Cinnamon Stick
¼ tsp Cloves
A pinch Nutmeg
A pinch Cardamom Seeds

Yogurt Sauce:

½ cup Whole Yogurt
¼ cup Water

1 tsp Arrowroot Flour

Beef:

¼ tbsp Olive oil
1 cup Sliced Onions

1 lb Beef Chuck Roast, cubed in 3 inch pieces

DIRECTIONS

Place all spices in a blender and blend until smooth. Add the spice mixture and yogurt ingredients; blend for a minute. Heat oil on Sauté, add the onions and beef; cook for 3 minutes.

Add the yogurt mixture and stir evenly. Seal the lid, select Soup mode and cook for 10 minutes on High pressure. Once done, allow for a natural release for 10 minutes.

Nutrition facts per serving: Calories 364, Protein 20g, Net Carbs 5.9g, Fat 25g

Beef and Broccoli

Prep + Cook Time: 35 minutes | Servings: 3 to 4

INGREDIENTS:

2 lb Chuck Roast, Boneless, cut into strips
4 cloves Garlic, minced
7 cups Broccoli Florets
1 tbsp Olive oil
1 cup Beef Broth

1 tbsp Arrowroot Starch
¾ cup sugar-free Soy Sauce
3 tbsp Swerve Sugar
Salt to taste

DIRECTIONS:

Select Sauté mode. Heat the olive oil, and add the beef and minced garlic. Cook the beef until browned. Then, add soy sauce, broth, and swerve sugar. Use a spoon to stir the ingredients well so that the sugar dissolves. Seal the lid, select Meat/Stew on High pressure for 15 minutes.

Meanwhile, put the broccoli in a bowl and steam in a microwave for 4 to 5 minutes. After, remove and set aside. Once ready, do a quick pressure release. Use a soup spoon to fetch out a quarter of the liquid into a bowl, add the arrowroot starch, and mix until well dissolved.

Pour the starch mixture into the pot and select Sauté mode. Stir the sauce and allow to thicken into a slurry. Add the broccoli into the pot and let simmer for 4 minutes. Turn off the pot. Dish the beef broccoli sauce into a bowl and serve with a side of squash spaghetti.

Nutrition facts per serving: Calories 232, Protein 14.8g, Net Carbs 3g, Fat 8.8g

Beef Hoagies

Prep + Cook Time: 65 minutes | Servings: 3

INGREDIENTS:

1 tbsp Olive oil
1 (14 oz) can French Onion Soup
1 lb Chuck Roast
1 Onion, sliced
2 tbsp sugar free Worcestershire Sauce

2 Cups Beef Broth
Salt and Black Pepper to taste
1 tsp Garlic Powder
3 Slices Provolone Cheese
3 Low Carb Hoagies, halved

DIRECTIONS:

Season the beef with garlic powder, salt, and pepper. Turn on the Instant Pot, open the lid, and select Sauté mode. Add the olive oil, once heated add the beef and brown on both sides for about 5 minutes. Remove the meat onto a plate.

Into the pot, add the onions and cook to soften. Then, pour the beef broth into the pot and use a spoon to stir while scraping the bottom of the pot off every stuck bit. Add the onion soup, Worcestershire sauce, and beef to the pot.

Seal the lid, select Meat/Stew mode on High pressure for 30 minutes. Once ready, do a natural pressure release for 20 minutes. Remove the meat onto a cutting board with tongs and use two forks to shred it.

Strain the juice in the pot through a sieve into a bowl to be used as Au Jus for serving. Spoon the shredded meat into the halved hoagies and top each hoagie with cheese. Serve with the Au Jus as a dip.

Nutrition facts per serving: Calories 265, Protein 26.3g, Net Carbs 3g, Fat 13.2g

Pepper Rolled Beef

Prep + Cook Time: 60 minutes | Servings: 4 to 6

INGREDIENTS:

2 lb Round Steak Pieces
½ Green Bell pepper, finely chopped
½ Red Bell pepper, finely chopped
½ Yellow Bell pepper, finely chopped
1 Yellow Onion, finely chopped
2 cloves Garlic, minced
Salt and Pepper to taste
¼ cup Almond flour
2 tbsp Olive oil
½ cup Water

DIRECTIONS:

Wrap the steaks in plastic wrap, place on a cutting board, and use a rolling pin to pound flat of about 2-inch thickness. Remove the plastic wrap and season them with salt and pepper. Set aside. Put the peppers, onion, and garlic in a bowl and mix them evenly with a spoon.

Spoon the bell pepper mixture onto the flattened steaks and roll them to have the peppers in it. Use some toothpicks to secure the beef rolls and dredge the steaks in the almond flour while shaking off any excess flour. Place them in a plate. Turn on the Instant Pot, open the lid, and select Sauté mode.

Add the oil, once has heated add the beef rolls and brown them on both sides, about 6 minutes. Then, pour the water over the meat, close the lid, secure the pressure valve, and select Meat/Stew mode on High pressure for 25 minutes.

Once ready, do a natural pressure release for 10 minutes, then a quick pressure release, and open the pot. Remove the meat onto a plate and spoon the sauce in the pot over it. Serve the stuffed meat rolls with a side of steamed veggies.

Nutrition facts per serving: Calories 190, Protein 46g, Net Carbs 4g, Fat 32.5g

Dairy Free Beef Stew

Prep + Cook Time: 90 minutes | Servings: 3

INGREDIENTS

1 lb Sirloin Tip Roast, cut in 3 large chunks
Salt and Black Pepper to taste
1 tsp Olive oil
1 large Onion, sliced
1 Red Bell pepper, sliced
1 Yellow Bell pepper, sliced
3 cloves Garlic, minced
1 tsp dried Oregano
1 tsp Cumin Powder
1 tsp Smoked Paprika
½ tsp Turmeric
1/6 cup Dry White Wine
1 cup Diced Tomatoes
1 Bay Leaf
1/6 cup Capers
1 Pimiento Pepper, minced
½ tbsp Plain Vinegar

DIRECTIONS

Season the beef with white pepper and salt. Heat oil on Sauté and brown the beef; remove to a plate. Add peppers and onion and cook for 4 minutes. Add garlic, spices, and oregano.

Add the wine, cook to reduce it for 3 minutes. Add the tomatoes and bay leaf, stir. Add the beef back. Seal the lid, select Manual and cook on High Pressure for 40 minutes. Once ready, do a natural pressure release for 20 minutes. Shred the meat, add the remaining ingredients, and simmer for 5 minutes on Sauté.

Nutrition facts per serving: Calories 271, Protein 24.2g, Net Carbs 3.9g, Fat 17g

Beef Brisket in Red Curry

Prep + Cook Time: 40 minutes | Servings: 4

INGREDIENTS:

1 ½ lb Beef Brisket, cut in cubes
1 tbsp Olive oil
2 cloves Garlic, minced
¼-inch Ginger, peeled and sliced
2 Bay Leaves
2 Star Anises
1 large Carrot, chopped
1 medium Onion, chopped

2 tbsp Red Curry Paste
1 cup Coconut Milk
1 Turnip, peeled and chopped
1 tbsp Swerve Sugar
2 tsp Oyster Sauce
2 tsp Coconut Flour
3 tbsp Water

DIRECTIONS:

Turn on the Instant Pot, open the lid, and select Sauté mode. Add the olive oil, once heated add the garlic, ginger, and red curry paste. Stir fry them for 1 minute. Add the onion and beef. Stir using a spoon and cook them for 4 minutes. Add the carrots, bay leaves, turnips, star anises, swerve sugar, and water. Stir.

Seal the lid, select Meat/Stew mode on High pressure for 25 minutes. Once ready, do a quick pressure release, and open the pot. In a bowl, add the coconut flour and 4 tablespoons of coconut milk. Mix them well with a spoon and pour in the pot along with the oyster sauce and remaining coconut milk. Stir gently so as to not break the turnips.

Cover the pot, select Sauté mode to allow the sauce to thicken for about 3 minutes. After, turn off the pot. Spoon the sauce into soup bowls and serve with a side of cauli rice.

Nutrition facts per serving: Calories 434, Protein 27.6g, Net Carbs 2.2g, Fat 15.6g

Pot Roast

Prep + Cook Time: 35 minutes | Servings: 4

INGREDIENTS:

2 lb Beef Chuck Roast
3 tbsp Olive oil, divided into 2
Salt to taste
1 cup Beef Broth

1 packet Onion Soup Mix
1 cup chopped Broccoli
2 Red Bell pepper, seeded and quartered
1 Yellow Onion, quartered

DIRECTIONS:

Season the chuck roast with salt and set aside. Turn on the Instant Pot, open the lid, and select Sauté mode. Add the olive oil, once heated add the chuck roast and sear for 5 minutes on each side. Then, add the beef broth to pot.

In a zipper bag add the broccoli, onions, bell peppers, the remaining olive oil, and onion soup. Close the bag and shake the mixture to coat the vegetables well. Use tongs to remove the vegetables into the pot and stir with a spoon.

Seal the lid, select Meat/Stew on High for 25 minutes. Once ready, do a quick pressure release, and open the pot. Remove the Beef onto a cutting board, let cool slightly, and then slice it. Plate and serve with the vegetables and a drizzle of the sauce in the pot.

Nutrition facts per serving: Calories 142, Protein 25.2g, Net Carbs 0g, Fat 3.8g

Bell pepper Beef Mix

Prep + Cook Time: 55 minutes | Servings: 4

INGREDIENTS:

2 lb Beef Chuck Roast
1 tbsp Onion Powder
1 tbsp Garlic Powder
1 tbsp Italian Seasoning
Salt and Black Pepper to taste

1 cup Beef Broth
1 White Onion, sliced
1 Green Bell pepper, sliced
1 Red Bell pepper, sliced
1 tbsp Olive oil

DIRECTIONS:

Place the beef in a plate and season them with pepper, salt, garlic powder, Italian seasoning, and onion powder. Set on Sauté mode. Add the oil, once heated add the beef pieces to it and sear them on both sides to brown which is about 5 minutes. Use a pair of tongs to remove them onto a plate after. Cook in 2 batches.

Pour the beef broth and fish sauce into the pot to deglaze the bottom while you use a spoon to scrape any stuck beef bit at the bottom. Add the meat back to the pot, close the lid, secure the pressure valve, and select Meat/Stew mode on High pressure for 40 minutes.

Once ready, do a quick pressure release, and open the pot. Remove the meat with tongs onto a plate and pour out the liquid in the pot out into a bowl. Use paper towels to wipe the inner part of the pot clean.

Use two forks to shred the beef. Set aside. Select Sauté mode on the Instant Pot, add the remaining oil, once heated, add the beef with onions and bell peppers. Sauté them for 3 minutes and adjust the taste with salt and pepper. Dish the stir-fried beef into serving plates.

Nutrition facts per serving: Calories 220, Protein 14g, Net Carbs 0g, Fat 17g

Beef and Beer Stew

Prep + Cook Time: 60 minutes | Servings: 4

INGREDIENTS:

2 lb Beef Stew, cut into pieces
Salt and Black Pepper to taste
¼ cup Almond flour
3 tbsp Butter
2 tbsp Worcestershire Sauce

2 cloves Garlic, minced
1 packet Dry Onion Soup Mix
2 cups Beef Broth
1 medium bottle Beer, low carb
1 tbsp Tomato Paste

DIRECTIONS:

In a zipper bag, add the beef, salt, almond flour, and pepper. Close the bag up and shake to coat the beef well with the mixture. Select Sauté mode and melt the butter.

Add the beef and brown them on both sides for 5 minutes. Add the beef to deglaze the bottom of the pot. Add the tomato paste, beer, Worcestershire sauce, and the onion soup mix. Stir.

Seal the lid, select Meat/Stew on High for 35 minutes. Once ready, do a natural pressure release for 10 minutes, and then a quick pressure release to let out any remaining steam. Spoon beef stew into bowls and serve with over a bed of vegetable mash.

Nutrition facts per serving: Calories 235, Protein 18.5g, Net Carbs 0.2g, Fat 10.2g

Unstuffed Cabbage Roll Soup

Prep + Cook Time: 35 minutes | Servings: 5 to 6

INGREDIENTS

3 tbsp Olive oil
3 cloves Garlic, minced
2 Onions, chopped
2 Shallots, minced
2 ½ lb Ground beef
2 tsp dried Parsley
1 tsp dried Oregano
Salt and Pepper to taste
1 cup Marinara Sauce
1 small Cauliflower, riced
6 cups Beef Broth
2 medium Cabbages, sliced

DIRECTIONS

Heat oil on Sauté, add shallots and onions, and cook for 3 minutes. Add the beef and brown; then add the seasonings, marinara sauce, and cauli rice. Cook for 5 minutes.

Add the cabbages, seal the lid, select Manual and cook on High Pressure mode for 15 minutes. Once done, quickly release the pressure, open the lid, and stir. Serve warm.

Nutrition facts per serving: Calories 312, Protein 31g, Net Carbs 5.8g, Fat 15.2g

Spicy Beef Stew

Prep + Cook Time: 50 minutes | Servings: 3

INGREDIENTS

1 lb Beef Brisket, cut in 1 ½ inch cubes
2 tbsp Red Habanero Paste
Salt and Black Pepper to taste
1 tbsp Butter
1 Onion, sliced thinly
½ tbsp Tomato Paste
3 cloves Garlic, crushed
¼ cup Tomato Salsa
¼ cup Beef Broth
¼ tsp Fish Sauce
¼ cup Minced Cilantro

DIRECTIONS

Mix beef, salt and pepper, in a bowl. Melt butter on Sauté, and stir-fry onions for 2 minutes. Stir in garlic and tomato paste; cook for 1 minute. Stir in beef, salsa, fish sauce and broth.

Seal the lid and cook on High Pressure mode for 35 minutes. Once ready, quickly release the pressure. Stir and serve stew garnished with cilantro.

Nutrition facts per serving: Calories 251, Protein 28g, Net Carbs 5g, Fat 11g

Green Beans Beef Soup

Prep + Cook Time: 45 minutes | Servings: 5

INGREDIENTS

2 tsp Olive oil
2 lb Ground beef
2 Onions, chopped
2 tbsp Minced Garlic
2 tsp Thyme
2 tsp Oregano
3 cups Green Beans, cut in short strips
2 cups Diced Tomatoes
2 cups Beef Broth
Salt and Black Pepper to taste
Parmesan Cheese, grated to garnish

DIRECTIONS

Heat oil on Sauté, and brown the beef. Stir in tomatoes, broth and green beans. Seal the lid, select Manual and cook on Low Pressure for 30 minutes. Once done, quickly release the pressure. Season with pepper and salt. Dish soup, sprinkle with Parmesan cheese and serve.

Nutrition facts per serving: Calories 186, Protein 14g, Net Carbs 3g, Fat 12g

Beef Taco Soup

Preparation Time: 45 minutes 1 Servings: 4 to 6

INGREDIENTS

2 tbsp Coconut Oil
2 medium Yellow Onions, chopped
5 mixed colored Bell peppers, chopped
2 ½ lb Ground beef
4 tbsp Chili Powder
3 tbsp Cumin Powder
Salt and Black Pepper to taste
2 tsp Paprika

2 tsp Cinnamon Powder
1 tsp Onion Powder
1 tsp Garlic Powder
½ Cayenne Powder
2 cups Diced Tomatoes
2 cups Beef Broth
1 cup Coconut Milk
2 Green Chilies, minced

DIRECTIONS

Heat oil on Sauté, add bell peppers and onion; cook for 5 minutes. Add beef, and brown, drain, and add it back to the pot. Stir in all spices. Top with tomatoes, chilies, milk, and broth.

Stir, seal the lid, select Soup and cook for 25 minutes on High pressure. Once done, quickly release the pressure. Dish the soup and garnish with jalapenos, cilantro and scallions.

Nutrition facts per serving: Calories 197, Protein 19g, Net Carbs 3.2g, Fat 5.3g

Meatballs in Spaghetti Sauce

Prep + Cook Time: 15 minutes | Servings: 4

INGREDIENTS:

2 lb Ground beef
1 cup Keto Breadcrumbs
1 Onion, finely chopped
2 cloves Garlic, minced
Salt and Pepper to taste
1 tsp dried Oregano

3 tbsp Milk
1 cup grated Parmesan Cheese
2 Eggs, cracked into a bowl
4 cups Spaghetti Sauce
1 tbsp Olive oil

DIRECTIONS:

In a bowl, put in the beef, onion, keto breadcrumbs, parmesan cheese, eggs, garlic, milk, salt, oregano, and pepper. Use hands to mix and make bite size balls out of the mixture.

Open the pot, add the spaghetti sauce, and the meatballs. Close the lid, secure the pressure valve, and select Meat/ Stew mode on High pressure for 6 minutes.

Once ready, do a natural pressure release for 5 minutes, then do a quick pressure release to let out any extra steam. Dish the meatball sauce over spaghetti squash and serve.

Nutrition facts per serving: Calories 194, Protein 7.3g, Net Carbs 0.1g, Fat 7.3g

Balsamic Beef Pot Roast

Prep + Cook Time: 70 minutes | Servings: 2

INGREDIENTS

1 Chuck Roast, Boneless and halved
Salt and Black Pepper to taste
2 tsp Garlic Powder
1/6 Balsamic Vinegar

2 cups Water
1 Onion, minced
¼ tsp Xantham Gum
Chopped Parsley to garnish

DIRECTIONS

Season the beef with pepper, salt and garlic. Set on Sauté and brown the beef on all sides. Add water, vinegar and onion. Stir lightly. Seal the lid and cook on Meat/Stew for 35 minutes.

Once done, quickly release the pressure. Remove the beef to a bowl and break it into large chunks. To the pot, set on Sauté and simmer the sauce for 10 minutes. Add the xantham gum and the beef. Stir and turn off the heat. Dish, garnish with parsley, and serve.

Nutrition facts per serving: Calories 393, Protein 30g, Net Carbs 3g, Fat 28g

Italian Pepperoncini Beef

Prep + Cook Time: 55 minutes | Servings: 3

INGREDIENTS:

2 lb Beef Roast, cut into cubes
14 oz jar Pepperoncini Peppers, with liquid

1 pack Brown Gravy Mix
1 pack Italian Salad Dressing Mix

DIRECTIONS:

To the pot, add in the beef, pepperoncini peppers, brown gravy mix, Italian salad dressing mix, and ½ cup water. Seal the lid, secure the pressure valve, and select Meat/Stew on High for 55 minutes.

Once ready, do a quick pressure release, and open the pot. Dish the ingredients to a bowl and use two forks to shred the beef. Serve the beef sauce in plates with a side of steamed veggies.

Nutrition facts per serving: Calories 161, Protein 27g, Net Carbs 0g, Fat 28g

Minute Steak and Cheese Stuffed Mushrooms

Prep + Cook Time: 10 minutes | Servings: 3

INGREDIENTS:

6 large White Mushrooms, stems removed
2 cups cooked Leftover Beef, cubed
2 tsp Garlic Salt

2 oz Cream Cheese, softened
1 cup shredded Cheddar Cheese
1 tsp Olive oil

DIRECTIONS:

In a bowl, add the chopped beef, garlic salt, cream cheese, and cheddar cheese. Use a spoon to mix them.Spoon the beef mixture into the mushrooms and place the stuffed mushrooms in. Drizzle them with the olive oil.

Seal the lid, select Meat/Stew on High for 5 minutes. Once ready, do a quick pressure release. Remove the mushrooms onto a plate. Serve hot with a side of steamed green veggies.

Nutrition facts per serving: Calories 120, Protein 4.3g, Net Carbs 0g, Fat 7.5g

Bacon Wrapped Beef with Green Beans

Prep + Cook Time: 30 minutes | Servings: 3

INGREDIENTS:

3 Rib Eye Steaks
6 strips Bacon
Salt to taste
1 tbsp Olive oil
2 cups long slices Green Beans
¼ cup Water

DIRECTIONS:

Season the rib eye steaks with salt. Roll around each steak with two bacon slices and secure the bacon ends with toothpicks. Turn on the Instant Pot, open the lid, and select Sauté mode. Add the wrapped steaks and brown on both sides for 8 minutes. Add the green beans and pour in water.

Seal the lid, select Meat/Stew on High for 15 minutes. Once ready, do a quick pressure release. Plate the wrapped beef with the green beans and serve with a side of parsnip mash.

Nutrition facts per serving: Calories 240, Protein 18g, Net Carbs 0g, Fat 12g

Coconut Beef Roast

Prep + Cook Time: 40 minutes | Servings: 4

INGREDIENTS:

1 lb Beef Roast, cut into cubes
Salt and Black Pepper to taste
¼ cup Coconut Milk, light
¼ cup Peanut Satay Sauce
2 cups diced Carrots

DIRECTIONS:

Open the Instant Pot and put the beef in it. In a bowl, add the coconut milk, salt, pepper, and satay sauce. Use a spoon to mix them well and pour them over the beef. Add the carrots too.

Seal the lid, select Meat/Stew mode on High pressure for 25 minutes. Once ready, do a quick pressure. Use a spoon to dish the meat into a serving plate and serve with a side of steamed greens.

Nutrition facts per serving: Calories 142, Protein 16.8g, Net Carbs 0g, Fat 7.8g

Sliced Meat with Mixed Mushrooms

Prep + Cook Time: 13 minutes | Servings: 4

INGREDIENTS:

1 lb Beef meat, sliced
2 tbsp Onion powder
1 cup Tomato puree
½ cup Thyme, chopped
½ cup Cheddar cheese, shredded
3 cups Mushrooms, chopped
½ large Onion, chopped
Parsley to garnish

DIRECTIONS:

Mix tomato paste and onion, in a bowl. Pour in the pot and add meat, thyme, mushrooms and cheese. Seal the lid, press Manual and cook for 9 minutes on High pressure.

When done, do a natural pressure release, for 10 minutes. Serve with fresh parsley.

Nutrition facts per serving: Calories 543, Protein 31.1g, Net Carbs 8.5g, Fat 36.5g

Beef Celeriac Soup

Prep + Cook Time: 60 minutes | Servings: 3

INGREDIENTS

2 tbsp Coconut Oil
1 Onion, diced
2 cups Diced Celeriac
2 Carrots, chopped
2 Celery Stalks, chopped
1 cup Diced Tomatoes

2 cups Bone Broth
1 lb Stew Beef
Salt and White Pepper to taste
1 tsp Herbs de Provence
½ tsp Onion Powder
¼ cup Green Beans, cut in ½ inch strips

DIRECTIONS

Heat oil on Sauté, add the celery, carrots, onion, and celeriac; cook for 10 minutes. Stir the remaining ingredients, seal the lid, select Meat/Stew and cook for 30 minutes on High. Once done, quickly release the pressure. Let it sit for 5 minutes before serving.

Nutrition facts per serving: Calories 204, Protein 21.7g, Net Carbs 6.7g, Fat 24g

Beef with Haricots vert

Prep + Cook Time: 17 minutes | Servings: 3

INGREDIENTS:

1 lb Ground Beef
1 tbsp Lemon juice
2 tbsp Butter
2 cups Haricots vert

1 Onion, chopped
2 Garlic cloves, minced
Salt and Pepper, to taste

DIRECTIONS:

Melt butter on Sauté and stir-fry onion and garlic for 2 minutes, until tender. Add lemon juice, beef, and Haricots vert; season with salt and pepper. Pour 1 cup of water; seal the lid. Cook for 15 minutes on High pressure. When ready, do a quick release and serve hot.

Nutrition facts per serving: Calories 386, Protein 42.5g, Net Carbs 6.1g, Fat 19.3g

Ground Beef with Peppers

Prep + Cook Time: 15 minutes | Servings: 3

INGREDIENTS:

1 tbsp Olive oil
½ cup Tomato sauce
1 lb Ground Beef
2 green Peppers, sliced

2 red Peppers, sliced
1 Onion, chopped
½ tbsp Chili powder
Salt and Pepper, to taste

DIRECTIONS:

Add onion and vegetable oil to the pot. Press Sauté and stir in the meat, tomato sauce, green peppers and red peppers. Season with salt, pepper and chili powder.

Pour half cup of water, seal the lid, and cook for 15 minutes on High pressure. When ready, allow for a natural pressure release for 10 minutes, and serve immediately.

Nutrition facts per serving: Calories 515, Protein 51.3g, Net Carbs 7.5g, Fat 22.4g

Cauliflower Meat

Prep + Cook Time: 45 minutes | Servings: 5

INGREDIENTS:

½ lb Beef meat, boiled
1 cup Cauliflower florets
1 Onion, chopped
2-3 Garlic cloves, minced
2 Tomatoes, chopped
¼ tbsp Turmeric powder
¼ tbsp Cumin powder

¼ tbsp Cinnamon powder
1 tbsp Salt
½ tbsp Chili powder
4 tbsp Olive oil
½ cup Chicken broth
1 Green Chili

DIRECTIONS:

Heat oil on Sauté and cook the cauliflower for 3-4 minutes; set aside. In the same oil, cook onion for 1 minute. Add tomatoes, chili, salt, and turmeric and cook for 3 minutes.

Add the beef and stir-fry for 15 minutes. Add the chicken broth and cauliflower, seal the lid and cook on Manual for 10 minutes on High pressure. When ready, do a quick pressure release and sprinkle with cumin powder and cinnamon powder; toss well.

Nutrition facts per serving: Calories 303, Protein 23.7g, Net Carbs 8.3g, Fat 14.1g

Ground Beef with Flax Seeds

Prep + Cook Time: 30 minutes | Servings: 4

INGREDIENTS

1 ½ lb ground Beef
1 package Sausage
2 tsp dried, chopped Onion
1 tsp Garlic powder
1 tsp dried Basil
1 tsp dried Parsley
½ cup Flax seed meal

½ tsp Salt
1 tsp ground fennel
1 cup dried Tomatoes, sliced
2 Eggs, beaten
1 Mango, cubed
1 tsp Coconut oil

DIRECTIONS

In a deep bowl, mix onion, garlic powder, dried basil, flax seed meal, salt, and fennel.

Squeeze the sausage out of any casings and place in the bowl; cut in very small pieces. Place the meat in the same bowl and mix the ingredients with hands.

Shape the meat into the form of two loaves. Heat a teaspoon of coconut oil on Sauté.

Transfer the meat loaves, brown for a few minutes. Add half cup of water, lower the trivet, and place the meatloaf on top. Seal the lid, press Meat/Stew and cook on High pressure for 30 minutes. When ready, do a quick pressure release and with mango cubes.

Nutrition facts per serving: Calories 487, Protein 51.2g, Net Carbs 3.1g, Fat 31.4g

Beef Meat with Shallots

Prep + Cook Time: 20 minutes | Servings: 4

INGREDIENTS

¾ lb halved, peeled shallots
1 ½ tbsp Olive oil
3 cups Beef broth
¾ cup red Wine
1 ½ tsp Tomato paste

2 lb trimmed Beef tenderloin roast
1 tsp dried Thyme
3 tbsp Coconut oil
1 tbsp Almond flour
Salt and Pepper, to taste

DIRECTIONS

Melt olive oil on Sauté. Roast shallots and mix in wine and broth. Season with salt and pepper. Seal the lid, press Manual and cook on High pressure for 20 minutes.

When ready, quick release the pressure. Add the tomato paste. Pat the beef dry and sprinkle with salt and pepper. Add the thyme, salt, pepper, and drizzle with coconut oil.

Pour ½ cup of water and sauté the beef per side for 10 minutes. Pour in broth mixture, 1½ tsp of coconut oil, flour and cook on Sauté for 10 minutes, until sauce thickens.

Nutrition facts per serving: Calories 576, Protein 67.5g, Net Carbs 8.1g, Fat 25.4g

Tamari Steak with Tomatoes

Prep + Cook Time: 25 minutes | Servings: 4

INGREDIENTS

2 tbsp low-carb Tamari
1 pound Beef Steak, sliced
2 Tomatoes, chopped
1 tsp Sweetener
1 tsp Vinegar

2 Garlic Cloves, minced
1 small Onion, diced
2 tbsp Olive oil
½ cup Beef Broth
Salt and Pepper, to taste

DIRECTIONS

Heat half of the oil on Sauté, and add the beef slices. Season with salt and pepper, and cook until browned, for 5 minutes. Remove to a plate. Add in the rest of the oil, onions and garlic; cook for 3 minutes. Stir in tomatoes and cook for 2 minutes. Add in the remaining ingredients and the beef.

Seal the lid, select Manual and cook on HIGH pressure for 5 minutes. When ready, press Cancel and do a quick pressure release. Serve immediately.

Nutrition facts per serving: Calories 312, Protein 28g, Net Carbs 7g, Fat 15g

Meatloaf with Cheddar

Prep + Cook Time: 40 minutes | Servings: 8

INGREDIENTS

1 ½ cups Water
2 tbsp Almond flour
2 pounds ground Beef
1 small Onion, grated
½ tsp minced Garlic
1 Egg
2 tbsp grated Parmesan Cheese

½ cup Cheddar Cubes
¼ tsp Smoked Paprika
¼ tsp Italian Seasoning
Salt and Pepper, to taste

DIRECTIONS

Pour in water and lower the trivet. Grease a baking dish with cooking spray; set aside. Place all ingredients, except for the cheddar cheese, in a large bowl. Mix until well combined. When fully incorporated, place half of the meat mixture inside the greased baking dish.

Flatten it out and top with cheddar cubes. Top with the rest of the beef mixture, flattening it to make an even layer. Place the dish on top of the trivet and seal the lid.

Select Manual and set the cooking time to 30 minutes. Cook on HIGH pressure. When ready, do a quick pressure release. Let the meatloaf sit for a few minutes before slicing.

Nutrition facts per serving: Calories 272, Protein 27g, Net Carbs 2g, Fat 17g

Beef with Cauliflower Pilaf

Prep + Cook Time: 24 minutes | Servings: 4

INGREDIENTS

1 pound Ground Beef
½ cup Beef Broth
1 small Onion, diced
¼ tsp Garlic Powder
3 cups Cauliflower Rice

1 tbsp Butter
2 tbsp Tomato Paste
¼ tsp dried Parsley
Salt and Pepper, to taste

DIRECTIONS

Melt butter on Sauté. Add the diced onion and cook for 2-3 minutes. When soft, stir in the beef. Season with salt and pepper and cook beef for a few minutes, until brown.

Stir in all the remaining ingredients and seal the lid. Press Manual and cook for 5 minutes on HIGH pressure. When the timer goes off, release the pressure quickly.

Nutrition facts per serving: Calories 291, Protein 32g, Net Carbs 4g, Fat 18g

Sesame Tamari Flank Strips

Prep + Cook Time: 20 minutes | Servings: 4

INGREDIENTS

1 pound Flank Steak, cut into strips
2 tbsp low-carb Tamari
1 tbsp Vinegar
1 ½ tbsp Sesame Seeds
1 tsp Granulated Swerve

¼ tsp Onion Powder
¼ tsp Garlic Powder
1 tbsp Coconut Oil
Salt and Pepper, to taste

DIRECTIONS

Set on Sauté and melt the coconut oil. Add the flank strips, season with salt and pepper, and cook until browned on all sides, for 6 minutes.

Add the remaining ingredients, except the seeds, to a bowl, and whisk together until smooth. Pour the mixture over the flank steak. Stir well to coat the meat fully. Cook on Sauté for 3-4 minutes, or until the meat becomes sticky. Sprinkle the seeds over and serve immediately!

Nutrition facts per serving: Calories 243, Protein 35g, Net Carbs 3g, Fat 24g

Cauliflower Rice with Ground Beef

Prep + Cook Time: 25 minutes | Servings: 5

INGREDIENTS

1 finely chopped Onion
5 tbsp Coconut oil
2 chopped cloves of Garlic
2 diced Tomatoes
1 pinch Salt
1 tsp Paprika
1 tsp Saffron

2 cups Cauliflower rice
3 cups Beef broth
1 cup dry white Wine
1 lb ground Beef
1 tsp ground Flax seeds
1 cup Green beans

DIRECTIONS

Melt the coconut oil on Sauté mode. Stir-fry onion until soft, for 2 minutes. Add garlic, tomatoes, salt, paprika, saffron, and beans; and keep stirring until tomatoes soften.

Add the ground beef and mix the ingredients. Add cauli rice, broth, flax seed powder, and salt. Seal the lid, press Manual and cook on High pressure for 25 minutes. Once ready, quickly release the pressure. Add the shallots and season with pepper and salt.

Nutrition facts per serving: Calories 349, Protein 31.6g, Net Carbs 6.9g, Fat 20.3g

Shredded Mexican Beef

Prep + Cook Time: 23 minutes | Servings: 6

INGREDIENTS

2 pounds Chuck Roast
1 tsp Chili Powder
½ tsp Smoked Paprika
½ tsp Cumin
¼ cup Butter

1 ½ cups canned diced Tomatoes
1 cup Beef Broth
Salt and Pepper, to taste
½ tsp Garlic Powder

DIRECTIONS

Melt butter on Sauté, add the beef and sear on all sides. Remove to a plate.

Place the tomatoes and all of the spices in the pot and cook for 2 minutes. Pour in broth and stir to combine. Return the beef to the pot. Close the lid on and turn it clockwise to seal.

Press Manual and set the cooking time to 20 minutes on HIGH pressure. When ready, press Cancel and release the pressure quickly. Grab two forks and shred the beef inside the pot.

Nutrition facts per serving: Calories 265, Protein 32g, Net Carbs 1g, Fat 15g

Beef Tenderloin with Tarragon Sauce

Prep + Cook Time: 50 minutes | Servings: 4

INGREDIENTS

1 pound Beef Tenderloin
1 ¼ cups Beef Broth
¼ cup Heavy Cream
¼ cup Balsamic Vinegar
1 Onion, diced

1 Garlic Clove, minced
1 ½ tbsp chopped Tarragon
1 tbsp Butter
1 tbsp Olive oil
Salt and Pepper, to taste

DIRECTIONS

Set on Sauté and heat the olive oil. Add the beef and season with salt and pepper. Sear the meat on all sides, until browned. Remove to a plate.

Melt the butter and cook the onions for 3 minutes. Stir in garlic and cook for 30 seconds. Pour the vinegar in and stir to deglaze the pot. Stir in the tarragon and stir-fry for 2 minutes.

When the vinegar is reduced by half, whisk in the rest of the ingredients. Return the beef to the pot and seal the lid. Select Meat/Stew mode and cook on HIGH pressure for 25 minutes. When ready, press Cancel and do a quick pressure release. Top with the sauce and serve.

Nutrition facts per serving: Calories 421, Protein 32g, Net Carbs 3.2g, Fat 27g

Keto Beef Chili

Prep + Cook Time: 23 minutes | Servings: 4

INGREDIENTS

1 pound ground Beef
2 (14-ounce) cans of diced Tomatoes
3 cups Cauliflower Rice
1 tbsp Chili Powder
½ cup Beef Broth
1 Onion, diced
1 tsp Cumin
1 tbsp Worcestershire Salt
1 tsp Garlic Powder
½ tsp Smoked Paprika
Salt and Pepper
1 tbsp Olive oil

DIRECTIONS

Set on Sauté and heat the oil. Add the beef and cook for a few minutes, until browned. Dump all remaining ingredients in the pot. Give the mixture a good stir and seal the lid.

Select Meat/Stew and cook for 15 minutes on HIGH pressure. When it goes off, press Cancel and allow for a natural pressure release, for 10 minutes. Serve with keto bread and enjoy.

Nutrition facts per serving: Calories 283, Protein 30g, Net Carbs 3.5g, Fat 24g

Beef Casserole with Veggies

Prep + Cook Time: 23 minutes | Servings: 4

INGREDIENTS

1 pound Ground Beef
1 Bell Pepper, chopped
1 Zucchini, chopped
4 cups Cauliflower Rice
14 ounces canned diced Tomatoes
¼ tsp Garlic Powder
½ tsp dried Basil
1 tbsp Olive oil
Salt and Pepper, to taste
1 ½ cups Water

DIRECTIONS

Set on Sauté and heat the oil. Add the ground beef and cook until browned, for 5 minutes. Remove a baking dish. Add the rest of the ingredients, except the water, and give it a good stir.

Pour the water in the Pot and lower the trivet. Place the dish on top of the trivet. Seal the lid. Press Manual and cook on HIGH pressure for 8 minutes. When it goes off, release the pressure naturally, by allowing the valve to drop on its own, for 10 minutes.

Nutrition facts per serving: Calories 460, Protein 24g, Net Carbs 9g, Fat 29g

Creamy Cauli & Beef Soup

Prep + Cook Time: 26 minutes | Servings: 4

INGREDIENTS

1 pound ground Beef
3 ½ cups Cauliflower Rice
1 cup Sour Cream
4 cups Beef Broth
1 tsp chopped Parsley
¼ cup grated Parmesan Cheese
Salt and Pepper, to taste
¼ Onion, diced
2 tbsp Butter

DIRECTIONS

Melt the butter on Sauté. Stir-fry the onions 2 minutes and add in the beef. Season with salt and pepper, and cook until the beef browns, for 4 minutes.

Pour in broth, cauliflower, and parsley. Adjust the seasoning, and seal the lid. Select Manual and cook on HIGH pressure for 10 minutes.

When ready, do a quick pressure release. Stir in the sour cream and Parmesan, and serve.

Nutrition facts per serving: Calories 322, Protein 27g, Net Carbs 3.8g, Fat 21g

No Carb Lasagna

Prep + Cook Time: 40 minutes | Servings: 2

INGREDIENTS

1 lb Ground beef
1 clove Garlic, minced
1 Onion,
1 cup Ricotta Cheese
¼ cup Parmesan Cheese
1 Egg
¼ cup Marinara Sauce
4 oz Mozzarella Slices

DIRECTIONS

Add the beef, garlic and onion, and brown the beef, on Sauté. Meanwhile, combine the egg, Parmesan and ricotta cheese, in a bowl. Drain grease from the pot and transfer beef to sizeable souffle dish.

Turn off the pot and clean. Stir in the marina sauce and spoon out half the meat sauce into a bowl. Top the meat sauce in the souffle dish with half of the mozzarella slices, and half of the egg mixture. Layer the remaining meat sauce on top, followed by mozzarella and egg mixture.

Cover with loose aluminum foil. Pour water in the Instant pot, lower the trivet, and place the dish on top. Seal the lid, select Manual and cook on High Pressure for 10 minutes.

Once done, quickly release the pressure. Transfer the dish to a flat surface, remove foil and sprinkle with extra Parmesan cheese. Let sit for 5 minutes until cheese melts.

Nutrition facts per serving: Calories 365, Protein 25g, Net Carbs 1g, Fat 25g

Lamb Leg

Prep + Cook Time: 55 minutes | Servings: 5

INGREDIENTS

1 (3 lb) Lamb Leg
Salt and Black Pepper to taste
2 tbsp Olive oil
2 cups Water
5 cloves Garlic, pureed
2 tbsp Chopped Rosemary

DIRECTIONS

Pat dry the lamb with paper towels; season with pepper and salt. Heat the oil on Sauté, and brown the lamb on all sides; then set aside. Rub garlic and rosemary on all side of the lamb.

Fit a rack in the Instant Pot and pour in the water. Place the lamb on the rack. Seal the lid, select Meat/Stew and cook on High for 35 minutes. Once ready, do a natural pressure release for 10 minutes. Remove the lamb onto a metal rack and sear on all sides to lightly brown.

Nutrition facts per serving: Calories 432, Protein 45g, Net Carbs 0g, Fat 26g

Minty Lamb "Rice"

Prep + Cook Time: 23 minutes | Servings: 4

INGREDIENTS

1 pound ground Lamb
4 cups Cauliflower Rice
2 tbsp chopped Mint
1 tsp chopped Parsley
1 tbsp Olive oil

14 ounces canned diced Tomatoes
¼ tsp Cayenne Pepper
Salt and Pepper, to taste
1 cup Beef Broth

DIRECTIONS

Heat the oil on Sauté. Add the lamb and season with salt and pepper. Cook for 4 minutes, or until browned. St r in the remaining ingredients and seal the lid. Select Manual and cook for 12 minutes on HIGH pressure. When ready, press Cancel and do a quick pressure release. Serve right away.

Nutrition facts per serving: Calories 335, Protein 29g, Net Carbs 4g, Fat 24g

Lamb Curry

Prep + Cook Time: 4 hours, 60 minutes | Servings: 4 to 6

INGREDIENTS

2 lb Lamb Spare Ribs
Salt to season

Sauce:

1 tbsp Olive oil
1 Onion, chopped
8 large Tomatoes, chopped
3 cloves Garlic, minced
1 tbsp Curry Powder

2 tbsp Curry Powder

Salt to taste
1 Lemon, juiced
¾ cup Chopped Cilantro, shared into 2
2 Scallions, chopped

DIRECTIONS

Season the lamb with salt and curry powder. Run well and marinate for 4 hours. Set the pot Sauté and brown the ribs on all sides; cook in 2 batches. Remove to a plate. Puree the onion and tomatoes in a blender; set aside. Stir-fry the minced garlic in the hot oil, for 3 minutes.

Add the tomatoes, stir and cook for 5 minutes. Stir in the curry, cilantro, salt, and lemon juice. Let boil, add back the lamb and coat with the sauce. Seal the lid, select Manual and cook on High Pressure for 20 minutes. Once done, do a natural pressure release for 20 minutes. Scoop off excess fat and discard. Stir in the scallions. Dish curry with parsley garnishing.

Nutrition facts per serving: Calories 257, Protein 29g, Net Carbs 1g, Fat 14g

Goulash Soup

Prep + Cook Time: 50 minutes | Servings: 3

INGREDIENTS

1 lb Ground beef
1 tsp + 1 tsp Olive oil
1 Red Bell pepper, cut in short strips
1 Onion, sliced
2 cloves Garlic, minced

1 tbsp Sweet Paprika
1 tbsp Hot Paprika
2 cups Beef Broth
1 cup Diced Tomatoes

DIRECTIONS

Heat half of the oil on Sauté and brown the beef, stirring occassionally. Remove to a plate. Add the remaining oil to the pot, add the bell pepper and onions. Cook for 4 minutes.

Add the sweet and hot paprika, stir and cook with the onions for 3 minutes. Add the remaining ingredients and the beef. Seal the lid, select Soup mode and cook for 15 minutes on High. Once ready, do a natural pressure release for 10 minutes. Serve with a dollop of sour cream.

Nutrition facts per serving: Calories 311, Protein 32.7g, Net Carbs 2.7g, Fat 15.4g

Lamb Shanks

Prep + Cook Time: 85 minutes | Servings: 5

INGREDIENTS

2 lb Lamb Shanks
Salt and Black Pepper to taste
1 tbsp + 1 tbsp Olive oil
1 Carrot, chopped
1 Celery Stalk, chopped
1 Onion, chopped
2 tbsp Tomato Paste

2 cloves Garlic, crushed
3 cups Diced Tomatoes
1 cup Beef Broth
1 tbsp Red Boat Fish Sauce
½ tbsp Balsamic Vinegar
Minced Parsley to garnish

DIRECTIONS

Season shanks with pepper and salt. Heat half of the oil on Sauté, and brown the shanks for 10 minutes. Transfer to a plate. Add the remaining oil and the vegetables.

Cook for 4 minutes with stirring. Stir in the tomato paste. Add the shanks back along with tomatoes and all liquid ingredients. Season extra black pepper. Stir and seal the lid.

Select Manual and cook on High Pressure mode for 45 minutes. Once ready, do a natural pressure release for 20 minutes. Serve shanks with a generous top of sauce.

Nutrition facts per serving: Calories 285, Protein 35g, Net Carbs 1.7g, Fat 11g

Lamb Stew

Prep + Cook Time: 50 minutes | Servings: 3

INGREDIENTS

1 lb Lamb Stew meat, cut in 1-inch pieces
1 Celeriac, peeled and chopped
2 Carrots, cut in 2 inch pieces
1 Onion, diced

2 small sprigs Rosemary
3 cloves Garlic, sliced
2 tbsp Water
Salt to taste

DIRECTIONS

Place all ingredients in the Instant Pot. Seal the lid, select Stew/Meat and cook for 35 minutes on High pressure. Once done, quickly release the pressure. Discard the bay leaf and serve.

Nutrition facts per serving: Calories 280, Protein 34.7g, Net Carbs 2.2g, Fat 10.8g

Greek Style Lamb Shoulder

Prep + Cook Time: 60 minutes | Servings: 3

INGREDIENTS

Lamb Seasoning:

1 lb Lamb Shoulder, without a joint
2 cloves Garlic, minced
3 sprigs Thyme

2 tsp Monk Fruit Syrup
Salt and Black Pepper to taste

In the Pot:

½ cup Water
2 cloves Garlic, crushed

2 sprigs Thyme

Garnishing:

Chopped Parsley
3 Lemon Wedges

1 tsp Lemon Zest

DIRECTIONS

Season the lamb with the seasoning ingredients, roll it up and secure with butcher's twines. Drizzle with the monk fruit syrup. Place the water, garlic and thyme in the Instant Pot.

Add the lamb in the pot. Seal the lid, select Manual and cook on High Pressure for 40 minutes. Once done, do a natural pressure release for 10 minutes. Place the lamb on a searing rack, cut the off the twines, and sear until brown on all sides. You may do this in an oven.

Nutrition facts per serving: Calories 239, Protein 25.4g, Net Carbs 0g, Fat 10.8g

Lamb Kofta in Tomato Sauce

Prep + Cook Time: 30 minutes | Servings: 4

INGREDIENTS

1 lb ground Lamb
¼ Onion, grated
2 tbsp grated Parmesan Cheese
2 tbsp Almond flour
1 Egg
¼ tsp Cayenne Pepper

¼ tsp Garlic Powder
1 cup Tomato Sauce
½ cup chopped Tomatoes
1 tbsp Olive oil
1 tbsp chopped Cilantro
Salt and Pepper, to taste

DIRECTIONS

Place lamb, onion, Parmesan, flour, egg and cayenne pepper in a large bowl. Mix with hands until well-combined. Shape into 4 koftas. Set your Instant Pot to Sauté and heat the olive oil.

Add the koftas and cook for 2 minutes per side. Stir the remaining ingredients in a bowl. Pour the sauce over the koftas and seal the lid. Select Manual and cook on HIGH pressure for 15 minutes. When ready, do a quick pressure release and serve hot.

Nutrition facts per serving: Calories 412, Protein 31g, Net Carbs 4g, Fat 23g

Chipotle Braised Lamb Shank

Prep + Cook Time: 90 minutes | Servings: 3

INGREDIENTS

3 Lamb Shanks
Salt and Black Pepper to taste
2 tsp Garlic Powder
2 tsp Cumin Powder
1 tsp Coriander Powder
1 tsp Mustard Powder
2 tbsp Olive oil
1 cup Diced Tomatoes
1 cup Water
1 tbsp Chipotle in Adobo Sauce
2 cloves Garlic
¼ White Onion, sliced
3 Carrots, chopped
Chopped Cilantro to garnish
1 Radish, sliced to garnish
1 Lime, cut in wedges

DIRECTIONS

Place the lamb on a flat surface and mix salt, pepper, oil and powders, in a bowl. Season the lamb with the mixture. Let sit for 30 minutes.

Heat the oil on Sauté, add the lamb and brown on all sides. Remove to a plate. In a blender, puree tomato, chipotle, salt and water, and pour the mixture in the pot.

Add garlic, onion, carrots, lamb shanks, and seal the lid, select Manual and cook on High Pressure for 45 minutes. Once ready, do a natural pressure release for 10 minutes. Remove the lamb onto a serving plate and select Sauté. Let the sauce thicken for 10 minutes.

Nutrition facts per serving: Calories 255, Protein 23g, Net Carbs 1g, Fat 10g

Cinnamon and Cocoa Lamb Shoulder

Prep + Cook Time: 50 minutes | Servings: 4

INGREDIENTS

1 pound Lamb Shoulder, boneless
1 tsp Cocoa Powder
¼ tsp Cinnamon Powder
½ tsp Sweetener
½ tsp Garlic Powder
½ tsp Onion Flakes
¼ tsp Cayenne Pepper
1 tbsp Olive oil
Salt and Pepper, to taste
1 ½ cups Beef Broth

DIRECTIONS

Heat the oil on Sauté. Meanwhile, combine all spices in a bowl. Rub the spice mixture onto lamb and place it in the pot. Sear on all sides for about 5 minutes in total. Pour in the broth and seal the lid. Select Mea/Stew and cook for 30 minutes on HIGH. When ready, do a quick pressure release.

Nutrition facts per serving: Calories 291, Protein 27g, Net Carbs 1g, Fat 25g

Butter Lamb

Prep + Cook Time: 90 minutes | Servings: 4

INGREDIENTS

2 lb Arm Roast, cut in 2-inch pieces
1 tbsp Olive oil
2 tbsp Ranch Mix Seasoning
3 Jalapenos, ringed
1 tbsp Italian Seasoning
6 tbsp Butter
1 cup Water

DIRECTIONS

Heat the oil on Sauté, and brown the lamb. Add the remaining ingredients, close the lid, secure the pressure valve, and select Manual on High Pressure for 60 minutes. Once ready, do a natural pressure release for 5 minutes. Shred the beef with forks and serve.

Nutrition facts per serving: Calories 542, Protein 34g, Net Carbs 41g, Fat 41g

Lamb Chops

Prep + Cook Time: 15 minutes | Servings: 3

INGREDIENTS

2 lb lamb Chops
Salt to taste
2 sprigs Rosemary, chopped
1 tbsp Olive oil

1 tbsp Butter, unsalted
1 tbsp Tomato Paste
½ cup Beef Stock
1 Shallot, halved

DIRECTIONS

Season the chops with salt and rosemary. Heat oil and butter on Sauté, and brown the lamb on each side. Remove to a plate. Add the shallot and tomatoes, and cook for 2 minutes.

Pour in broth and add the lamb chops with resulting juices. Seal the lid, select Manual and cook on High mode for 2 minutes. Once ready, quickly release the pressure. Serve the chops with juices.

Nutrition facts per serving: Calories 226, Protein 16g, Net Carb 0g, Fat 18g

Braised Oxtail

Prep + Cook Time: 75 minutes | Servings: 4

INGREDIENTS

Oxtail:

2 lb Oxtail
1 medium Onion, chopped

1 Carrot, chopped in large chunks
2 tbsp Olive oil

Braising:

⅓ cup Soy Sauce
⅓ cup Dry White Wine
2 cloves Garlic, minced
2 inch Ginger, grated

2 tbsp Monk Fruit Syrup
1 tbsp Swerve Sweetener
Black Pepper to taste

DIRECTIONS

Heat the oil on Sauté, add the oxtail and slightly brown them. Mix the braising ingredients and pour over the oxtail. Add the veggies, seal the lid, select Meat/Stew and cook for 45 minutes.

Once done, allow for a natural release, for 10 minutes. Remove excess fat and serve hot.

Nutrition facts per serving: Calories 264, Protein 12.5g, Net Carbs 0g, Fat 20.3g

Oxtail Soup

Prep + Cook Time: 1 hour 35 minutes | Servings: 5

INGREDIENTS

2 lb Oxtail
3 tbsp Olive oil
1 sprig Thyme
1 sprig Rosemary
1 Bay Leaf
⅓ tsp Clove Powder
1 Lemon, 2 tbsp juice

2 cups Bone Broth
1 Rutabaga, diced
1 Tomato Puree
1 cup Green Beans
1 cup Chopped Carrots
1 Celery Stalk, chopped
Salt and Black Pepper to taste

DIRECTIONS

Season oxtail with salt and pepper. Heat the oil on Sauté, add oxtail and brown on each side. Add the herbs, spices and lemon juice. Stir and cook for 3 minutes.

Remove oxtail and set aside. Stir in the remaining ingredients and cook for 10 minutes. Add the meat back, seal the lid, select Manual and cook on High pressure for 1 hour.

Once done, quickly release the pressure. Remove the oxtail, shred it and add back to the pot. Select Sauté and cook the sauce for 5 minutes to thicken.

Nutrition facts per serving: Calories 371, Protein 32.6g, Net Carbs 8.2g, Fat 21.5g

Easy Osso Buco

Prep + Cook Time: 4 hours 40 minutes | Servings: 6 to 8

INGREDIENTS

2 cups Chopped Onion
1 cup Chopped Carrots
1 cup Chopped Celery
1.5 cup Beef Broth
2 cups Diced Tomatoes
6 cloves + 1 clove Garlic, minced

Salt and Black Pepper to taste
6 tsp Olive oil
8 (2-inch thick) Veal chops
½ cup Dry White Wine
½ cup fresh Chopped Parsley
2 tsp Orange Zest

DIRECTIONS

Mix all ingredients, except veal and wine, in a bowl. Season the meat with pepper and salt, and brown for 3 minutes on all sides on Sauté. Pour wine to deglaze the bottom.

Add in the bowl ingredients, seal the lid, select Slow Cook mode for 4 hours. Once done, quickly release the pressure. Remove the meat to a plate. Serve with saffron risotto.

Nutrition facts per serving: Calories 315, Protein 34g, Net Carbs 1g, Fat 10g

Oxtail Ragout

Prep + Cook Time: 55 minutes | Servings: 4

INGREDIENTS

1 tbsp Butter
1 medium Onion, chopped
1 Celery Stalk, chopped
1 Carrot, chopped

¾ cup Beef Broth
½ cup Diced Tomatoes
1 Bay Leaf
1 tsp dried Thyme

1 tsp dried Rosemary
Salt and Black Pepper to taste

2 Oxtail Joints, separated
1 tsp Plain Vinegar

DIRECTIONS

Melt butter on Sauté, and cook the onion, celery and carrots for 3 minutes. Add the remaining ingredients, except the meat. Cook for 2 minutes and add the oxtail. Seal the lid.

Select Manual and cook on High Pressure for 30 minutes. Once ready, do a natural pressure release for 10 minutes. Remove any excess fat, stir and serve.

Nutrition facts per serving: Calories 168, Protein 12.7g, Net Carbs 6.1g, Fat 13g

Rosemary Veal Stew

Prep + Cook Time: 50 minutes

INGREDIENTS

2 sprigs Rosemary, chopped
1 tbsp Olive oil
1 tbsp Butter
18 Shallots, pureed
1 Carrot
1 Celery Stalk

1 tbsp Arrowroot Flour
2 lb Veal, cut in 2 inch pieces
¼ cup Dry White Wine
1 cup Water
Salt to taste

DIRECTIONS

Heat oil and butter on Sauté, stir-fry the shallots and veggies for 3 minutes. Add meat and wine, and cook for 5 minutes. Pour in water to almost cover. Seal the lid, and cook on Manual on High Pressure for 20 minutes. Once done, do a natural pressure release for 10 minutes.

Nutrition facts per serving: Calories 244, Protein 31.7g, Net Carbs 3.8g, Fat 9g

Spicy Pulled Pork

Prep + Cook Time: 23 minutes | Servings: 4

INGREDIENTS

2 pounds Pork Shoulder
1 tsp Chili Powder
½ tsp Smoked Paprika
½ tsp Cumin
½ tsp Onion Powder

½ tsp Garlic Salt
¼ tsp Pepper
1 ½ cups Beef Broth
1 tbsp Coconut Oil

DIRECTIONS

Melt coconut oil on Sauté. Combine all spices in a bowl, and massage the pork with the mixture. Add the pork to the Instant Pot. Sear well on all sides, until browned.

Pour in broth and seal the lid. Select Meat/Stew and cook on HIGH pressure for 35 minutes. When it goes off, do a quick pressure release. Transfer the pork to a cutting board. Grab two forks and shred the meat. Serve with hot sauce and mashed broccoli.

Nutrition facts per serving: Calories 295, Protein 28g, Net Carbs 0g, Fat 21g

Brown Gravy Pork Roast

Prep + Cook Time: 25 minutes | Servings: 4

INGREDIENTS:

- 2 lb Pork Roast, cut into slabs
- 1 tbsp Italian Seasoning
- 1 tbsp Ranch Dressing
- 1 tsp Red Wine Vinegar
- 2 cloves Garlic, minced
- Salt and Pepper to taste
- 1 small Onion, chopped
- 1 tbsp Olive oil
- 2 tsp Onion Powder
- ½ tsp Paprika
- 4 tbsp Brewed Coffee
- 1 ½ cups Beef Broth
- 2 tbsp Xanthan Gum
- 2 tbsp Water
- Chopped Parsley to garnish

DIRECTIONS:

Season the pork roast with salt and pepper and set aside. In a bowl, add the Italian seasoning, ranch dressing, red wine vinegar, garlic, onion powder, paprika, and coffee. Set on Sauté.

Add the oil to the pot and sauté the onion until translucent. Pour the gravy coffee mixture and broth in; add the pork roast. Seal the lid, select Meat/Stew and cook on High for 12 minutes. Once ready, do a quick pressure release. Remove the pork roast with a slotted spoon onto a serving plate.

Mix the xanthan gum with the water in a small bowl and add to the sauce. Select Sauté mode. Stir and cook the sauce to thicken which is about 4 minutes. Once the gravy is ready, turn off the pot and spoon the gravy over the pork. Garnish with parsley and serve with a turnip mash.

Nutrition facts per serving: Calories 190, Protein 19g, Net Carbs 2g, Fat 10g

Pork Strips with Tomatoes

Prep + Cook Time: 25 minutes | Servings: 4

INGREDIENTS

- 1 pound Pork Loin, cut into strips
- 14 ounces canned diced Tomatoes
- 2 tbsp Ketchup
- 1 tsp Italian Seasoning
- ¼ tsp Garlic Powder
- 1 ½ cups Beef Broth
- 1 tbsp Coconut Oil
- Salt and Pepper, to taste

DIRECTIONS

Set your Instant Pot to Sauté and melt the coconut oil. Add the pork and season with salt and pepper. Cook until browned on all sides.

Grease a baking dish with cooking spray and transfer the pork to it. Stir in the tomatoes, ketchup, Italian seasoning, and garlic powder.

Pour the broth into the Instant Pot and lower the trivet. Place the dish on top of the trivet and seal the lid. Cook on HIGH pressure for 10 minutes. After the beep, do a quick pressure release and open the lid carefully. Serve with keto bread and cheese.

Nutrition facts per serving: Calories 285, Protein 25g, Net Carbs 6g, Fat 20g

Bangers and Mash with Onion Gravy

Prep + Cook Time: 30 minutes | Servings: 2

INGREDIENTS:

2 lb Turnips, peeled and halved
5 Pork Sausages
1 cup Water + 2 tbsp Water
⅓ cup Green Onion, sliced
Salt and Pepper to taste
4 tbsp Milk

¼ cup + 4 tbsp Unsalted Butter
1 tbsp Arrowroot Starch
3 tbsp Balsamic Vinegar
1 Onion, sliced thinly
1 cup + 2 tbsp Beef Broth

DIRECTIONS:

Place the turnips in the pot and pour the water over. Seal the lid, secure the pressure valve, and select Steam on High pressure for 5 minutes. Once ready, do a quick pressure release.

Remove the turnips to a bowl. Add a quarter cup butter to the turnip and use a masher to mash the turnips until the butter is well mixed into the turnip. Slowly add the milk and mix using a spoon. Add green onions, season with pepper and salt and fold in with the spoon. Set aside.

Pour out the liquid in the Instant Pot and use paper towels to wipe inside the pot dry. Select Sauté and melt 2 tbsp of butter. Add sausages and brown them on each side for 3 minutes.

After they are browned, remove them onto the turnip mash and cover with aluminium foil to keep warm. Set aside. Back into the pot add the two tablespoons of the beef broth to deglaze the bottom of the pot while stirring and scraping the bottom with a spoon.

Add the remaining butter and onions. Sauté the onions until they are translucent then pour in the balsamic vinegar. Stir for another minute. In a bowl, mix the arrowroot starch with water and pour into the pot.

Stir and add the remaining beef broth. Allow the sauce to thicken and adjust the taste with salt and pepper. Turn off the heat once a slurry is formed. Dish the mashed potatoes and sausages in serving plates. Spoon the gravy over and serve with steamed green beans.

Nutrition facts per serving: Calories 300, Protein 12g, Net Carbs 3g, Fat 16g

Herby Cuban Pork Roast

Prep + Cook Time: 55 minutes | Servings: 8

INGREDIENTS

3 pounds Pork Shoulder
3 tbsp Olive oil
1 tsp Vinegar
Juice of 1 Lime
½ tsp Onion Flakes
1 tsp dried Parsley

1 tsp Cumin seeds
1 tsp Garlic Powder
Salt and Pepper, to taste
1 ½ cups Beef Broth
1 Red Chilli, deseeded and chopped
1 tbsp fresh Cilantro, chopped to garnish

DIRECTIONS

In a bowl, combine the olive oil, lime juice, vinegar, and spices and herbs. Rub the mixture on the meat. Add the pork inside the Pot and cover with the remaining marinade.

Pour the broth around the pork and seal the lid. Select the Meat/mode and cook on HIGH pressure for 40 minutes. When it goes off, do a quick pressure release. Slice or shred the meat before serving.

Nutrition facts per serving: Calories 305, Protein 32g, Net Carbs 2g, Fat 13g

Pork Stew

Prep + Cook Time: 60 minutes | Servings: 4

INGREDIENTS

1 lb Pork Loin, cut into cubed
1 cup Cauliflower Florets
1 cup Broccoli Florets
1 Celery Stalk, chopped
½ Onion, diced
2 Garlic Cloves, minced
14 ounces diced canned Tomatoes
3 cups Beef Broth
1 cup Snap Peas, chopped
Salt and Black Pepper, to taste
1 tsp dried Thyme
1 tbsp Arrowroot mixed with 1 tbsp Water
2 tbsp Coconut Oil

DIRECTIONS

Melt half of the coconut oil on Sauté. Add the pork and season with salt and pepper. Cook for a few minutes, until browned on all sides. Remove to a plate.

Add the remaining coconut oil and cook the onions for 2 minutes. Then, stir in garlic and celery, and cook for 1 minute. Add in the remaining ingredients, except the arrowroot mixture.

Seal the lid, press Meat/Stew and cook for 15 minutes on HIGH pressure. When it goes off, do a natural pressure release, for 10 minutes. Stir in the arrowroot mixture and set to Sauté. Cook for a few minutes or until slightly thickened. Serve immediately.!

Nutrition facts per serving: Calories 385, Protein 28g, Net Carbs 6.2g, Fat 22g

Lemony Pork Belly

Prep + Cook Time: 55 minutes | Servings: 4

INGREDIENTS

2 pounds Pork Belly
1 tbsp Sweetener
2 tbsp Lime Juice
1 Onion, chopped
½ cup Chicken Broth
2 cups Water

DIRECTIONS

Combine the pork belly and water in your Instant Pot and seal the lid. Press Manual and cook for 25 minutes on HIGH pressure. Meanwhile, place the remaining ingredients in a food processor and pulse until pureed.

When the timer goes off, do a quick pressure release. Remove the pork to a baking dish and pour the puree over. Do not discard the water in the pot. Lower the trivet in the pot. Place the dish on top and seal the lid. Cook for 15 minutes on HIGH pressure.Do a quick pressure release.

Nutrition facts per serving: Calories 453, Protein 25g, Net Carbs 6g, Fat 35g

Ham with Collard Greens

Prep + Cook Time: 10 minutes | Servings: 4

INGREDIENTS:

20 oz Collard Greens, chopped
5 tbsp Chicken Bouillon
4 cups Water
½ cup diced Sweet Onion
2 ½ cups diced Ham

DIRECTIONS:

Place the ham at the bottom of the pot. Add the collard greens and onion. Then, add the chicken cube to the water and dissolve it. Pour the mixture into the pot. Seal the lid, select Steam mode on Low pressure for 5 minutes. Once ready, do a quick pressure release.

Spoon the vegetables and the ham with sauce into a serving platter. Serve with a steak dish.

Nutrition facts per serving: Calories 128, Protein 6.5g, Net Carbs 0g, Fat 3.5g

Pork in Mushroom Gravy

Prep + Cook Time: 35 minutes | Servings: 4

INGREDIENTS:

4 Pork Chops
1 tbsp Olive oil
3 cloves Garlic, minced
Salt and Pepper to taste
1 tsp Garlic Powder
1 (10 oz) Mushroom Soup

8 oz Mushrooms, sliced
1 small Onion, chopped
1 cup Beef Broth
1 sprig Fresh Thyme
Chopped Parsley to garnish

DIRECTIONS:

Heat oil on Sauté, and add mushrooms, garlic, and onion. Sauté stirring occasionally until translucent, for 3 minutes. Season pork chops with salt, garlic powder, and pepper.

Add into the pot followed by the thyme and broth. Seal the lid, select Meat/Stew and cook on High pressure for 15 minutes. Once ready, do a natural pressure release for about 10 minutes, then a quick pressure release to let the remaining steam out.

Select Sauté and add mushroom soup. Stir until the mixture thickens. Dish the pork and gravy into a serving bowl and garnish with parsley. Serve with a side of creamy squash mash.

Nutrition facts per serving: Calories 227, Protein 15.5g, Net Carbs 0g, Fat 15.5g

Pork Tenderloin with Ginger Soy Sauce

Prep + Cook Time: 20 minutes | Servings: 4

INGREDIENTS:

2 lb Pork Tenderloin
½ cup sugar-free Soy Sauce
¼ cup Monk Fruit Sugar
½ cup Water + 2 tbsp Water
3 tbsp grated Ginger

2 cloves Garlic, minced
2 tbsp Sesame Oil
2 tsp Arrowroot Starch
Chopped Scallions to garnish
Sesame Seeds to garnish

DIRECTIONS:

Add soy sauce, monk fruit sugar, half cup of water, ginger, garlic, and sesame oil; stir. Then, add the pork. Seal the lid, and select Meat/Stew mode on High for 10 minutes. Once ready, do a quick pressure release and remove the pork onto a serving plate.

In a bowl, mix the arrowroot starch with the remaining water until smooth and pour into the pot. Select Sauté mode, stir the sauce frequently and cook until it thickens. Once the sauce is ready, serve the pork with a side endive salad and spoon the sauce all over it.

Nutrition facts per serving: Calories 240, Protein 21g, Net Carbs 3g, Fat 9g

Beef Bourguignonne

Prep + Cook Time: 45 minutes | Servings: 4

INGREDIENTS:

2 lb Stewing Beef, cut in chunks
Salt and Pepper to taste
2 ½ tbsp Olive oil
¼ tsp Red Wine Vinegar
¼ cup Pearl Onion
3 tsp Tomato Paste
½ lb Turnips, peeled and halved
2 Carrots, peeled and chopped

1 Onion, sliced
2 cloves Garlic, crushed
1 cup Red Wine
2 cups Beef Broth
1 bunch Thyme
½ cup Cognac
2 tbsp Almond flour

DIRECTIONS:

Season the beef with salt, pepper, and a light sprinkle of flour. Heat oil on Sauté, and brown the beef on all sides. This can be done in batches but after all the meat should be returned to the pot. Pour the cognac into the pot and stir the mixture to deglaze the bottom of the pot.

Add the thyme, red wine, beef broth, tomato paste, garlic, turnips, onion, and pearl onions. Stir with a spoon. Seal the lid, select Meat/Stew on High for 25 minutes. Once ready, do a quick pressure release to let out the remaining steam.

Use the spoon to remove the thyme, adjust the taste with salt and pepper, and add the vinegar. Stir the sauce and dish in a serving bowl. Serve with a side of cauli rice or low carb bread.

Nutrition facts per serving: Calories 339, Protein 36.3g, Net Carbs 0.1g, Fat 11.7g

Beef Burger

Prep + Cook Time: 20 minutes | Servings: 4

INGREDIENTS:

1 lb Ground Beef
1 (1 oz) packet Dry Onion Soup Mix

1 cup Water

Assembling:

4 low carb Burger Buns
4 Tomato Slices
4 Cheddar Cheese Slices
4 small leaves Lettuce

Mayonnaise
Mustard
Sugar-Free Ketchup

DIRECTIONS:

In a bowl, add the beef and onion mix, and combine them well together with your hands.

Make 4 patties with your hands and wrap them in each foil paper. Pour the water into the Instant Pot and fit the steamer rack in it. Place the wrapped patties on the trivet, close the lid, and secure the pressure valve. Select Meat/ Stew mode on High pressure for 10 minutes.

Once ready, do a quick pressure release to let out the remaining steam,. Use a set of tongs to remove the wrapped beef onto a flat surface and carefully unwrap them.

Assemble the burger:

In each half of the buns, put a lettuce leaf, then a beef patty, a slice of cheese, and a slice of tomato. Top with the other halves of buns. Serve with some ketchup, mayonnaise, and mustard.

Nutrition facts per serving: Calories 580, Protein 28g, Net Carbs 2g, Fat 42g

Pork Carnitas Lettuce Cups

Prep + Cook Time: 30 minutes | Servings: 6

INGREDIENTS:

3 lb Pork Shoulder
2 tbsp + 2 tbsp Olive oil
1 small head Butter Lettuce, dried
2 Limes, cut in wedges
2 Carrots, grated
1 ½ cup Water
1 Onion, chopped
½ tsp Cayenne Pepper

½ tsp Coriander Powder
1 tsp Cumin Powder
1 tsp Garlic Powder
1 tsp White Pepper
2 tsp dried Oregano
1 tsp Red Pepper Flakes
Salt to taste
1 tbsp Cocoa Powder, unsweetened

DIRECTIONS:

In a bowl, add the onion, cayenne pepper, coriander powder, garlic powder, white pepper, dried oregano, red pepper flakes, salt, and cocoa powder. Mix them well with a spoon.

Sprinkle the spice mixture on the pork and use your hands to rub the spice well onto the meat. Then, wrap the meat in plastic wrap and refrigerate overnight. The next day, turn on the Instant Pot, open the pot, and select Sauté mode.

Pour 2 tablespoons of olive oil in the pot and once is heating, remove the pork from the fridge, remove the wraps and put in the pot. Brown on both sides for 6 minutes and then pour the water on it. Seal the lid, select Meat/ Stew mode on High pressure for 20 minutes.

Once ready, do a quick pressure release. Use a set of tongs to remove the pork onto a cutting board and use two forks to shred it. Empty the pot and wipe clean. Set the pot on Sauté mode and add the remaining olive oil. Once has heated, add the shredded pork to and fry until browns lightly for 5 minutes. Turn off the heat and begin assembling.

Arrange double layers of lettuce leaves on a flat surface, make a bed of grated carrots, and spoon the pulled Pork on top.

Nutrition facts per serving: Calories 315, Protein 28.2g, Net Carbs 0g, Fat 18.5g

Easy BBQ Ribs

Prep + Cook Time: 40 minutes | Servings: 2 to 3

INGREDIENTS:

½ lb rack Baby Back Ribs
Salt and Pepper to season

½ cup sugar-free Barbecue Sauce
3 tbsp Apple Cider Vinegar

DIRECTIONS:

Heat oil on Sauté, and season the ribs with salt and pepper. Brown the ribs in the oil for 1 to 2 minutes per side. Pour the barbecue sauce and apple cider vinegar over the ribs and use tongs to turn to be well coated. Seal the lid, set on Steam on High for 30 minutes.

Once the timer goes off, do a natural pressure release for 15 minutes, then a quick pressure release to let out the remaining steam. Remove the ribs onto a serving platter and set the pot on Sauté to simmer until the sauce thickens, for 6 minutes. Use a knife to slice the ribs and pour the sauce all over. Serve the ribs with a generous side of steamed crunchy green beans.

Nutrition facts per serving: Calories 310, Protein 21g, Net Carbs 3g, Fat 10g

Braised Pork Neck Bones

Prep + Cook Time: 40 minutes | Servings: 6

INGREDIENTS:

3 lb Pork Neck Bones
3 to 4 tbsp Olive oil
Salt and Black Pepper to taste
2 cloves Garlic, smashed
1 tbsp sugar-free Tomato Paste

1 tsp dried Thyme
1 White Onion, sliced
½ cup Red Wine
1 cup Beef Broth

DIRECTIONS:

Turn on the Instant Pot, open the lid, and select Sauté mode. Pour in the olive oil and while heats, quickly season the pork neck bones with salt and pepper; brown on all sides. You can work in batches for the best browning result. Each batch should take about 5 minutes.

After, use a set of tongs to remove them onto a plate. Add the onion and sprinkle with some salt as desired. Stir with a spoon and cook the onions until they have softened. Then, add the smashed garlic, thyme, pepper, and tomato paste. Cook them for 2 minutes but with constant stirring to prevent the tomato paste from burning.

Next, pour the red wine into the pot to deglaze the bottom of the pot. Add the pork neck bones back to the pot and pour the beef broth over it. Close the lid, secure the pressure valve, and select Meat/Stew mode on High pressure for 5 to 15 minutes.

Once ready, let the pot sit for 10 minutes before doing a quick pressure release. Open the pot. Dish the pork neck soup into a serving bowl and serve with a good amount of broccoli mash.

Nutrition facts per serving: Calories 106, Protein 13.4g, Net Carbs 0g, Fat 6.5g

Pork Roast Sandwich

Prep + Cook Time: 20 minutes | Servings: 4

INGREDIENTS:

2 lb Chuck Roast
¼ cup Monk Fruit Sugar
1 tsp Paprika
1 tsp Garlic Powder

1 White Onion, sliced
3 2 cups Beef Broth
Salt to taste
2 tbsp Apple Cider Vinegar

Assembling:

3 Low Carb Buns, halved

White Cheddar Cheese, grated

DIRECTIONS:

Place the pork roast on a clean flat surface and sprinkle with paprika, garlic powder, monk fruit sugar, and salt. Use your hands to rub the seasoning on the meat. Add beef broth to it, onions, pork, and apple cider vinegar. Seal the lid, select Meat/Stew and cook on High for 15 minutes.

Once ready, do a quick pressure release, and open the pot. Turn off the pot. Remove the roasts with tongs and place them on a cutting board. Use two forks to shred.

In the buns, add the shredded pork with as much meat as desired, add some cooked onions from the pot, and top with the cheese. Serve warm with cheese.

Nutrition facts per serving: Calories 305, Protein 45g, Net Carbs 0g, Fat 35g

Balsamic Pork Tenderloin

Prep + Cook Time: 30 minutes | Servings: 4

INGREDIENTS:

2 lb Pork Tenderloin
2 tbsp Olive oil
¼ cup Monk Fruit Sugar
½ cup Chicken Broth
Salt and Black Pepper to taste
1 clove Garlic, minced
1 tsp Sage Powder
1 tbsp Dijon Mustard
¼ cup Balsamic Vinegar
1 tbsp sugar-free Worcestershire Sauce
½ tbsp Xanthan Gum
4 tbsp Water

DIRECTIONS:

Season the pork with salt and pepper. Select Sauté mode. Heat oil on Sauté, and brown the pork on both sides for 4 minutes in total. Remove to a plate and set aside.

Add the monk fruit sugar, chicken broth, balsamic vinegar, garlic, Worcestershire sauce, mustard, and sage. Stir the ingredients and return pork to the pot. Seal the lid, select Meat/Stew and cook on High pressure for 10 minutes. Once done, do a quick pressure release.

Remove the pork with tongs onto a plate and wrap in aluminum foil. Next, mix the xanthan gum with water and pour into the pot. Select Sauté mode, stir the mixture and cook to thicken. Then, turn the pot off after the desired thickness is achieved.

Unwrap the pork and use a knife to slice with 3 to 4-inch thickness. Arrange the slices on a serving platter and spoon the sauce all over it. Serve with a sautéed Brussels sprouts and red onion chunks.

Nutrition facts per serving: Calories 154, Protein 23.3g, Net Carbs 2g, Fat 10.1g

Tender Greek Pork

Prep + Cook Time: 60 minutes | Servings: 6

INGREDIENTS:

3 lb Pork Roast, cut into pieces
3 tbsp Cavender's Greek Seasoning
1 tsp Onion Powder
¼ cup Beef Broth
¼ cup fresh Lemon Juice
Salt to taste

DIRECTIONS:

Open the Instant Pot and put the pork chunks in it. In a bowl, add the greek seasoning, onion powder, beef broth, lemon juice, and some more salt as desired.

Mix them using a spoon and pour the sauce over the pork in the Instant Pot. Close the lid, secure the pressure valve, and select Meat/Stew mode on High pressure for 45 minutes.

Once ready, do a natural pressure release for 10 minutes then do a quick pressure release to let out any more steam, and open the pot. Use a slotted spoon to remove the pork chunks onto a chopping board and use forks to shred. Add the shredded pork to a salad and serve.

Nutrition facts per serving: Calories 210, Protein 22.9g, Net Carbs 0g, Fat 12.4g

Pork in Vegetable Sauce

Prep + Cook Time: 40 minutes | Servings: 4

INGREDIENTS:

2 lb Pork Loin Roast
Salt and Pepper to taste
3 cloves Garlic, minced
1 medium Onion, diced
2 tbsp Butter
3 stalks Celery, chopped
3 Carrots, chopped
1 cup Chicken Broth
2 tbsp sugar-free Worcestershire Sauce
½ tbsp Monk Fruit Sugar
1 tsp Yellow Mustard
2 tsp dried Basil
2 tsp dried Thyme
1 tbsp Arrowroot Starch
¼ cup Water

DIRECTIONS:

Turn on the Instant Pot, open the lid, and select Sauté mode. Pour the oil in and while heats quickly season the pork with salt and pepper. Put the pork to the oil and sear to golden brown on both sides. This is about 4 minutes.

Then, include the garlic and onions and cook them until they are soft for 4 minutes too.

Top with the celery, carrots, chicken broth, Worcestershire sauce, mustard, thyme, basil, and monk fruit sugar. Use a spoon to stir it. Seal the lid, select Meat/Stew mode on High pressure for 20 minutes. Once ready, do a quick pressure release.

Remove the meat from the pot onto a serving platter. Add the arrowroot starch to the water, mix with a spoon, and add to the pot. Select Sauté and cook the sauce to become a slurry with a bit of thickness. Season with salt and pepper and spoon the sauce over the meat in the serving platter.Serve with a side of steamed almond garlicky rapini mix.

Nutrition facts per serving: Calories 326, Protein 25.7g, Net Carbs 0g, Fat 16.1g

Creamy Pork with Bacon

Prep + Cook Time: 23 minutes | Servings: 4

INGREDIENTS

⅓ cup Heavy Cream
1 cup Chicken Broth
1 ½ tsp Arrowroot
1 tbsp Water
3 Bacon Slices, chopped
1 tsp Olive oil
1 pound Pork Tenderloin, cut into strips
1 tsp dried Thyme
¼ tsp Garlic Powder
Salt and Pepper, to taste

DIRECTIONS

Set your Instant Pot to Sauté, add the bacon and cook for 5-6 minutes, until crispy. Remove to a plate lined with paper towel to drain excess oil and set aside.

Heat the olive oil in the pot until sizzling. Add the pork strips and season with salt and pepper; cook until browned on all sides, for 6 minutes. Pour the broth over and stir in the spices.

Seal the lid, select Manual and cook on HIGH pressure for 15 minutes. After the beep, do a quick pressure release. Stir in the heavy cream and cook on Sauté for 2 minutes.

Whisk together arrowroot and water, and stir the mixture into the sauce. Adjust the seasoning.

Nutrition facts per serving: Calories 355, Protein 28g, Net Carbs 2g, Fat 25g

Pulled Pork in Lettuce Wraps

Prep + Cook Time: 50 minutes | Servings: 4

INGREDIENTS

3 lb Pork Roast
1 tbsp Olive oil
1 head Lettuce, washed, pat dry

Spice Mix:

1 tbsp unsweetened Cocoa Powder
Salt to taste
White Pepper to taste
½ tsp Garlic Powder
½ tsp Red Pepper Flakes

1 large avocado, chopped
½ cup mayonnaise
2 cups Water

2 tsp Oregano
½ tsp Cumin
¼ tsp Coriander Powder
¼ tsp Cayenne Pepper
1 large red Onion, chopped finely

DIRECTIONS

Mix the spices and rub onto pork. Wrap the pork in plastic wrap, and marinate in the refrigerator overnight. Heat oil on Sauté, and brown the pork on all sides. Pour the water, seal the lid and cook on High for 50 minutes. Once ready, do a natural pressure release for 20 minutes. Remove to a platter.

Press Sauté and simmer the juices down. Shred the pork and set aside. Place a pan over medium heat, heat the olive oil and add the pork. Drizzle some of the cooking liquid on the pork, stir and turn off. Arrange lettuce wraps on a flat surface, fill each wrap with a bit of avocado and mayonnaise and top with pork.

Nutrition facts per serving: Calories 350, Protein 39g, Net Carbs 6g, Fat 15g

Coconut Ginger Pork

Prep + Cook Time: 45 minutes | Servings: 4

INGREDIENTS:

3 lb Shoulder Roast
1 tbsp Olive oil
Salt and Black Pepper to season
2 cups Coconut Milk
1 tsp Coriander Powder

1 tsp Cumin Powder
3 tbsp grated Ginger
3 tsp minced Garlic
1 Onion, peeled and quartered
Parsley Leaves (unchopped), to garnish

DIRECTIONS:

In a bowl, add the coriander, salt, pepper, and cumin. Use a spoon to mix them. Season the pork with the spice mixture. Then, use your hands to rub the spice on the meat.

Turn on the Instant Pot and open the pot. Add the olive oil and pork to it. Add the onions, ginger, garlic, and coconut milk. Seal the lid, select Meat/Stew mode and cook on High pressure for 40 minutes.

Once ready, do a quick pressure release. Dish the meat with the sauce into a serving bowl, garnish with the parsley, and serve with a side of keto bread.

Nutrition facts per serving: Calories 267, Protein 38g Net Carbs 0g, Fat 11g

Sweet Spicy Pork Chops

Prep + Cook Time: 25 minutes | Servings: 4

INGREDIENTS

- 4 Pork Chops, Boneless and cubed
- 6 cloves Garlic, minced
- 1 Onion, cut in big chunks
- 2 Zucchinis, chopped in big chunks
- 2 tbsp Sesame Oil
- 1 tsp Red Chili Flakes
- ½ tsp Ginger Juice
- ½ tsp Orange Zest
- 1 tbsp Tahini
- 2 tbsp Monk Fruit Syrup
- 1 tbsp Plain Vinegar
- ½ tbsp Arrowroot Powder
- 1 tsp Sriracha Sauce
- 1/6 cup Water
- Salt and Pepper to taste

DIRECTIONS

Season the pork with pepper and salt. Heat half of the oil on Sauté. Add the garlic and pork. Brown the pork on all sides. Mix the remaining oil, ginger juice, zest, tahini, flakes, monk syrup and vinegar.

Mix evenly and pour over the pork. Seal the lid and cook on High Pressure for 12 minutes. Once done, quickly release the pressure. Add in zucchinis and onion, seal the lid and cook for 5 minutes on High pressure. Once done, release the pressure quickly. Mix the arrowroot powder with water and pour in the pot. Stir in the sriracha sauce and serve.

Nutrition facts per serving: Calories 231, Protein 15.1g, Net Carbs 0.7g, Fat 8.3g

Green Chile Pork Carnitas

Prep + Cook Time: 55 minutes | Servings:

INGREDIENTS

- 4 lb Pork Shoulder, cut 3 pieces
- 3 tbsp Olive oil
- Salt and Black Pepper to taste
- 2 Jalapenos, seeded, minced
- 2 Green Bell peppers, seeded, chopped
- 2 Poblano Peppers, seeded, minced
- 1 ½ lb Tomatillos, husked, quartered
- 4 cloves Garlic, peeled
- 2 medium Red Onions, chopped
- 2 tsp Cumin Powder
- 2 tsp Dried Oregano
- 2 ½ cups Pork Broth
- 3 Bay Leaves

Toppings:

- Red Onion, chopped
- Queso Fresco
- Cilantro, roughly chopped

DIRECTIONS

Season the pork with pepper and salt. Heat oil on Sauté, and brown pork on all sides for 6 minutes. Add bell pepper, peppers, tomatillo, onion, cumin, garlic, oregano, bay leaves and broth.

Stir, close the lid, secure the pressure valve and select Manual mode on High Pressure for 10 minutes. Once done, do a natural pressure release for 15 minutes.

Remove the meat from the pot, shred it in a plate; set aside. Puree the remaining ingredients in the pot using a stick blender. Add the pork back. Set on Sauté and simmer for 5 minutes. Stir twice and serve in keto tacos with the toppings.

Nutrition facts per serving: Calories 690, Protein 27g, Net Carbs 1g, Fat 48g

Pork in Peanut Sauce

Prep + Cook Time: 50 minutes | Servings: 4

INGREDIENTS:

3 lb Pork Roast
1 cup Hot Water
1 large Red Bell pepper, seeded and sliced
Salt and Pepper to taste
1 large White Onion, sliced
½ cup sugar-free Soy Sauce

1 tbsp Plain Vinegar
½ cup Peanut Butter
1 tbsp Lime Juice
1 tbsp Garlic Powder
1 tsp Ginger Puree

To Garnish:

Chopped Peanuts
Chopped Green Onions

Lime Wedges

DIRECTIONS:

Pour soy sauce, vinegar, peanut butter, lime juice, garlic powder, and ginger puree to a bowl. Use a whisk to mix them together and even. Add a few pinches of salt and pepper, and mix it.

Open the Instant Pot and put the pork in it. Pour the hot water and peanut butter mixture over. Close the lid, secure the pressure valve, and select Meat/Stew mode on High pressure for 20 minutes. Once ready, do a quick pressure release.

Use a slotted spoon or a set of tongs to remove the meat onto a cutting board and use two forks to shred it. Return to the sauce and select Sauté mode. Let simmer for about 2 minutes, then turn the Instant Pot off. On a bed of broccoli cauli rice, spoon the meat with some sauce and garnish with the chopped peanuts, green Onions, and the Lemon wedges.

Nutrition facts per serving: Calories 243, Protein 27g, Net Carbs 0g, Fat 6.6g

Carrot and Pork Stew

Prep + Cook Time: 45 minutes | Servings: 6

INGREDIENTS:

1 Onion, chopped
2 Tomatoes, chopped
2 Carrots, sliced
½ lb Pork meat, pieces, boiled
2 cups Chicken broth
½ tbsp Garlic paste
½ tbsp Ginger paste

½ tbsp Cumin powder
½ tbsp Cinnamon powder
½ tbsp Chili powder
¼ tbsp Salt
¼ tbsp Turmeric powder
3 tbsp Olive oil
2 Jalapeño peppers, whole

DIRECTIONS:

Heat oil on Sauté, and sauté onion for 2 minutes. Add in tomatoes, ginger, garlic, salt, chili, and turmeric; stir-fry for 1 minute. Add pork and cook for 10 minutes.

Add carrots and cook until the meat lightly tender, about 4-5 minutes. Next, add the chicken broth and jalapeños. Seal the lid and cook on High pressure for 30 minutes.

When ready, do a quick pressure release and stir in cinnamon and cumin powder.

Nutrition facts per serving: Calories 151, Protein 8g, Net Carbs 1.5g, Fat 5.2g

Kalua Pork

Prep + Cook Time: 2 hours 2 minutes | Servings: 2

INGREDIENTS

6 lb Pork Shoulder, cut in to 2
3 tbsp Olive oil
1 cup Water

2 tbsp Hickory Liquid Smoke
Salt to season

DIRECTIONS

Heat oil on Sauté, brown the pork each side for 8 minutes. Press Cancel and remove to a platter. Add in water and hickory smoke liquid. Stir and add the roasts with juices.

Sprinkle salt on top of the pork roasts. Seal the lid and cook on High Pressure 90 minutes. Once done, do a natural pressure release for 20 minutes. Remove the pork and shred it.

Discard fats that come off the meat while shredding.

Nutrition facts per serving: Calories 260, Protein 24g, Net Carbs 0g, Fat 18g

Coconut Pork Shoulder

Prep + Cook Time: 20 minutes | Servings: 2

INGREDIENTS

¼ lb cubed Pork Shoulder
2 tbsp Coconut oil
1 lb of halved Brussels Sprouts
½ chopped Onion
1 pinch of Salt

1 pinch of Black Pepper
1 tsp Flax seed powder
¼ cup toasted and chopped Almonds
1 Lemon zest
½ cup Coconut Milk

DIRECTIONS

Set on Sauté mode and heated the oil; add the pork and cook for 2-3 minutes. Add the onions, flax seed, Brussels sprouts, ½ cup of coconut milk and seal the lid.

Cook to Manual on High pressure for 15 minutes. When ready, do a quick pressure release. Season with pepper and salt. Serve with almonds and lemon zest.

Nutrition facts per serving: Calories 457, Protein 24.1g, Net Carbs 7.3g, Fat 30.4g

Prosciutto Wrapped Asparagus Canes

Prep + Cook Time: 25 minutes | Servings: 4

INGREDIENTS

1 lb Asparagus,
1 lb Bacon Strips

1 cup Water

DIRECTIONS

Pour in water and place a steamer basket. Wrap each asparagus with a bacon strip. Arrange the canes in the basket. Seal the lid, and cook on High Pressure for 3 minutes. Once done, quickly release the pressure. Remove the canes and serve warm.

Nutrition facts per serving: Calories 242, Protein 20g, Net Carbs 1g, Fat 18g

Hot Shredded Pork

Prep + Cook Time: 30 minutes | Servings: 4

INGREDIENTS:

2 Pork fillets, boiled, shredded
½ tbsp Garlic paste
½ tbsp Salt
½ tbsp Soy sauce
2 tbsp Lemon juice
2 tbsp Barbecue sauce
½ cup Chili Garlic sauce
2 tbsp Vinegar
½ tbsp Chili powder
2 tbsp Olive oil

DIRECTIONS:

Heat oil on Sauté, and cook garlic for 1 minute. Add the pork and brown for 10 minutes per side. Add soy sauce, chili sauce, vinegar, barbecue sauce, salt, and chili powder and cook for another 5 minutes. Transfer to a serving dish and drizzle lemon juice.

Nutrition facts per serving: Calories 351, Protein 45.1g, Net Carbs 5.1g, Fat 14.9g

Bacon Brussel Sprout Dish

Prep + Cook Time: 17 minutes | Servings: 2 to 3

INGREDIENTS

2 cups Brussel Sprouts, trimmed and halved
4 slices Bacon Slices, chopped
Salt to taste
1 tsp Monk Fruit Syrup

DIRECTIONS

Chop the bacon into small squares. Set the pot on Sauté. Add the bacon and cook until brown and crumbly. Add the brussels sprout and cook for 5 minutes. Add ¼ cup of water and stir.

Seal the lid, and cook on High Pressure mode for 2 minutes. Once ready, quickly release the pressure. Remove to a plate, drizzle with the syrup and salt.

Nutrition facts per serving: Calories 83, Protein 3g, Net Carbs 0g, Fat 5.3g

Spicy Pork Chops

Prep + Cook Time: 2 minutes | Servings: 3

INGREDIENTS

2 lb Pork Chops, Boneless
Salt to taste
1 tbsp Coconut Oil
3 tbsp Hot Sauce
1 Onion, sliced
2 cloves Garlic, minced
½ tsp Dried Thyme
½ cup Chicken Broth
2 Carrots, julienned
1 cup String Beans

DIRECTIONS

Heat oil on Sauté, add the chops, season with salt, and brown them on each side. Remove to a plate. Add the onions, thyme, hot sauce, and garlic. Stir and cook for 3 minutes.

Add the pork chops back to the pot with the chicken broth, string beans and carrots. Seal the lid, and cook on High Pressure for 10 minutes. Once ready, quickly release the pressure.

Nutrition facts per serving: Calories 320, Protein 26g, Net Carbs 5g, Fat 19g

Sausage and Pepper Sauce

Prep + Cook Time: 35 minutes | Servings: 3

INGREDIENTS

10 Pork Sausages
2 large Green Bell peppers, diced
2 large Yellow Bell peppers, diced
2 large Red Bell peppers, diced
1 cup Diced Tomatoes
¼ cup Tomato Sauce
1 cup Water
3 Basil Leaves
3 cloves Garlic, minced
1 tbsp Italian Seasoning
Salt to taste

DIRECTIONS

Place all ingredients in the pot with peppers arranged on top; don't stir. Seal the lid and cook on High Pressure for 15 minutes. Once ready, quickly release the pressure. Stir and serve.

Nutrition facts per serving: Calories 173, Protein 9g, Net Carbs 0g, Fat 15g

Pork Roll Soup

Prep + Cook Time: 45 minutes | Servings: 4

INGREDIENTS

2 tbsp Olive oil
1 ½ lb Minced Pork
1 Onion, diced
4 cups Beef Broth
1 small Cabbage, chopped
1 cup Carrots, shredded
1 tsp Garlic Powder
1 tsp Onion Powder
Salt to taste
1 tsp Ginger Paste
½ cup Coconut Aminos

DIRECTIONS

Heat oil on Sauté, add the pork and brown for 9 minutes. Stir in the remaining ingredients. Seal the lid, and cook on High Pressure for 25 minutes. Once ready, quickly release the pressure.

Nutrition facts per serving: Calories 101, Protein 3.8g, Net Carbs 0.5g, Fat 10g

Easy Pork Ribs

Prep + Cook Time: 55 minutes | Servings: 3

INGREDIENTS

3 lb Pork Ribs, cut in section

Dry Rub:

1 tbsp Swerve Sweetener
Salt to taste
Black Pepper to taste
2 tsp Garlic Powder
2 tsp Onion Powder
2 tsp Paprika
1 tsp Allspice
1 tsp Coriander Powder

For the sauce:

1 cup Keto Ketchup
1 tbsp Swerve Sweetener
1 tbsp Plain Vinegar
¼ cup Water
¼ tsp Liquid Smoke
¼ tsp Allspice
¼ tsp Onion Powder

DIRECTIONS

Mix the dry ingredients in a bowl and season the ribs. Arrange the ribs at the bottom of the Instant Pot. Mix the sauce ingredients and pour over the ribs. Seal the lid, select Manual and cook on High Pressure for 35 minutes. Once done, quickly release the pressure.

Transfer the ribs to a flat platter. Select Sauté mode and simmer the sauce to thicken.

Nutrition facts per serving: Calories 90, Protein 6.2g, Net Carbs 1.2g, Fat 6.4g

Fall-Apart Pork Butt with Garlic Sauce

Prep + Cook Time: 55 minutes | Servings: 5

INGREDIENTS

2 pounds Pork Butt
¼ cup Worcestershire Sauce

For garlic sauce
2 Garlic cloves, chopped
1 tbsp olive oil, plus 2 tsp extra
1 onion, minced

½ tsp Onion Flakes
Salt and Pepper, to taste

1 tbsp Lemon juice
½ cup Beef stock
1 tbsp double cream

DIRECTIONS

Brush the pork with Worcestershire sauce, and let it sit at room temperature for 90 minutes. Then, transfer to the pot, season with salt and pepper, and pour in the water.

Seal the lid, hit the Manual and set the cooking time to 45 minutes on HIGH pressure.

Meanwhile, in a bowl, combine the ingredients for the garlic sauce, adjust the seasoning, and set aside. After the beep, do a quick pressure release and open the lid carefully.

Pour the garlic mixture over the meat. Select Sauté, and simmer for 10 minutes or until thickened.

Nutrition facts per serving: Calories 680, Protein 25g, Net Carbs 8g, Fat 56g

Bacon Onion Jam

Prep + Cook Time: 6 hours 40 minutes | Servings: 6

INGREDIENTS

1 lb Bacon strips, cut in ½-inch pieces
4 Onions, chopped
2 cloves Garlic
¼ cup Monk Fruit Powder
¼ cup Starfruit Juice

¼ cup Plain Vinegar
1 tsp fresh Thyme Leaves
1/6 tsp Cinnamon Powder
A pinch Cayenne Pepper

DIRECTIONS

Add bacon and fry until slightly cooked but not crispy, on Sauté. Remove to a paper-towel-lined plate and refrigerate. Scoop out the grease from the pot leaving a tablespoon of oil.

Add the garlic and onion and cook for 5 minutes. Stir in the remaining ingredients, seal the lid, and cook on Slow Cook mode for 6 hours. Once done, quickly release the pressure.

Stir in the bacon, and cook on Sauté for 10 minutes. Scoop into an airtight container, refrigerate and use for up to a week.

Nutrition facts per serving: Calories 40, Protein 22g, Net Carbs 0g, Fat 26g

Pork and Tofu Toscana Soup

Prep + Cook Time: 40 minutes | Servings: 4

INGREDIENTS

2 tbsp Olive oil
2 lb Pork Sausage, cut in 2 inch chunks
1 Sweet Onion, diced
1 tsp dried Oregano
½ lb Tofu, pressed

8 cups Chicken Broth
1 cup chopped Kale Leaves
1 ½ cups Heavy Cream
Salt and Pepper to taste
½ cup Parmesan Cheese, grated

DIRECTIONS

Heat oil on Sauté, add sausage and tofu. Cook until brown for 6 minutes. Stir in garlic, onion, and oregano and cook for 3 minutes. Stir in broth and scrape the bottom of the pot to deglaze.

Stir in salt and pepper, seal the lid, select Manual and cook on High Pressure for 5 minutes. Check to make sure the contents don't go over the Max Fill line marked on the inner liner.

Once done, do a natural pressure release for 10 minutes and then quickly release the remaining pressure. Stir in kale and cook on Sauté mode for 3 minutes. Stir in heavy cream and serve.

Nutrition facts per serving: Calories 132, Protein 13g, Net Carbs 2.9g, Fat 2.3g

Coconut Ginger Pork

Prep + Cook Time: 55 minutes | Servings: 4

INGREDIENTS

1 tbsp Olive oil
2 lb Pork Shoulder
1 tsp Coriander Powder
1 tsp Cumin Powder
Salt to taste
Black Pepper to taste

1 inch Ginger, grated
2 cloves Garlic, minced
1 Onion, cut in large chunks
¼ can Coconut Milk
Lime Wedges to garnish

DIRECTIONS

Combine pepper, salt, cumin, and coriander and rub onto meat. Heat oil on Sauté, add the meat, ginger, garlic, onion, and milk. Seal the lid and cook on High Pressure for 45 minutes.

Once ready, quickly release the pressure. Garnish with lemon wedges, to serve.

Nutrition facts per serving: Calories 78, Protein 11g, Net Carbs 0.8g, Fat 3g

Pork Meatballs

Prep + Cook Time: 55 minutes | Servings: 3

INGREDIENTS

2 Eggs, beaten
2 tsp Macadamia Nuts, grounded
2 cloves Garlic, minced
⅓ cup Parmesan Cheese, grated
Salt to taste

⅓ tsp Parsley Flakes
Pepper to taste
½ lb Ground Pork
1 cup Beef Broth

DIRECTIONS

Combine all ingredients, except the meat and broth, in a bowl. Mix in the meat to the mixture. Shape 2-inch balls and press Sauté on the Instant Pot. Pour in the broth and let boil.

Add the meatballs to the broth and simmer for 15 minutes, turning once. Cook the meat until hardened and cooked through. Serve with tomato sauce.

Nutrition facts per serving: Calories 47, Protein 5.5g, Net Carbs 0.1g, Fat 1.9g

Southern Pork Roast

Prep + Cook Time: 45 minutes | Servings: 4

INGREDIENTS

- 1 stick Butter, sliced
- 1 cup Beef Broth
- ¼ cup Banana Pepper Ring Brine
- 3 pounds Pork Roast
- 1 tbsp Dill
- 1 tbsp Onion Powder
- ½ tbsp Garlic Powder
- 4 tbsp Banana Pepper Rings
- Salt and Pepper, to taste

DIRECTIONS

In the pot, pour the broth, and add pork, brine, garlic, onion, and dill. Stir to combine. Season with salt and pepper. Arrange banana pepper rings on top and cover with butter slices.

Seal the lid, select Manual and set the cooking time to 35 minutes. Cook on HIGH pressure. When it goes off, do a quick pressure release. Let the pork sit for 10 minutes before slicing.

Nutrition facts per serving: Calories 411, Protein 32g, Net Carbs 3g, Fat 30g

Bacon Cheddar Egg Bites

Prep + Cook Time: 30 minutes | Servings: 3

INGREDIENTS

- 6 Eggs
- 6 Bacon Strips, cooked and chopped
- ½ cup Cheddar Cheese
- ½ cup Cottage Cheese
- 6 tbsp Heavy Cream
- 2 tbsp Chopped Parsley
- 1 cup Water

DIRECTIONS

Place all ingredients except the bacon and parsley, and puree until smooth. Add the parsley and stir.

Grease egg bite molds with cooking spray, add the bacon in each mold and pour the egg mixture in each cup two thirds up way to the top. Cover each mold with a foil.

Pour water in the Instant Pot and fit a trivet in it. Place the egg molds on the trivet, seal the lid, secure the pressure valve, and select Steam mode for 8 minutes.

Once ready, do a quick release. Remove the egg mold and let sit for 5 minutes.

Nutrition facts per serving: Calories 310, Protein 19g, Net Carbs 5g, Fat 22g

Tandoori BBQ Pork Ribs

Prep + Cook Time: 40 minutes | Servings: 4 to 6

INGREDIENTS

1 ½ lb Pork Ribs
1 Bay Leaf
1 inch Ginger, grated
3 cloves Garlic
2 tbsp Tandoori Spice Mix
1 cup Water
Salt to taste
¼ cup BBQ Sauce

DIRECTIONS

Line ribs flat in the Instant Pot, add water, ginger, garlic, bay leaf, one tbsp of Tandoori spice mix and salt. Seal the lid, select Manual and cook on High Pressure for 20 minutes.

Once done, do a natural pressure release for 10 minutes. Carefully remove the ribs and place on a flat surface.

Wrap the bony sides with foil, pat dry the meaty sides and coat with the BBQ sauce. Sear with a torch or broil for 5 minutes per side. Serve immediately.

Nutrition facts per serving: Calories 296, Protein 22g, Net Carbs 0g, Fat 23g

Sweet Chipotle Pork

Prep + Cook Time: 35 minutes | Servings: 4

INGREDIENTS

1 pound Pork Tenderloin
2 tbsp Chipotle Powder
2 tbsp Sweetener
½ tsp Smoked Paprika
¼ tsp Garlic Powder
¼ tsp Onion Powder
½ tsp Cumin
1 tbsp Olive oil
Salt and Pepper, to taste
1 ½ cups Beef Broth

DIRECTIONS

Heat the oil on Sauté. Combine all spices in a bowl, and rub the pork with the mixture. Sear the meat on all sides, until browned. Pour in the broth and seal the lid.

Select Manual and cook on HIGH pressure for 20 minutes. After the beep, press Cancel and do a quick pressure release. Serve warm with mashed cauliflower.

Nutrition facts per serving: Calories 243, Protein 28g, Net Carbs 1g, Fat 25g

Creamy Ranch Pork Chops

Prep + Cook Time: 20 minute | Servings: 2

INGREDIENTS:

4 Pork Loin Chops
1 (15 oz) can Mushroom Soup Cream
1 oz Ranch Dressing and Seasoning Mix
½ cup Chicken Broth
Chopped Parsley to garnish

DIRECTIONS:

Add pork, mushroom soup cream, ranch dressing and seasoning mix, and chicken broth. Seal the lid, select Meat/Stew mode on High pressure for 10 minutes.

Once ready, do a natural pressure release for 10 minutes, then a quick pressure release. Serve the pork and the sauce with well-seasoned sautéed cremini mushrooms.

Nutrition facts per serving: Calories 318, Protein 26.1g, Net Carbs 2g, Fat 18.9g

Pork Roast with Mushroom Gravy

Prep + Cook Time: 65 minutes | Servings: 3

INGREDIENTS

1 lb Pork Roast
Salt to taste
Black Pepper to taste
1 small head Cauliflower
1 medium Onion, diced
3 cloves Garlic, minced

1 Celery Rib, cut in big chunks
1 cup Chicken Broth
1 cup Portobello Mushrooms
1 tbsp Olive oil
1 cup Water

DIRECTIONS

Place all vegetables and broth in the pot, add the pork roast on top and sprinkle with pepper and salt. Seal the lid, secure the pressure valve and cook on High Pressure for 40 minutes.

Once done, quickly release the pressure. Remove the pork to a baking dish. Preheat an oven to 400 F and bake the pork for 10 minutes. Meanwhile, select Sauté on the pot and simmer the gravy until it boils down. Place the pork roasts in a plate and dish the gravy over, to serve.

Nutrition facts per serving: Calories 364, Protein 31.9g, Net Carbs 5g, Fat 30.9g

No-Pressure Cumin Pork Chops

Prep + Cook Time: 28 minutes | Servings: 4

INGREDIENTS

4 Pork Chops
½ tbsp Cumin
1 tsp Chili Powder

2 tbsp Coconut Oil
Salt and Pepper, to taste

DIRECTIONS

Combine the oil and all spies, in a bowl. Rub this mixture onto the meat. Set the Instant Pot on Sauté and add in the pork. Cook for about 15 minutes, flipping once halfway through cooking. Serve the pork chops with steamed broccoli and keto mayo.

Nutrition facts per serving: Calories 305, Protein 30g, Net Carbs 0g, Fat 19.5g

FISH AND SEAFOOD

Sweet & Spicy Mahi Mahi

Prep + Cook Time: 10 minutes | Servings: 4

INGREDIENTS:

4 Mahi Mahi Fillets, fresh
4 cloves Garlic, minced
1 ¼ -inch Ginger, grated
Salt and Black Pepper
2 tbsp Chili Powder

1 tbsp Sriracha Sauce
1 ½ tbsp Monk Fruit Syrup
1 Lime, juiced
1 cup

DIRECTIONS:

Place the mahi mahi on a plate and season with salt and pepper on both sides. In a bowl, add the garlic, ginger, chili powder, sriracha sauce, monk fruit syrup, and lime juice. Use a spoon to mix it. With a brush, apply the hot sauce mixture on the fillet.

Open the Instant Pot, pour the water into and fit the trivet at the bottom of the pot. Put the fillets on the trivet. Close the lid, secure the pressure valve, and select Steam mode on High pressure for 5 minutes. Once ready, do a quick pressure release. Use a set of tongs to remove the mahi mahi onto serving plates. Serve with steamed or braised asparagus.

Nutrition facts per serving: Calories 130, Protein 34g, Net Carbs 0g, Fat 2g

One Pot Monk Fish with Greens

Prep + Cook Time: 25 minutes | Servings: 4

INGREDIENTS:

1 tbsp Coconut Oil
1 tbsp Olive oil
4 (8 oz) Monk Fish Fillets, cut in 2 pieces each
½ cup chopped Green Beans
2 cloves Garlic, sliced

1 cup Kale Leaves
½ lb Baby Bok Choy, stems removed, chopped
1 Lemon, zested and juiced
Lemon Wedges to serve
Salt and White Pepper to taste

DIRECTIONS:

Turn on the Instant Pot, open the lid, and select Sauté mode. Pour in the coconut oil, garlic, red chili, and green beans. Stir fry them for 5 minutes. Add the kale leaves, and cook them to wilt which is about 3 minutes. Meanwhile, place the fish on a plate and season them with salt, white pepper, and lemon zest. After, remove the green beans and kale into a plate and set aside.

Back to the pot, add the olive oil and fish to it. Cook them to brown on each side for about 2 minutes and then add the bok choy to it.

Pour the lemon juice over the fish and gently stir. Cook for 2 minutes and then turn off the Instant Pot. Spoon the fish with bok choy over the green beans and kale. Serve with a side of lemon wedges, and there, you have a complete meal.

Nutrition facts per serving: Calories 95, Protein 2g, Net Carbs 3g, Fat 7g

Fennel Alaskan Cod with Turnips

Prep + Cook Time: 20 minutes | Servings: 4

INGREDIENTS:

2 (18 oz) Alaskan Cod, cut into 4 pieces each
4 tbsp Olive oil
2 cloves Garlic, minced
2 small Onions, chopped
½ cup Olive Brine
2 cups Chicken Broth
Salt and Black Pepper to taste
½ cup sugar-free Tomato Puree
1 head Fennel, quartered
2 Turnips, peeled and quartered
1 cup Green Olives, pitted and crushed
1/2 cup Basil Leaves
Lemon Slices to garnish

DIRECTIONS:

Turn on the Instant Pot, open the pot, and select Sauté mode. Add the olive oil, once heated add the garlic and onion. Stir fry them until the onion has softened. Pour the chicken broth in and tomato puree. Let simmer for about 3 minutes.

Add the fennel, olives, turnips, salt, and pepper. Close the lid, secure the pressure valve, and select Steam mode on Low pressure for 8 minutes. Once ready, do a quick pressure release. Transfer the vegetables onto a plate with a slotted spoon.

Adjust broth's taste with salt and pepper and add the cod pieces. Close the lid again, secure the pressure valve, and select Steam mode on Low pressure for 3 minutes. Once ready, do a quick pressure release.

Remove the cod into soup plates, top with the veggies and basil leaves, and spoon the broth over them. Serve with a side of low carb crusted bread.

Nutrition facts per serving: Calories 64, Protein 14.8g, Net Carbs 5g, Fat 4.3g

Salmon with Lime Sauce

Prep + Cook Time: 10 minutes | Servings: 4

INGREDIENTS:

4 (5 oz) Salmon Filets
1 cup Water
Salt and Black Pepper to taste
2 tsp Cumin Powder
1 ½ tsp Paprika
2 tbsp chopped Parsley
2 tbsp Olive oil
2 tbsp Hot Water
1 tbsp Monk fruit Syrup
2 cloves Garlic, minced
1 Lime, juiced

DIRECTIONS:

In a bowl, add the cumin, paprika, parsley, olive oil, hot water, monk fruit syrup, garlic, and lime juice. Mix them together with a whisk. Set aside.

Open the Instant Pot and pour the water into it. Then, fit the steamer rack in it. Season the salmon with pepper and salt; place them on the steamer rack in the pot.

Close the lid, secure the pressure valve, and select Steam mode on High pressure for 5 minutes. Once ready, do a quick pressure release, and open the pot.

Use a set of tongs to transfer the salmon to a serving plate and drizzle the lime sauce all over it. Serve with steamed swiss chard.

Nutrition facts per serving: Calories 200, Protein 14g, Net Carbs 0g, Fat 12g

Scottish Seafood Curry

Prep + Cook Time: 45 minutes | Servings: 4

INGREDIENTS:

Seafood:

½ lb Squid, trimmed and cut into rings
½ lb Langoustine Tall Meat
½ lb Scallop Meat
½ lb Mussel Meat

Curry:

4 tbsp Olive oil
2 cups ShellFish Stock
2 Curry Leaves
2 tbsp Shallot Puree
3 tbsp Yellow Curry Paste
2 tbsp Ginger Paste
2 tbsp Garlic Paste
1 ½ tbsp Chili Powder
1 ½ tbsp Chili Paste
2 tbsp Lemongrass Paste
½ tsp Turmeric Powder
2 tsp Shrimp Powder
1 tsp Shrimp Paste
1 ½ cups Coconut Milk
1 cup Milk, full fat
1 tbsp Grants Scotch Whiskey
2 tbsp Fish Curry Powder
Salt to taste

Vegetables:

¼ cup diced Tomatoes
¼ cup chopped Onion
¼ cup chopped Okra
¼ cup chopped Aubergine

DIRECTIONS:

Turn on the Instant Pot, open the lid, and select Sauté mode. Add the olive oil, shallot paste, yellow curry paste, ginger puree, garlic paste, lemongrass paste, chili paste, shrimp paste, and curry leaves. Stir fry them for 10 minutes until well combined and aromatic.

Next, top with the turmeric powder, fish curry powder, and shrimp powder. Stir fry them for 1 minute. Pour in the shellfish stock and let boil for 10 minutes.

Then, add the scallops, squid, chopped onion, okra, tomatoes, and aubergine. Stir lightly. Close the lid, secure the pressure valve, and select Steam mode on High pressure for 5 minutes. Once ready, do a quick pressure release.

Add the milk, coconut milk, scotch whisky, and salt. Stir carefully so as to not mash the aubergine. Select Sauté mode and add the mussel meat and langoustine. Stir carefully again. Simmer the sauce for 3 minutes and then turn off the Instant Pot. Dish the seafood with sauce and veggies into serving bowls. Serve with a side of broccoli mash.

Nutrition facts per serving: Calories 566, Protein 59g, Net Carbs 0g, Fat 8g

Carolina Crab Soup

Prep + Cook Time: 45 minutes | Servings: 4

INGREDIENTS:

2 lb Crabmeat Lumps
6 tbsp Butter
6 tbsp Almond flour
Salt to taste
1 White Onion, chopped
3 tsp minced Garlic
2 Celery Stalk, diced
1 ½ cup Chicken Broth
¾ cup Heavy Cream
½ cup Half and Half Cream
2 tsp Hot Sauce
3 tsp sugar free Worcestershire Sauce
3 tsp Old Bay Seasoning
¾ cup Muscadet
Lemon Juice to serve
Chopped Dill to serve

DIRECTIONS:

Turn on the Instant Pot, open the lid, and select Sauté mode. Put the butter in to melt and then add the almond flour and mix in a fast motion to make a rue. Add the celery, onion, and garlic. Stir and cook until the onion softens for 3 minutes.

While whisking, gradually adds the half and half cream, heavy cream, and broth. Let simmer for 2 minutes. Then, add the Worcestershire sauce, old bay seasoning, Muscadet, and hot sauce. Stir and let simmer for 15 minutes.

Mix the crabmeat into the sauce. Leave the Instant Pot in Sauté mode and let the soup simmer for an additional 15 minutes. Press Cancel. Dish the soup into serving bowls, garnish with dill and drizzle squirts of lemon juice over. Serve with a side of keto garlic crusted bread.

Nutrition facts per serving: Calories 256, Protein 18.4g, Net Carbs 0g, Fat 14.5g

Seared Scallops with Butter Caper Sauce

Prep + Cook Time: 20 minutes | Servings: 4

INGREDIENTS:

2 lb Sea Scallops, foot removed
10 tbsp Butter, unsalted
4 tbsp Capers, drained

4 tbsp Olive oil
1 cup Dry White Wine
3 tsp Lemon Zest

DIRECTIONS:

Melt butter on Sauté, until caramel brown. Use a soup spook to fetch the butter out into a bowl. Next, add the oil to the pot; once heated add the scallops and sear on both sides to golden brown for 5 minutes. Use a set of tongs to remove them to a plate. Set aside.

Pour in wine to deglaze while using a spoon to scrape the bottom of the pot of any scallop bits. Add the capers, butter, and lemon zest. Use a spoon to gently stir the mixture once. After 40 seconds, spoon the sauce with capers over scallops. Serve with a side of braised asparagus.

Nutrition facts per serving: Calories 135, Protein 2.9g, Net Carbs 1.7g, Fat 5.8g

Oyster Stew

Prep + Cook Time: 10 minutes | Servings: 4

INGREDIENTS:

2 cups Heavy Cream
2 cups chopped Celery
2 cups Bone Broth
3 (10 oz) jars Shucked Oysters in Liqueur
3 Shallots, minced

3 tbsp Coconut Oil
Salt and White Pepper to taste
3 cloves Garlic, minced
3 tbsp chopped Parsley

DIRECTIONS:

Add the coconut oil, garlic, shallot, and celery. Stir-fry for 2 minutes on Sauté, and add heavy cream, broth, and oysters. Stir twice. Seal the lid, select Steam on Low pressure for 6 minutes.

When ready, do a quick pressure release. Season with salt and white pepper. Stir and dish the oyster soup into soup bowls. Garnish with parsley and top with low carb croutons.

Nutrition facts per serving: Calories 33, Protein 17g, Net Carbs 0g, Fat 1.2g

Fish Soul-Satisfying Soup

Prep + Cook Time: 35 minutes | Servings: 2

INGREDIENTS:

1 tbsp saffron
1 tbsp Garlic paste
Salt and black Pepper to taste
2 Fish fillets, cut into pieces
1 cup Cream
1 pinch Chili powder
1 cup Almond Milk
2 tbsp Olive oil

DIRECTIONS:

Heat oil in on Sauté mode and cook garlic and onion for 2 minutes. Add the fish and cook until golden brown, for 5 minutes. Season with salt and chili powder.

Shred the fish with a fork. Add in the cream and milk, mix well. Cook for 10 minutes on Manual mode on High pressure. When ready, do a quick pressure release.

Top with chili powder and saffron, to serve.

Nutrition facts per serving: Calories 587, Protein 29.1g, Net Carbs 4.7g, Fat 51.4g

Fish Tamarind Gravy

Prep + Cook Time: 45 minutes | Servings: 4

INGREDIENTS:

4 white Fish fillets, pieces
½ tbsp Salt
½ tbsp Chili powder
¼ cup Tamarind pulp
½ cup Tomato Curry
1 clove of Garlic, minced
1 Onion, chopped
2 tbsp Olive oil

DIRECTIONS:

In a bowl, add the fish fillets. Sprinkle with salt and black pepper. Heat oil on Sauté mode and fry the fish until golden. Cut into chunks and set aside.

Then heat 2 tbsp of oil and onion and garlic; stir-fry for 1-2 minutes. Add tomato puree, tamarind, salt, and paprika, stir well and cook for 8-10 minutes. Add fish chunks and pour in ½ cup of water. Seal the lid and cook for 10 minutes on high pressure.

Once ready, allow the pressure to release naturally for 10 minutes and serve hot.

Nutrition facts per serving: Calories 259, Protein 28.5g, Net Carbs 8.1g, Fat 12.3g

Salmon with Broccoli

Prep + Cook Time: 10 minutes | Servings: 4

INGREDIENTS

Juice from half lemon
1 tbsp Stevia
2 tbsp Soy sauce
1 tbsp Coconut oil
2 Skinned Salmon fillets
6 oz. Broccoli
4 oz. green Beans
2 peeled, stoned, and sliced Avocados
6 halved Cherry Tomatoes
6 oz. baby Spinach
2 oz. Walnut halves
2 oz. Almonds

DIRECTIONS

Mix the lemon juice, stevia, and soy sauce. Heat the coconut oil in the Instant Pot on Sauté mode. Add the broccoli and stir for 2 minutes.

Add the salmon filets and green beans and sauté the mixture for 3 more minutes. Add the rest of the ingredients, seal the lid and cook for 4 minutes on High pressure. Once ready, do a quick release and serve immediately.

Nutrition facts per serving: Calories 576, Protein 41.2g, Net Carbs 6.1g, Fat 39.4g

Teriyaki Salmon with Ginger

Prep + Cook Time: 10 minutes | Servings: 3

INGREDIENTS

¾ cup Teriyaki Marinade
2 tbsp Stevia
1 tsp grated fresh Ginger root
3 Salmon steaks
½ cup Chicken Broth
1 tbsp Coconut oil

DIRECTIONS

In your Instant Pot, combine the Kikkoman Teriyaki, marinade, stevia, coconut oil, and grated ginger root. Add the salmon and stir well. Seal the lid.

Press Manual and cook for 10 minutes on High pressure. Once ready, do a natural pressure release for 10 minutes and serve immediately with steamed asparagus.

Nutrition facts per serving: Calories 465, Protein 65.1g, Net Carbs 5.1g, Fat 15.4g

Fish with Coconut and Cauliflower Rice

Prep + Cook Time: 25 minutes | Servings: 3

INGREDIENTS

2 tbsp Coconut oil
¼ cup Chia seeds
3 thinly sliced Onions
3 crushed Garlic cloves
1 piece fresh, finely grated Ginger
2 tbsp Curry paste
1 can diced Tomatoes
½ cup Coconut Milk
1 lb white Fish filets, cut into pieces
½ cup frozen green Beans
¼ cup fresh Coriander leaves
Steamed Cauliflower rice for serving
1 Lemon cut into wedges

DIRECTIONS

Heat the oil on Sauté and cook the onion for 2 minutes until tender. Add the garlic and ginger and cook for a minute. Add the tomato and keep stirring until well combined.

Pour in coconut milk and a cup of cold water. Press Manual and seal the lid. Set on High pressure for 5 minutes. Once ready, do a quick pressure release.

Add the fish and the green beans; keep stirring. Cook for 10 minutes, lid off, on Sauté mode. Once the fish is cooked, add coriander leaves. Serve with cooked cauli rice.

Nutrition facts per serving: Calories 373, Protein 32.1g, Net Carbs 6.8g, Fat 21.4g

Duo Seafood Medley

Prep + Cook Time: 45 minutes | Servings: 4

INGREDIENTS

12 oz Sea Bass Filets, cut in 2 inch chunks
1 lb large Fresh Shrimp, peeled, deveined with tails on
1 ½ tbsp Olive oil
1 ½ tbsp Cajun Seasoning
1 White Onion, chopped
1 Green Bell pepper, diced
2 Celery Ribs, diced
14 oz Tomatoes, diced
1/6 cup Tomato Puree
1 Bay Leaf
⅓ cup Seafood Broth
Salt to taste
Pepper to taste

DIRECTIONS

Season the fish with salt, Cajun seasoning, and pepper; coat well. Heat oil on Sauté, and add the fish. Cook until close to doneness. Remove onto a plate and set aside.

Add the onion, celery, extra Cajun seasoning, and pepper, stir and cook for 1 minute. Add the tomatoes, tomato paste, broth, fish and bay leaf. Gently, stir well. Seal the lid.

Select Manual and cook on High Pressure for 5 minutes. Once done, quickly release the pressure. Hit Sauté and stir-fry shrimp for 4 minutes. Season with pepper and salt and serve.

Nutrition facts per serving: Calories 170, Protein 22g, Net Carbs 1g, Fat 6g

Tilapia with Chia Seeds

Prep + Cook Time: 15 minutes | Servings: 4

INGREDIENTS

½ lb Tilapia filets
2 tsp Coconut oil, melted
3 tbsp Chia seeds
¼ tsp Old Bay Seasoning
½ tsp Garlic, minced
½ tsp Salt
1 sliced Lemon
1 tsp grated Ginger
1 package frozen Cauliflower with red Pepper and Broccoli
1 cup Water

DIRECTIONS

Place the filets on a baking dish. Season with the Old Bay, garlic, ginger, salt, and pepper; sprinkle chia seeds and top with lemon slices.

Arrange the frozen vegetables around the fish. Pour water in the pot and insert the trivet. Place the baking dish on the trivet. Seal the lid and cook on High pressure for 10 minutes. Once ready, quickly release the pressure serve immediately!

Nutrition facts per serving: Calories 112, Protein 12.6g, Net Carbs 1.6g, Fat 5.4g

Steamed Crab Legs

Prep + Cook Time: 10 minutes | Servings: 3

INGREDIENTS

1 lb large Crab Legs, sharp ends chopped off
½ cup Water
Salt to taste
¼ cup Salted Pastured Butter
3 Lemon Slices
Chopped Parsley to garnish

DIRECTIONS

Fit the trivet in the Pot and pour the water in. Add the crab legs and sprinkle with salt. Seal the lid and cook on High pressure for 3 minutes. Once ready, quickly release the pressure.

Place a pan over medium heat, and melt half of the butter. Add the crab legs and toss them quickly in the butter. Turn heat off and transfer the crab legs to a plate. Drizzle with lemon juice and garnish with parsley. Enjoy with remaining melted butter.

Nutrition facts per serving: Calories 215, Protein 35g, Net Carbs 0g, Fat 12g

Cheesy Tilapia

Prep + Cook Time: 20 minutes | Servings: 4

INGREDIENTS

1 tbsp Butter
12 ounces Tilapia Fillets
¼ Onion, diced
½ cup Heavy Cream

¼ tsp Garlic Powder
5 ounces shredded Cheddar Cheese
Salt and Pepper, to taste

DIRECTIONS

Melt butter on Sauté. Add the onions and cook for 3 minutes, until soft. Add the tilapiAnd season with salt and pepper. Cook for 2 minutes on both sides, or until slightly golden.

Pour in heavy cream, sprinkle with garlic powder and top with cheese. Seal the lid and cook on HIGH pressure for 5 minutes. After the beep, do a quick pressure release. Serve immediately.

Nutrition facts per serving: Calories 195, Protein 18g, Net Carbs 5.5g, Fat 18g

Crab Quiche

Prep + Cook Time: 65 minutes | Servings: 4 to 6

INGREDIENTS

6 Eggs
1 ¼ cups Half and Half
Salt to taste
Pepper to taste
2 tsp Smoked Paprika

1 ¼ Herbes de Provence
1 ½ cups Parmesan Cheese, grated
1 cup Scallions, chopped
3 cups Crab Meat
2 cups Water

DIRECTIONS

Break eggs into a bowl and add half and half. Beat to incorporate evenly. Add pepper, salt, herbs, paprikAnd cheese; stir evenly. Add scallions and mix; add crab meat and stir evenly.

Cover the bottom part of a spring form pan with aluminum foil. Pour the crab mixture into the pan and level the surface flat. Fit a trivet in the Instant Pot and pour water.

Place the pan on the trivet, seal the lid and cook on High Pressure for 40 minutes. Once ready, quickly release the pressure. Remove the pan carefully, run around the edges of the quiche in the pan, and remove the quiche. Cut in slices and serve.

Nutrition facts per serving: Calories 395, Protein 22g, Net Carbs 7g, Fat 25g

Salmon in Spicy Lime Sauce

Prep + Cook Time: 20 minutes | Servings: 6

INGREDIENTS

Salmon:
3 Salmon Fillets, cut into 2
1 cup Water

Spicy Lime Sauce:
2 Jalapenos, seeded and diced
2 Limes, juices
3 cloves Garlic, minced
1 tbsp Monk Fruit Syrup
2 tbsp Olive oil

Salt to taste
Black Pepper to taste

2 tbsp Hot Water, (make a quick one in the microwave)
2 sprigs Parsley, minced
1 tsp Paprika
1 tsp Cumin

DIRECTIONS

Place all sauce ingredients in a bowl, mix well and set aside. Pour water in the pot and fit a steamer basket in. Arrange salmon in the basket and sprinkle with pepper and salt; don't mix.

Seal the lid, select Manual and cook on High Pressure mode for 5 minutes. Once ready, quickly release the pressure. Transfer the salmon to a plate and drizzle the spicy sauce over.

Nutrition facts per serving: Calories 415, Protein 29g, Net Carbs 1g, Fat 25g

Gingery and Orange Mackerel

Prep + Cook Time: 15 minutes | Servings: 4

INGREDIENTS

3 Spring Onions, chopped
4 Mackerel Fillets
1 cup White Wine
1-inch piece of Ginger, thinly sliced

Juice and Zest of 1 Orange
1 tbsp Olive oil
Salt and Pepper, to taste

DIRECTIONS

Pour in wine and juice t and stir in zest, ginger, and spring onions. Brush the fish fillets with olive oil and sprinkle them with salt and pepper. Place the mackerel in the steamer basket and lower the basket into the pot.

Seal the lid and cook on HIGH pressure for 6 minutes. After the beep, press Cancel and do a quick pressure release. Serve with steamed asparagus to enjoy.

Nutrition facts per serving: Calories 243, Protein 35g, Net Carbs 3.5g, Fat 5g

Steamed Shrimp with Asparagus

Prep + Cook Time: 20 minutes | Servings: 3

INGREDIENTS

1 lb Shrimp, peeled and deveined
1 cup Water
½ lb Asparagus, hard ends cut off
1 tsp Olive oil

Salt to taste
Pepper to taste
1 Lemon, juiced

DIRECTIONS

Pour water into the Instant Pot and fit in a steamer. Arrange the asparagus at the bottom of the steamer and arrange the shrimp on top. Drizzle with oil and sprinkle with salt and pepper.

Stir shrimp lightly. Seal the lid, select Steam for 3 minutes, and cook on High Pressure mode. Once ready, quickly release the pressure. Serve with garlic mayo or hot sweet sauce.

Nutrition facts per serving: Calories 163, Protein 21.6g, Net Carbs 3.1g, Fat 1.2g

Stewed Shellfish

Prep + Cook Time: 25 minutes | Servings: 4

INGREDIENTS

1 cup Scallops
2 cups Mussels
1 Onion, diced
1 tbsp Butter
2 Bell Peppers, diced

2 cups Cauliflower Rice
2 cups Fish Stock
A pinch of Saffron
Salt and Pepper, to taste

DIRECTIONS

Melt butter on Sauté. Add the onions and bell peppers and cook for 3 minutes, until soft. Stir in the saffron and scallops, and cook for an additional 2 minutes.

Add the rest of the ingredients, give the mixture a good stir and seal the lid. Select Manual mode and cook for 6 minutes on HIGH pressure. After the beep, allow the pressure valve to drop on its own for a natural pressure release, for about 5 minutes. Serve immediately.

Nutrition facts per serving: Calories 195, Protein 20g, Net Carbs 7.6g, Fat 7g

Creamy Prawn Scampi

Prep + Cook Time: 30 minutes | Servings: 2

INGREDIENTS

1 tbsp Butter
½ lb Jumbo Prawns, peeled, deveined, tail on
2 cloves Garlic, minced
¼ tbsp Red Pepper Flakes
¼ tsp Paprika
¼ cup Chicken Broth

¼ cup Half and Half
¼ cup Parmesan Cheese, grated
Salt to taste
Pepper to taste
1 Zucchini, spiralized

DIRECTIONS

Melt butter on Sauté, add pepper flakes and garlic and sauté for 1 minute. Add prawns, pepper, and paprika. Stir and pour in chicken broth. Seal the lid, select Manual mode on Low Pressure mode for 3 minutes. Once ready, press Cancel and do a quick release.

Select Sauté. Add cheese and half and half. Stir and once melted and fully incorporated, add the zoodles, stir gently not to break the zoodles. Cook for 1 minute and press Cancel.

Nutrition facts per serving: Calories 312, Protein 24g, Net Carbs 1g, Fat 9g

Lobster Tails with Dill Butter Sauce

Prep + Cook Time: 10 minutes | Servings: 4

INGREDIENTS

10 Lobster Tails, frozen
2 tsp Seafood Seasoning, of your choice
1 cup Water
6 tbsp Butter
2 tsp Minced Garlic

Salt to taste
Black Pepper to taste
1 Lemon, juiced
2 tsp Dill Weed, chopped

DIRECTIONS

Cut a line through the shell of the lobster tails. Set aside. Add the water and seafood seasoning to the Instant Pot. Fit a trivet over the water and place a steamer basket on top.

Arrange the lobster tails with shell side down in the basket. Seal the lid, select Manual and cook on High Pressure for 4 minutes.

Meanwhile make the butter sauce, by placing a pan over low heat and melting the butter. Add the remaining ingredients, stir and turn off the heat. Pour into a sauce dish and set aside.

Back to the pot, do a quick pressure release. Carefully remove the lobster tails onto a serving plate. Serve with lemon butter sauce immediately.

Nutrition facts per serving: Calories 114, Protein 23.9g, Net Carbs 1.5g, Fat 0.7g

One Pot Tuna & Veggies Dish

Prep + Cook Time: 15 minutes | Servings: 2

INGREDIENTS

2 (5 oz) Tuna Fillets
2 + 1 cloves Garlic, minced
1 inch Ginger, grated
1 Red Chili, minced
Salt to taste
Black Pepper to taste
2 tbsp Soy Sauce

½ tsp Monk Fruit Syrup
½ lb Mixed Veggies
2 Carrots, julienned
1 Lime, juiced
2 tbsp Olive oil
1 cup Water

DIRECTIONS

Pour water in the Instant Pot and fit in a trivet. In a bowl, mix ginger, 2 cloves of garlic, chili pepper, black pepper, salt, monk fruit syrup and 1 tbsp of soy sauce.

Arrange the tuna in a cake tin that will fit in the Pot. Pour the soy sauce mixture over the tuna. Place the cake tin on top of the trivet. Seal the lid, and cook on nHigh Pressure for 3 minutes.

Once ready, quickly release the pressure. Place a steamer basket on the tunAnd add the vegetables. Sprinkle remaining garlic, soy sauce, lime juice, salt, pepper, and olive oil.

Seal the lid, and cook on High Pressure mode for 10 minutes. Once ready, quickly release the pressure. Serve veggies with tuna, and drizzle juice over the tuna.

Nutrition facts per serving: Calories 180, Protein 40g, Net Carbs 0g, Fat 1.5g

Simple Steamed Clams

Prep + Cook Time: 10 minutes | Servings: 3

INGREDIENTS

¼ cup White Wine
¼ cup Water
1 tsp Minced Garlic
1 lb Clams

DIRECTIONS

Pour water and wine in the Instant Pot, add garlic and stir evenly. Fit a steamer basket in the in and arrange the clams in the basket.

Seal the lid, select Manual mode on High Pressure mode for 4 minutes. Once ready, quickly release the pressure. Serve clams with steamed veggies.

Nutrition facts per serving: Calories 26, Protein 4.4g, Net Carbs 0.8g, Fat 0.3g

Lemon Pepper Salmon

Prep + Cook Time: 5 minutes | Servings: 2

INGREDIENTS

2 (7 oz) Salmon Fillets, with skin
1 cup Water
2 sprigs Parsley
2 sprigs Dill
2 sprigs Tarragon
2 leaves Basil
4 tbsp Butter, divided into 2
Salt to taste
Pepper to taste
1 Lemon, sliced thinly

DIRECTIONS

Add water and herbs to the Instant Pot and fit a steamer basket. Arrange the salmon with skin side down in the basket. Sprinkle with pepper and salt, and add half of the butter on top.

Cover with lemon slices, seal the lid, select Steam and cook for 3 minutes on High pressure. Once ready, quickly release the pressure. Carefully remove the salmon on a serving plate, melt the remaining butter and drizzle it over the salmon.

Nutrition facts per serving: Calories 133, Protein 23g, Net Carbs 0g, Fat 4g

Shrimp in Coconut Milk Sauce

Prep + Cook Time: 20 minutes | Servings: 3

INGREDIENTS

1 lb Shrimp, peeled and deveined
1-inch Ginger piece, minced
2 cloves Garlic, minced
½ tsp Turmeric
Salt to taste
½ tsp Chili Powder
1 tsp Curry Powder
½ cup Coconut Milk, unsweetened
¼ cup Water

DIRECTIONS

Place all ingredients in a bowl, and mix until powders are well incorporated. Pour them into the Instant Pot, seal the lid, and cook on Low Pressure for 4 minutes. Once ready, quickly release the pressure.

Nutrition facts per serving: Calories 192, Protein 16g, Net Carbs 3g, Fat 12g

Simple Fish Curry

Prep + Cook Time: 20 minutes | Servings: 3

INGREDIENTS

1 ½ lb Tilapia Filets, cut in 2 inch chunks
2 tbsp Olive oil
2 ½ cups Coconut Milk
2 tbsp Garlic Ginger Paste
8 Curry Leaves
1 Onion, sliced
1 Green Bell pepper, sliced
1 Orange Bell pepper, sliced

Salt to taste
½ tsp Turmeric Powder
1 tsp Cayenne Powder
1 tsp Coriander Powder
½ tsp Cumin Powder
3 sprigs Cilantro
6 Mint Leaves
1 Lime, juiced

DIRECTIONS

Heat oil on Sauté. Add the ginger garlic paste and curry leaves. Cook for 30 seconds while stirring. Add the bell peppers and onions. Stir and cook for 30 seconds. Add the remaining listed spices, stir and cook for 30 seconds. Add the coconut milk, stir and cook for 30 seconds.

Add the fish and cilantro and coat the fish with the coconut mixture. Drop mint leaves on top. Seal the lid, and cook on High Pressure mode for 3 minutes. Once ready, quickly release the pressure. Drizzle lime juice over the sauce, stir gently and serve.

Nutrition facts per serving: Calories 206, Protein 22.4g, Net Carbs 0.1g, Fat 8.3g

Haddock in Creamy Tomato Broth

Prep + Cook Time: 45 minutes | Servings: 3

INGREDIENTS

2 lb Haddock Fillets
4 tbsp Butter
2 Onion, chopped
2 Carrots, chopped
2 cloves Garlic, minced
3 cups Chicken Broth
3 cups Diced Tomatoes

¼ tsp Cayenne Pepper
Salt to taste
Black Pepper to taste
3 cups Kale, chopped
1 cup Coconut Cream
2 sprigs Parsley, chopped
5 Basil Leaves, chopped

DIRECTIONS

Heat oil on Sauté, and cook the garlic and onion for 3 minutes. Add tomatoes, chicken broth, herb, peppers and salt. Stir and cook for 5 minutes.

Place a steamer basket in the Instant Pot over the tomato sauce. Arrange the fish in the steamer basket and season with salt and pepper. Seal the lid and select Manual mode.

Cook on High Pressure for 6 minutes. Once ready, quickly release the pressure. Remove the steamer basket with fish; set aside. Puree tomato sauce in the pot with a stick blender.Stir in the remaining ingredients. Hit Keep Warm and cook for 9 minutes. Serve fish drizzled sauce.

Nutrition facts per serving: Calories 197, Protein 34g, Net Carbs 0.5g, Fat 5.7g

Spicy Herbed Tuna

Prep + Cook Time: 15 minutes | Servings: 3

INGREDIENTS

4 sprigs each Parsley, Tarragon, Basil and Thyme
2 cloves Garlic, crushed
1 lb Tuna Steaks
1 tbsp Red Chili Flakes
1 tbsp Olive oil
Salt to taste

1 tsp Garlic Powder
½ tsp dried Thyme, Parsley, Basil and Tarragon
5 Lemon Slices
3 tbsp Butter
½ lb Asparagus, hard ends cut off
1 cup Water

DIRECTIONS

Add the water, crushed garlic and fresh herbs to the Instant Pot. Place the trivet at the bottom and arrange tuna steaks on top; season with peppers, salt and garlic powder.

Drizzle with olive oil and arrange lemon slices on top of the fish. Seal the lid and cook on High Pressure mode for 4 minutes. Once ready, quickly release the pressure.

Remove the tuna to a plate. Remove the inner pot of the Instant Pot and discard the water and herbs. Place it back to the pot and set on Sauté. Melt the butter, add the asparagus and sauté for 3 minutes. Season with salt and add the dried herbs; toss. Serve immediately.

Nutrition facts per serving: Calories 132, Protein 17g, Net Carbs 2g, Fat 4.2g

Ginger Steamed Scallion Fish

Prep + Cook Time: 15 minutes | Servings: 4

INGREDIENTS

2 lb Tilapia Fillet
4 tbsp Soy Sauce
2 inch Ginger, grated
2 cloves Garlic, minced
2 tbsp Olive oil

3 tbsp Ginger, julienned
½ cup Scallions, cut in long strips
½ cup Cilantro chopped
2 cups Water

DIRECTIONS

Mix the soy sauce, garlic, and minced ginger in a bowl. Place the fish and pour the mixture over it. Marinate for 30 minutes. Pour water in the Instant Pot and fit a steamer basket in.

Remove and place the fish in the steamer basket, but reserve the marinade. Seal the lid, select Manual and cook on Low Pressure for 2 minutes.

Once ready, quickly release the pressure. Set aside and wipe the pot clean. Heat oil on Sauté and stir-fry the scallions, ginger and cilantro for 3 minutes. Add the reserved marinade. Cook for 2 minutes. Press Cancel. Pour the sauce over the fish and serve warm.

Nutrition facts per serving: Calories 171, Protein 23g, Net Carbs 0g, Fat 5g

White Fish Stew

Prep + Cook Time: 25 minutes | Servings: 4

INGREDIENTS

- 2 lb Cod Fish, cut into 2 inch chunks
- 2 Limes, juiced
- 3 tbsp Olive oil
- 2 Jalapeno Peppers, seeded and chopped
- 2 medium Onions, chopped
- 2 medium Red Bell peppers, diced
- 2 medium Yellow Bell peppers, diced
- 3 cloves Garlic, minced
- 2 tsp Paprika
- 3 cups Chicken Broth
- 3 cups Chopped Tomatoes
- Salt to taste
- Black Pepper to taste
- 3 cups Coconut Milk

DIRECTIONS

Place the fish in a bowl, add lime juice and toss; set aside. Heat oil on Sauté, add the onions and bell peppers. Sauté for 2 minutes. Add the jalapenos, paprikAnd black pepper; stir.

Add the tomatoes and broth, stir and allow to boil for 5 minutes. Add the fish and coconut milk. Stir, seal the lid and cook on High Pressure for 3 minutes.

Once ready, quickly release the pressure. Adjust the salt and pepper and serve warm.

Nutrition facts per serving: Calories 146, Protein 15g, Net Carbs 0.7g, Fat 7.5g

Hot Anchovies

Prep + Cook Time: 20 minutes | Servings: 4

INGREDIENTS

- 1 Chili, sliced
- 1 tsp Chili Powder
- ½ tsp Red Chili Flakes
- 10 ounces Anchovy
- 4 tbsp Butter
- ⅓ cup ground Almonds
- 1 tsp Dill
- Salt and Pepper, to taste

DIRECTIONS

Melt butter on Sauté. Meanwhile, combine the chili and all spices in a bowl. Coat the anchovy with the mixture well.

When the butter is melted, add the anchovy and cook until browned, for about 4-5 minutes per side. Serve with keto bread and tangy tomato dip.

Nutrition facts per serving: Calories 331, Protein 28g, Net Carbs 3g, Fat 25g

Sea Bass in Tomato Sauce

Prep + Cook Time: 10 minutes | Servings: 3 to 4

INGREDIENTS

- 1 cup Coconut Milk
- 1 Lime, juiced
- 1 tbsp Tomato Puree
- 1 tsp Fish Sauce
- 2 cups Tomatoes, chopped
- 1 tsp Hot Sauce
- 3 cloves Garlic, minced
- 1 inch Ginger, grated
- Salt to taste
- White Pepper to taste
- 1 lb Sea Bass, cut in 2 inch chunks
- ½ cup Cilantro, chopped
- 4 Lime Wedges

DIRECTIONS

In a bowl, mix all ingredients, except the fish, lime wedges and cilantro. Place fish chunks in the pot and pour tomato mixture over. Seal the lid and cook on High Pressure for 3 minutes.

Once ready, quickly release the pressure. Dish the sauce into serving bowls, sprinkle with equal amounts of cilantro and lime wedges.

Nutrition facts per serving: Calories 111, Protein 21.2g, Net Carbs 1.4g, Fat 2.3g

Dill Spiced Salmon

Prep + Cook Time: 15 minutes | Servings: 3

INGREDIENTS

2 Lemons, 1 sliced and 1 juiced
½ cup Water
3 Salmon Fillets, frozen with skin
1 bunch Dill, chopped

2 tsp Unsalted Butter, melted
Salt to taste
Black Pepper to taste

DIRECTIONS

Pour half of the lemon juice and the water in the Instant Pot. Fit a steamer basket inside. Place the salmon in the basket and sprinkle with salt, pepper, dill, and top with lemon slices.

Seal the lid and cook on High Pressure for 5 minutes. Once ready, quickly release the pressure. Remove salmon. Drizzle with butter, remaining lemon juice, extra dill, pepper and serve.

Nutrition facts per serving: Calories 480, Protein 45g, Net Carbs 1g, Fat 26g

Cod Fish Packets

Prep + Cook Time: 10 minutes | Servings: 3

INGREDIENTS

3 Cod Fillets
Salt to taste
Black Pepper to taste
2 tsp Garlic Powder

3 sprigs Dill Leaves
6 Lemon Slices
3 tbsp Butter

DIRECTIONS

Cut out 3 sizable parchment papers for the fillets and lay them on a flat surface. Place each fillet at the center of each paper. Generously season with garlic powder, pepper, and salt.

Place a dill sprig, 2 slices of lemon and 1 tbsp of butter on each fish. Fit a trivet at the bottom of the Instant Pot; pour 1 cup of water. Close up and seal the parchment paper to make fish packets and place them on the trivet.

Seal the lid and cook on High Pressure for 5 minutes. Once ready, quickly release the pressure. Remove the fish packets carefully and serve warm.

Nutrition facts per serving: Calories 90, Protein 19g, Net Carbs 1.8g, Fat 2.5g

Simple Steamed Cod

Prep + Cook Time: 10 minutes | Servings: 4

INGREDIENTS

2 large fresh Cod Fillets, cut in 3 pieces each
1 cup Cherry Tomatoes
Salt to taste
Pepper to taste
4 tbsp Butter
1 cup Water

DIRECTIONS

In an oven-safe dish to fit in the Instant Pot, make a bed of tomatoes at the bottom of the dish. Season the fish with the pepper and salt and place them on the tomatoes.

Add butter on the fish. Pour the water in the Instant Pot and fit in a trivet. Place the dish in the pot, seal the lid, and cook on High Pressure for 5 minutes. Once ready, quickly release the pressure. Serve fish with tomatoes and steamed green veggies.

Nutrition facts per serving: Calories 116, Protein 26g, Net Carbs 2g, Fat 0.9g

Mackerel Packets

Prep + Cook Time: 25 minutes | Servings: 6

INGREDIENTS:

3 large Whole Mackerel, cut into 2 pieces
6 medium Tomatoes, quartered
1 large Brown Onion, sliced thinly
1 Orange Bell pepper, seeded and chopped
Salt and Black Pepper to taste
2 ½ tbsp Pernod
3 cloves Garlic, minced
2 Lemons, halved
1 ½ cups Water

DIRECTIONS:

Cut out 6 pieces of parchment paper a little longer and wider than a piece of fish with kitchen scissors. Then, cut out 6 pieces of foil slightly longer than the parchment papers.

Lay the foil wraps on a flat surface and place each parchment paper on each aluminium foil. In a bowl, add the tomatoes, onions, garlic, bell pepper, pernod, salt, and pepper. Use a spoon to mix them.

Place each fish piece on the layer of parchment and foil wraps. Spoon the tomato mixture on each fish. Then, wrap the fish and place the fish packets in the refrigerator to marinate for 2 hours. After 2 hours, remove the fish onto a flat surface.

Open the Instant Pot, pour the water into and fit the trivet at the bottom of the pot. Put the packets on the trivet. Close the lid, secure the pressure valve, and select Steam on High pressure for 5 minutes. Once ready, do a quick pressure release. Remove the trivet with the fish packets onto a flat surface.

Carefully open the foil and use a spoon to dish the soup with vegetables and sauce onto serving plates. Serve with a side of roasted daikon radish and the lemon wedges.

Nutrition facts per serving: Calories 95, Protein 10.9g, Net Carbs 0g, Fat 5.3g

Chili Black Mussels

Prep + Cook Time: 45 minutes | Servings: 4

INGREDIENTS:

1 ½ lb Black Mussels, cleaned and de-bearded
3 tbsp Olive oil
3 large Chilies, seeded and chopped
3 cloves Garlic, peeled and crushed
1 White Onion, chopped finely
10 large Tomatoes, skin removed and chopped

4 tbsp reduced sugar Tomato Paste
1 cup Dry White Wine
3 cups Vegetable Broth
⅓ cup fresh Basil Leaves
1 cup fresh Parsley Leaves

DIRECTIONS:

Turn on the Instant Pot, open the lid, and select Sauté mode. Add the olive oil, once heated add the onion and cook to soften. Then, add the chilies and garlic, and cook for 2 minutes while stirring frequently. Add the tomatoes and tomato paste, stir and cook for 2 minutes. Then, add the wine and vegetable broth. Let simmer for 5 minutes.

Now, add the mussels, close the lid, secure the pressure valve, and select Steam mode on High pressure for 5 minutes. Once ready, do a natural pressure release for 15 minutes, then a quick pressure release. Remove and discard any unopened mussels. Then, add half of the basil and parsley, and stir.

Dish the mussels with sauce in serving bowls and garnish with the remaining basil and parsley. Serve with a side of low carb crusted bread.

Nutrition facts per serving: Calories 120, Protein 10g, Net Carbs 1g, Fat 8g

VEGETABLES, VEGAN & SIDE DISHES

Cauli Rice Stuffed Peppers

Prep + Cook Time: 30 minutes | Servings: 4

INGREDIENTS:

4 Red Peppers
2 large Tomatoes, chopped
1 small Onion, chopped
2 cloves Garlic, minced
1 tbsp Olive oil
½ cup Cauli Rice
1 small Zucchini, chopped
1 cup Water, divided
½ tsp Smoked Paprika
½ cup chopped Mushrooms
Salt and Black Pepper to taste
1 cup grated Gouda Cheese

DIRECTIONS:

Turn on the pot and select Saute mode. Add the olive oil to heat and then add the onion and garlic. Saute for 3 minutes to soften, stirring occasionally.

Include the tomatoes, cook for 3 minutes and then add the cauli rice, zucchinis, and mushrooms. Season with paprika, salt, and black pepper and stir with a spoon. Cook for 5 to 7 minutes.

Use a knife to cut the bell peppers in halves (lengthwise) and remove their seeds and stems. Spoon the cauli rice mixture into the bell peppers leaving about a quarter space at the top of the bell peppers for the cheese. Sprinkle with the gouda cheese.

Once the content in the pot is finished, wipe the pot clean with some paper towels, and pour the water into it. After, fit the steamer rack at the bottom of the pot.

Place the stuffed peppers on top of the steamer rack, close the lid, secure the pressure valve, and select Steam mode on High pressure for 3 minutes.

Once ready, do a quick pressure release. Serve as they are or with a side of a meat dish.

Nutrition facts per serving: Calories 109, Protein 9.8g, Net Carbs 0g, Fat 1.9g

Creamy Broccoli Mash

Prep + Cook Time: 10 minutes | Servings: 4

INGREDIENTS:

3 heads Broccoli, chopped
6 oz Cream Cheese
2 cloves Garlic, crushed
2 tbsp Butter, unsalted
Salt and Black Pepper to taste
1 cup Water

DIRECTIONS:

Turn on the Instant Pot, open the lid, and select Sauté mode. Drop in the butter, once melts add the garlic and cook for 30 seconds while stirring frequently to prevent the garlic from burning. Then, add the broccoli, cream cheese, water, salt, and pepper.

Close the lid, secure the pressure valve, and select Steam mode on High pressure for 1 minute. Once ready, do a quick pressure release and use a stick blender to mash the ingredients until smooth to your desired consistency and well combined. Adjust the taste with salt and pepper and serve as a side dish to a sauce of your choice.

Nutrition facts per serving: Calories 166, Protein 16.7g, Net Carbs 2.6g, Fat 13g

Easy Spaghetti Squash

Prep + Cook Time: 10 minutes | Servings: 4

INGREDIENTS:

4 lb Spaghetti Squash

1 cup Water

DIRECTIONS:

Put the squash on a flat surface and use a knife to slice in half lengthwise. Use a spoon to scoop out all seeds and discard them.

Next, open the Instant Pot, pour the water into and fit the trivet at the bottom. Place the squash halves on the trivet, close the lid, secure the pressure valve, and select Steam mode on High pressure for 6 minutes. Once ready, do a quick pressure release. Remove the squash halves onto a cutting board and use a fork to separate the pulp strands into spaghetti-like pieces.

Nutrition facts per serving: Calories 75, Protein 1.2g, Net Carbs 3.9g, Fat 4.1g

Basic Steamed Asparagus

Prep + Cook Time: 5 minutes | Servings: 4

INGREDIENTS:

1 ½ lb Asparagus, ends trimmed
Salt and Pepper to taste

1 cup Water

DIRECTIONS:

Open the Instant Pot, pour the water into and fit the steamer rack at the bottom. Place the asparagus on the steamer rack, close the lid, secure the pressure valve, and select Steam mode on High pressure for 1 minute. Once ready, do a quick pressure release. Remove the asparagus with tongs onto a plate and sprinkle with salt and pepper. Serve with a sauce of your choice or varying meat dishes.

Nutrition facts per serving: Calories 22, Protein 2g, Net Carbs 1g, Fat 0g

Coconut Cauli Rice

Prep + Cook Time: 8 minutes | Servings: 4

INGREDIENTS:

2 heads Cauliflower
1 cup Coconut Milk

Salt to taste
1 ½ tsp Arrowroot Starch

DIRECTIONS:

Inside a bowl, place a grater and grate the cauliflower into rice-like pieces. Open the Instant Pot, add the cauli rice, salt, and coconut milk in it. Close the lid, secure the pressure valve, and select Steam mode on High pressure for 1 minute. Once ready, do a quick pressure release.

Add the arrowroot starch and use a spoon to stir the ingredients until thickened. Spoon the cauli rice into a serving bowl and serve as a side dish to a sauce or meat dish of your choice.

Nutrition facts per serving: Calories 247, Protein 2.1g, Net Carbs 1.1g, Fat 21.9g

Spicy Zoodle and Bok Choy Soup

Prep + Cook Time: 35 minutes | Servings: 6

INGREDIENTS:

1 lb Baby Bok Choy, stems removed
6 oz Shitake Mushrooms, stems removed and sliced to a 2-inch thickness
2 Zucchinis, spiralized

2 Sweet Onion, chopped
2-inch Ginger, chopped
2 cloves Garlic, peeled
2 tbsp Sesame Oil
2 tbsp sugar free Soy Sauce

3 Carrots, peeled and sliced diagonally

2 tbsp Chili Paste
6 cups Water
Salt to taste
Chopped Green Onion to garnish
Sesame Seeds to garnish

DIRECTIONS:

In a food processor, add the chili paste, ginger, onion, and garlic; and process them until they are pureed. Turn on the Instant Pot, open the pot, and select Sauté mode.

Pour in the sesame oil, once it has heated add the onion puree and cook for 4 minutes while stirring constantly to prevent burning. Add the water, mushrooms, soy sauce, and carrots. Stir.

Close the lid, secure the pressure valve, and select Steam mode on High pressure for 2 minutes. Once ready, do a quick pressure release.

Add the zucchini noodles and bok choy, and stir them to ensure that they are well submerged in the liquid. Adjust the taste with salt, cover the pot, and let the vegetables sit for 10 minutes. Use a soup spoon to dish the soup with veggies into soup bowls. Sprinkle with green onions and sesame seeds. Serve as a complete meal.

Nutrition facts per serving: Calories 121, Protein 2.1g, Net Carbs 5.2g, Fat 4.1g

Leafy Green Sauté

Prep + Cook Time: 5 minutes | Servings: 4

INGREDIENTS:

2 lb Baby Spinach
1 lb Kale Leaves
½ lb Swiss Chard
1 tbsp dried Basil

Salt and Black Pepper to season
½ tbsp Butter
½ cup Water

DIRECTIONS:

Turn on the Instant Pot, open it, add the water to it, and fit the trivet at the bottom of the pot. Put the spinach, swiss chard, and kale on the trivet. Close the lid, secure the pressure valve, and select Steam on High pressure for 1 minute. Once ready, do a quick pressure release.

Remove the trivet with the wilted greens onto a plate and discard the water in the pot. Select Sauté mode on the pot and add the butter. Once melts, add the spinach and kale back to the pot, and the dried basil. Season with salt and pepper and stir it. Turn off the pot and dish the sautéed greens into serving plates and serve as a side dish.

Nutrition facts per serving: Calories 30, Protein 3g, Net Carbs 2g, Fat 0.5g

Greek-Style Eggplant Lasagne

Prep + Cook Time: 20 minutes | Servings: 4

INGREDIENTS:

3 large Eggplants, sliced in uniform ¼ inches
4 ¼ cups sugar free Marinara Sauce
1 ½ cups shredded Mozzarella Cheese
Cooking Spray
Chopped Fresh Basil to garnish

DIRECTIONS:

Open the pot and grease with cooking spray. After, arrange the eggplant slices in a single layer in the bottom of the pot and sprinkle some cheese all over it.

Arrange another layer of eggplant slices on the cheese, sprinkle this layer with cheese also, and repeat the layering of eggplant and cheese until both ingredients are exhausted.

Lightly spray the eggplant with cooking spray and pour the marinara sauce all over it. Close the lid and pressure valve, and select Steam mode on High pressure for 8 minutes.

Once ready, do a quick pressure release. With two napkins in hand, gently remove the inner pot of the Instant Pot. Then, place a plate to cover this pot and turn the eggplant over on the plate. Garnish the eggplant and cheese with basil and serve them as a side dish.

Nutrition facts per serving: Calories 288, Protein 9g, Net Carbs 5.4, Fat 5g

Tofu Soup

Prep + Cook Time: 20 minutes | Servings: 4

INGREDIENTS:

16 oz firm Tofu, Water- packed
7 cloves Garlic, minced
1 tbsp Monk Fruit Sugar
1 tbsp Olive oil
2 tbsp Ginger Paste
¼ cup sugar free Soy Sauce
3 cup sliced Bok Choy
1 large Zucchini, spiralized
4 cups Vegetable Broth
1 cup sliced Shitake Mushrooms
½ cup chopped Cilantro

DIRECTIONS:

Drain the liquid out of the tofu, pat the tofu dry with paper towels, and use a knife to cut them into 1-inch cubes. Turn the Instant Pot on, open the pot, and select Sauté mode.

Pour the oil to heat, add the garlic and ginger, and sauté them for 1 minute. Add the monk fruit sugar, broth, and soy sauce. Stir the mixture and cook for 30 seconds.

Include the tofu and bok choy, close the lid, secure the pressure valve, and select Steam mode on High pressure for 2 minutes. Once ready, do a quick pressure release. Add the zucchini noodles, give it a good stir using a spoon, and close the lid.

Let the soup sit for 4 minutes. Add the cilantro and stir in with the spoon. Use a soup spoon to fetch the soup into soup bowls and enjoy.

Nutrition facts per serving: Calories 214, Protein 12g, Net Carbs 0.9g, Fat 5g

Winter Vegetable Soup

Prep + Cook Time: 20 minutes | Servings: 4

INGREDIENTS:

- 1 small Parsnip, peeled and sliced in a 2-inch thickness
- 1 Kohlrabi, peeled and diced
- 1 Carrot, peeled and chopped
- 1 cup chopped Butternut Squash
- 2 small Red Onions, cut in wedges
- 1 cup chopped Celery
- 1 tbsp chopped Fresh Rosemary
- 8 Sage Leaves, chopped finely
- 1 Bay Leaf
- 5 cups Vegetable Broth
- Salt and Pepper to taste
- 2 tsp Olive oil
- 2 tbsp chopped Parsley

DIRECTIONS:

Open the Instant Pot and add the parsnip, kohlrabi, carrot, squash, onion, celery, rosemary, sage leaves, Bay Leaf, vegetable broth, salt, pepper, and olive oil.

Seal the lid, select Steam mode on High pressure for 5 minutes. Once ready, do a quick pressure release. Add the parsley and stir in with a spoon. Use a soup spoon to fetch the soup into soup bowls. Serve it as it is or with a side of low crusted bread.

Nutrition facts per serving: Calories 98, Protein 4.1g, Net Carbs 4.9g, Fat 4.4g

Creamy Kale Soup

Prep + Cook Time: 15 minutes | Servings: 4

INGREDIENTS:

- 1 ½ lb Kale Leaves
- 1 tbsp Olive oil
- 1 Onion, chopped
- 4 cloves Garlic, minced
- 4 cups Vegetable Broth
- 1 ¼ cup diced Kohlrabi
- 1 ¼ cup Almond Milk
- Salt and Pepper to taste
- 1 ½ tbsp. White Wine Vinegar
- Chopped Peanuts to garnish

DIRECTIONS:

Turn on the Instant Pot, open the pot, and select Sauté mode. Add the olive oil, once it has heated add the onion and garlic and sauté them for 1 minute.

Add the kohlrabi, kale, and vegetable broth. Close the lid, secure the pressure valve, and select Steam mode on High pressure for 5 minutes. Once ready, do a quick pressure release.

Add the white wine vinegar, almond milk, salt, and pepper. Use a stick blender to puree the ingredients in the pot. Spoon the soup into bowls, sprinkle with peanuts, and serve with a side of low carb bread.

Nutrition facts per serving: Calories 69, Protein 2.5g, Net Carbs 1.8g, Fat 4.2g

Mini Pesto Cake

Prep + Cook Time: 6 minutes | Servings: 1

INGREDIENTS

- 1 ½ tbsp Pesto Sauce
- 1 Egg
- 2 tbsp Butter
- 3 tbsp Almond flour
- ½ tsp Baking Powder
- A pinch of Salt
- A pinch of Red Pepper Flakes
- 1 cup Water

DIRECTIONS

Pour in the water and lower the trivet. Whisk together the remaining ingredients in a small jar. Seal the jar and place it on top of the trivet. Seal the lid and cook on High pressure for 3 minutes.

When it goes off, release the pressure quickly. Let the cake cool for 5 minutes before serving.

Nutrition facts per serving: Calories 431, Protein 12g, Net Carbs 5g, Fat 38g

Mediterranean Pasta with Avocado

Prep + Cook Time: 13 minutes | Servings: 2

INGREDIENTS

1 tbsp chopped Oregano
1 cup Baby Spinach
¼ cup grated Parmesan Cheese
2 tbsp chopped Capers
¼ cup chopped Sun-Dried Tomatoes
1 tsp minced Garlic

1 tsp fresh rosemary, chopped
1 tbsp fresh parsley, roughly chopped
½ cup chopped Kalamata Olives
1 avocado, pitted and sliced
2 Zucchinis, spiralized
2 tbsp Butter

DIRECTIONS

Melt butter on Sauté. When sizzling, add the garlic and cook for 45 seconds, until fragrant.

Stir in the spinach and zucchini, and cook for about 5 minutes. Add the rest of the ingredients except Parmesan cheese and avocado, stir well to combine, and cook for 2 more minutes.

Finally, sprinkle with Parmesan cheese and avocado slices, and enjoy!

Nutrition facts per serving: Calories 315, Protein 15g, Net Carbs 6.5g, Fat 28g

Feta-Stuffed Mushrooms with Walnuts

Prep + Cook Time: 30 minutes | Servings: 2

INGREDIENTS

4 Portobello Mushrooms
1 Garlic Clove, minced
1 cup crumbled Feta Cheese
1 Onion, chopped
¼ cup Walnuts, roughly chopped

2 tap fresh Dill, chopped
1 egg, beaten
Salt and Pepper, to taste
1 tbsp Olive oil
1 ½ cups Water

DIRECTIONS

Pour in the water and lower the trivet. Grease a baking dish with cooking spray and set aside.

Prepare the mushrooms by removing the stems and washing them well. In a bowl, combine garlic, feta, onion, walnuts, and dill well. Fill the mushrooms with the feta mixture and then drizzle with the oil; season to taste. Arrange the stuffed portobellos in the baking dish.

Place the dish on top of the trivet and seal the lid. Cook on High pressure for 20 minutes.When the timer goes off, do a quick pressure release and open the lid carefully.

Nutrition facts per serving: Calories 326, Protein 15g, Net Carbs 5g, Fat 29g

Tofu and Swiss Chard Bowl

Prep + Cook Time: 60 minutes | Servings: 4

INGREDIENTS

1 Green Onion, diced
9 ounces Swiss Chard, chopped
3 tbsp Olive oil
2 tbsp Tamari

Tofu:

2 tsp minced Garlic
15 ounces Tofu, cubed
1 tbsp Tamari
1 tbsp Water

1 tsp Sweetener
Juice of ½ Lime
1 tbsp chopped Parsley

1 tbsp Sesame Oil
1 tbsp Vinegar
1 ½ cups Water

DIRECTIONS

Pour in the water and lower the trivet. Place all tofu ingredients in a Ziploc bag. Shake well to incorporate everything, and let the mixture sit for about 30 minutes to marinate.

After 30 minutes, grease a baking dish with cooking spray and arrange the tofu on it, evenly. Place the dish on top of the trivet and seal the lid. Cook on High pressure for 20 minutes.

After the beep, do a quick pressure release. Remove the dish and let it sit for 2 minutes to cool a bit. Meanwhile, combine all remaining ingredients in a bowl. Stir in the tofu.

Nutrition facts per serving: Calories 415, Protein 24g, Net Carbs 6.6g, Fat 31g

Peppery and Cheesy Pizza

Prep + Cook Time: 43 minutes | Servings: 2

INGREDIENTS

½ cup halved Cherry Tomatoes
⅓ cup shredded Cheddar Cheese
1 Bell Pepper, sliced
1 tsp Italian Seasoning
2 tbsp Parmesan Cheese
2 tbsp Psyllium Husk
6 ounces shredded Mozzarella Cheese

1 tbsp chopped Oregano
½ tsp Black Pepper
¼ tsp Salt
½ cup Almond flour
¼ cup Low-Carb Pizza Sauce
1 ½ cups Water

DIRECTIONS

Pour in the water and lower the trivet. Line a round baking dish with parchment paper and set aside. Place the mozzarella in a heat-proof bowl and then inside the microwave. Microwave to melt. Transfer to a bowl and let cool until it is safe to handle. Add the almond flour, Psyllium Husk, Italian seasoning, salt, and Parmesan cheese. Stir well. Knead the dough with hands and divide in half. Roll the halves into two rounds.

Place one round on top of the lined dish and place on top of the trivet. Seal the lid, and set the cooking time to 6 minutes. Cook on High. When the timer goes off, do a quick pressure release. Remove the dish from the pot and spread half of the pizza sauce on top. Sprinkle with half of the pepper and oregano, and top with half of the toppings.Return the dish on the trivet and seal the lid. Cook for 8 minutes on High pressure. Do a quick pressure release. Repeat the process with the remaining pizza.

Nutrition facts per serving: Calories 521, Protein 31g, Net Carbs 3.7g, Fat 15g

Spinach Ricotta Pie

Prep + Cook Time: 35 minutes | Servings: 8

INGREDIENTS

½ cup chopped Onions
6 cups chopped Spinach
2 cups Ricotta Cheese
3 Eggs
1 tbsp Olive oil
¼ cup grated Parmesan Cheese
1 Garlic Clove, minced
1 cup shredded Mozzarella Cheese
Salt and Pepper, to taste
1 ½ cups Water

DIRECTIONS

Heat the oil on Sauté, and when and add the onions. Sauté for 3 minutes, until softened; add the garlic and cook for a minute, until fragrant. Stir in the spinach and cook for another minute, until wilted. Transfer the mixture to a bowl.

Pour water in the pot and lower the trivet. Beat the eggs in the same bowl with the spinach, and then stir in the remaining ingredients. Grab a dish that fits inside the Instant Pot and spray with cooking spray. Pour the ricotta and spinach mixture into the dish. Place the dish on top of the trivet and seal the lid. Cook on High pressure for to 20 minutes.

When the timer goes off, do a quick pressure release. Remove the dish, and let cool for 5 minutes before slicing.

Nutrition facts per serving: Calories 250, Protein 8g, Net Carbs 4g, Fat 15g

Smoked Paprika Cauliflower Cakes

Prep + Cook Time: 18 minutes | Servings: 4

INGREDIENTS

1 lb Cauliflower Rice
1 tsp Smoked Paprika
½ tsp Baking Powder
½ cup Almond flour
1 tsp Pepper
¼ tsp Garlic Powder
¼ tsp Onion Powder
3 Eggs
½ tsp Salt
½ cup Parmesan Cheese
2 tbsp Butter

DIRECTIONS

Place all ingredients, except the butter, in a large bowl and mix with hands to combine. Shape the mixture into 4 cakes. Melt butter on Sauté, and add 2 of the cauliflower cakes inside the pot.

Cook on all sides until crispy. Melt the remaining tablespoon of butter and repeat the process with the other two cakes. Serve and enjoy!

Nutrition facts per serving: Calories 215, Protein 9g, Net Carbs 4.5g, Fat 15g

Three-Cheese Stuffed Peppers

Prep + Cook Time: 40 minutes | Servings: 4

INGREDIENTS

½ cup Cottage Cheese
½ cup grated Parmesan Cheese
½ cup shredded Mozzarella Cheese
¼ cup chopped Spinach
4 Bell Peppers
4 Eggs
1 tbsp olive oil
2 tbsp scallions, chopped
Salt and Pepper, to taste
1 ½ cups Water

DIRECTIONS

Pour in the water and lower the trivet. Grease a baking dish that fits inside the Instant Pot with cooking spray and set aside.

Cut the bell peppers in half lengthwise and remove the seeds. Place all remaining ingredients in a bowl, and mix to combine. Divide the cheese mixture between the bell peppers.

Arrange the stuffed peppers in the baking dish and then place on top of the trivet. Seal the lid and cook on High pressure for 20 minutes. After the beep, do a quick pressure release and serve immediately with yogurt dip.

Nutrition facts per serving: Calories 245, Protein 18g, Net Carbs 6g, Fat 16g

Beet and Pecan Bowl

Prep + Cook Time: 25 minutes | Servings: 4

INGREDIENTS

4 Large Beets, chopped
½ Shallot, minced
2 Garlic Cloves, minced
½ cup chopped Walnuts
1 cup Veggie Broth
1 tbsp Olive oil
½ cup grated Parmesan Cheese

DIRECTIONS

Place the beets in a food processor and pulse until a rice-like consistency is formed. Heat olive oil on Sauté. When sizzling, add the shallots and cook for 2 minutes.

Stir in the garlic and cook for an additional minute. Pour the broth over and stir in the beet rice. Seal the lid and cook on High pressure for 12 minutes.

When it goes off, do a quick release. If the liquid hasn't been absorbed fully, drain the beets a bit. Stir in the Parmesan cheese. Divide among 4 bowls and top with walnuts, to serve.

Nutrition facts per serving: Calories 273, Protein 9g, Net Carbs 8.5g, Fat 22g

Broccoli with Tomatoes

Prep + Cook Time: 23 minutes | Servings: 4

INGREDIENTS

1 Broccoli Head, broken into florets
2 (14-ounce) cans diced Tomatoes
½ Onion, diced
1 tsp Garlic Powder
½ tsp Celery Seeds
1 tbsp Olive oil
Salt and Pepper, to taste

DIRECTIONS

Heat the oil on Sauté. When hot and sizzling, add the onions and cook for 3 minutes. Stir in the tomatoes and spices, and cook for 2 more minutes.

Add the broccoli, stir to combine, and seal the lid. Select Manual and cook on HIGH pressure for 8 minutes. When it goes off, do a quick pressure release. Serve chilled.

Nutrition facts per serving: Calories 153, Protein 9g, Net Carbs 5g, Fat 12g

Asparagus Zoodles with Pesto & Soft Boiled Eggs

Prep + Cook Time: 15 minutes | Servings: 2

INGREDIENTS

4 Asparagus Spears, sliced
2 Zucchinis, spiralized
1 Garlic Clove, minced
2 tsp Olive oil
¼ cup Pesto Sauce

4 eggs
1 cup Water
Salt and Pepper, to taste
1 tbsp fresh chopped Dill to garnish

DIRECTIONS

Pour in the water and lower the trivet. Arrange the eggs in a steamer basket. Seal the lid and cook on Low pressure for 3 minutes. Once ready, do a quick release.

Allow the eggs to cool. Peel the eggs halve and set aside. Add olive oil on Sauté. When hot and sizzling, add the garlic. Cook the garlic for just a minute, until fragrant. Stir in the asparagus and zoodles and cook for about 3 minutes. Season with some salt and pepper.

Stir in the pesto sauce and cook just until it becomes heated through. Transfer to a serving plate, top with the halved eggs and fresh dill.

Nutrition facts per serving: Calories 312, Protein 8g, Net Carbs 4g, Fat 25g

Squash Spaghetti with Mint and Almond Pesto

Prep + Cook Time: 9 minutes | Servings: 2

INGREDIENTS

1 Celery Stalk, diced
1 tbsp Olive oil
¼ tsp Lemon Zest, grated
Juice of ½ Lemon
3 Yellow Summer Squashes, spiralized

2 tbsp finely chopped Mint
1 tbsp Almonds, toasted and chopped
¼ cup Olive oil
Salt and Pepper, to taste
1 ½ cups Water

DIRECTIONS

Add half of the almonds, celery, oil, lemon juice, and mint to your food processor and blend until combined, but not entirely smooth. Season and set aside.

Pour in the water and lower the trivet. Grease a baking dish with cooking spray and place the spiralized squash inside. Place the dish on top and seal the lid.

Cook for 4 minutes on HIGH pressure. When ready, do a quick pressure release and transfer the squash noodles to a large bowl. Top with the pesto, the remaining almonds, and lemon zest.

Nutrition facts per serving: Calories 174, Protein 5g, Net Carbs 5g, Fat 8g

Radish Hash Browns

Prep + Cook Time: 15 minutes | Servings: 4

INGREDIENTS

4 Eggs
1 pound Radishes, shredded
⅓ cup grated Parmesan Cheese
¼ tsp Garlic Powder
Salt and Pepper, to taste
1 ½ cups Water

DIRECTIONS

Pour the water in and lower the trivet. Grease a baking dish with cooking spray and set aside.

In a large bowl, beat the eggs along with the garlic powder, salt, and pepper. Stir in the radishes and the Parmesan cheese. Pour the mixture into the greased baking dish and place the dish on top of the trivet.

Seal the lid and cook for 20 minutes on HIGH pressure. When it goes off, release the pressure quickly. Open the lid carefully. Cut the hash browns into 4 squares, and serve with aioli.

Nutrition facts per serving: Calories 80, Protein 7g, Net Carbs 5g, Fat 5g

Cheese Sandwich with Chimichurri

Prep + Cook Time: 15 minutes | Servings: 1

INGREDIENTS

2 tbsp Almond flour
2 Eggs
3 tbsp Butter
½ tsp Baking Powder
1 ½ tbsp Psyllium Husk Powder
2 slices Swiss Cheese
1 tsp Lime juice
1 tbsp fresh chives, finely chopped
½ tsp garlic powder
1 tsp Avocado oil
Crushed red pepper, to taste
1 tsp fresh Cilantro, chopped
Salt and Pepper, to taste

DIRECTIONS

In a small bowl, mix avocado oil, chives, garlic powder, and cilantro; season with salt and red pepper to taste and set aside.

Add the flour, 2 tbsp of the butter, eggs, baking powder, psyllium husk powder, and salt and pepper, in a microwave-safe bowl with a square shape. Beat until smooth and fully combined.

Place in the microwave and microwave for about 90 seconds. Invert the 'bun' onto a cutting board and cut it in half.

Melt a tbsp of butter on Sauté. Lay in one 'bread' slice, cover with the cheese and top with the other slice. Press with a spatula and cook for about 2-3 minutes. Flip over and cook for a couple of minutes until the cheese melts and sandwich is golden. Drizzle with the chimichurri.

Nutrition facts per serving: Calories 621, Protein 32g, Net Carbs 6g, Fat 65g

Cheesy Jalapeno Lunch 'Waffles'

Prep + Cook Time: 11 minutes | Servings: 2

INGREDIENTS

1 tbsp Coconut Flour
3 Eggs
1 Jalapeno, seeded and diced
1 ounce grated Cheddar Cheese
3 ounces Cream Cheese

1 tsp Baking Powder
1 tbsp Butter
A pinch of Salt
1 tsp Psyllium Husk Powder

DIRECTIONS

Place everything in a food processor. Process the mixture until smooth and well-incorporated.

Melt the butter on Sauté, add half of the previously processed batter and cook until golden on both sides. Set aside and do the same with the other 'waffle'. Serve with chicken breast.

Nutrition facts per serving: Calories 331, Protein 16g, Net Carbs 4.3g, Fat 25g

Fake Mac and Cheese

Prep + Cook Time: 11 minutes | Servings: 4

INGREDIENTS

1 Cauliflower Head, finely chopped
½ cup shredded Cheddar Cheese
¼ cup shredded Mozzarella Cheese

2 tbsp grated Parmesan Cheese
⅔ cup Heavy Cream
Salt and Pepper, to taste

DIRECTIONS

Combine the heavy cream, cauliflower, cheddar, and mozzarella, in the Instant Pot. Season with salt and pepper. Seal the lid on and cook on HIGH pressure for 6 minutes.

Do a quick pressure release and open the lid carefully. Sprinkle with the Parmesan cheese and divide between 4 serving bowls, to serve.

Nutrition facts per serving: Calories 230, Protein 7g, Net Carbs 2.5g, Fat 12g

Mushroom Cream Soup

Prep + Cook Time: 23 minutes | Servings: 4

INGREDIENTS

12 ounces Mushrooms, sliced
¼ cup Butter
1 Garlic Clove, minced

5 ounces Crème Fraiche
4 cups Vegetable Broth
Salt and Pepper, to taste

DIRECTIONS

Melt the butter on Sauté, add garlic and cook for a minute, until fragrant. Stir in the mushrooms and cook for 4 minutes. Season the veggies with salt and pepper and pour in broth.

Stir well and seal the lid. Select MANUAL and cook for 8 minutes on HIGH pressure. Release the pressure quickly. Open the lid and blend with a hand blender. Stir in the crème fraiche. Ladle to serving bowls and enjoy hot.

Nutrition facts per serving: Calories 280, Protein 6g, Net Carbs 5.8g, Fat 25g

Kale and Cauliflower Stew

Prep + Cook Time: 17 minutes | Servings: 4

INGREDIENTS

2 Celery Stalks, diced
3 cups Cauliflower Rice
2 tbsp Olive oil
2 Garlic Cloves, minced
2 Carrots, sliced
2 cups Kale, chopped

1 Onion, diced
4 cups Veggie Broth
14 ounces canned diced Tomatoes
2 tsp Cumin
Salt and Pepper, to taste

DIRECTIONS

Heat the olive oil on Sauté. Add the celery, onions, and carrots, and cook for a few minutes, until softened. Then, stir in the garlic and cook for 45 seconds more.

Add the rest of the ingredients to the pot and stir to combine. Seal the lid and cook on High pressure for 8 minutes. When the timer goes off, let the pressure valve drop on its own for a natural pressure release. Open the lid gently and ladle into serving bowls.

Nutrition facts per serving: Calories 320, Protein 12g, Net Carbs 4g, Fat 14g

Flax and Swiss Chard Patties

Prep + Cook Time: 22 minutes | Servings: 4

INGREDIENTS

1 cup shredded Mozzarella Cheese
1 tbsp Flaxseed Meal
2 Green Onions, chopped
½ Cauliflower Head
1 cup chopped Swiss Chard
1 tbsp Olive oil

1 tsp chopped Thyme
2 Eggs
⅓ cup grated Parmesan Cheese
2 tbsp Butter
Salt and Pepper, to taste

DIRECTIONS

Place the cauliflower in a food processor and blend it until rice-like consistency forms. Stir in the thyme, Swiss chard, and green onions. Process until smooth and transfer the mixture to a bowl. Stir in the remaining ingredients.

Melt half of the butter on Sauté. Place ¼ of the batter in the pot and cook for a few minutes on both sides, until golden and crispy. Repeat the process one more time. Then, melt the remaining batter and do the same with the remaining batch. Serve with garlic-yogurt sauce.

Nutrition facts per serving: Calories 281, Protein 16g, Net Carbs 3.5g, Fat 20g, Fiber 1g, Sodium 180mg

Portobello Burgers

Prep + Cook Time: 17 minutes | Servings: 2

INGREDIENTS

2 Portobello Mushrooms
2 Keto Buns
2 Eggs, whisked
2 tbsp Butter

2 tbsp Mayonnaise
2 Lettuce Leaves
Salt and Pepper, to taste

DIRECTIONS

Melt half of the butter on Sauté. Add the eggs and season with salt and pepper. Cook on until set, for a few minutes. Transfer the eggs to a plate. Melt the remaining butter and add in the portobellos. Cook for about 3 minutes per side. Season with salt and pepper.

Cut the buns open and place a lettuce leaves inside. Add a portobello mushroom and spread the mayo over. Top with the eggs and close the sandwich. Serve right away.

Nutrition facts per serving: Calories 531, Protein 23g, Net Carbs 7.4g, Fat 50g

Dill and Artichoke Salad

Prep + Cook Time: 20 minutes | Servings: 4

INGREDIENTS

6 Baby Artichokes
1 ½ cups Water
1 ½ tbsp chopped Dill
1 tbsp Lemon Juice
½ tsp Lemon Zest

¼ cup Olive oil
1 tbsp chopped Capers
½ tsp Capers Brine
A pinch of Sweetener
Salt and Pepper, to taste

DIRECTIONS

Pour the water into the Instant Pot and add the artichokes. Seal the lid, select Manual and cook on HIGH pressure for 10 minutes. When the timer goes off, do a quick pressure release.

Transfer the artichokes to a cutting board. Chop finely and place in a bowl. Add the rest of the ingredients to the bowl and toss with hands until everything is combined and the artichokes are well coated. Serve with chicken breast.

Nutrition facts per serving: Calories 173, Protein 1g, Net Carbs 5g, Fat 13g

Eggplant and Parmesan Burgers

Prep + Cook Time: 25 minutes | Servings: 4

INGREDIENTS

1 Large Eggplant
½ cup grated Parmesan Cheese
2 tbsp Olive oil

2 tbsp Mustard
1 ½ cups Water

For the Slaw

½ cup white Cabbage, shredded

½ cup red cabbage, shredded

DIRECTIONS

Pour the water into the Instant Pot. Wash the eggplants and slice into 4 rounds. Place them in the pot, and seal the lid. Cook on HIGH pressure for 2 minutes.

When the timer goes off, do a quick pressure release. Drain the eggplants and discard the cooking liquid. Brush the eggplants with mustard and coat with Parmesan cheese.

Set to Sauté and heat the olive oil. When sizzling, add the eggplant burgers. Cook for a few minutes per side, or until golden. Serve with yogurt or tomato sauce.

Nutrition facts per serving: Calories 183, Protein 5g, Net Carbs 3.5g, Fat 5g

Tomato Soup with Goat Cheese Topping

Prep + Cook Time: 16 minutes | Servings: 6

INGREDIENTS

1 cup Olive oil
2 tbsp Lemon Juice
2 tbsp Apple Cider Vinegar
1 Cucumber, chopped
2 Red Peppers, roasted and chopped
1 Small Red Onion, chopped
2 Green Peppers, chopped
4 Tomatoes, chopped
2 Spring Onions, chopped
2 Garlic Cloves
7 ounces Goat Cheese, crumbled
2 Avocados, flesh scooped out
6 cups water

DIRECTIONS

Dump all the ingredients, except the cheese, in a food processor and pulse until smooth. Pour the mixture into your Instant Pot and seal the lid. Cook for 15 minutes on HIGH pressure.

When the timer goes off, do a quick pressure release and ladle into 6 serving bowls. Top with goat cheese, to serve.

Nutrition facts per serving: Calories 532, Protein 18g, Net Carbs 6.5g, Fat 50g, Fiber 3g, Sodium 310mg

Pumpkin Chipotle Soup

Prep + Cook Time: 19 minutes | Servings: 6

INGREDIENTS

2 cups Pumpkin Puree
½ cups chopped Onions
1 tsp chopped Parsley
32 ounces Veggie Broth
½ cup Heavy Cream
2 tbsp Olive oil
1 tbsp chopped Chipotle
½ tbsp Red Wine Vinegar
2 tsp Swerve
1 tsp minced Garlic
½ tsp Cumin
Salt and Pepper, to taste

DIRECTIONS

Heat oil on Sauté, and when hot and sizzling, add the onions and cook until soft. Stir in the garlic and cook for 45 seconds more.

Add the rest of the ingredients to the pot, except for the vinegar, and give it a good stir. Seal the lid and cook on High pressure for 5 minutes.

After the beep, move the handle to "Venting" for a quick pressure release. Stir in the vinegar just before ladling into serving bowls.

Nutrition facts per serving: Calories 140, Protein 2g, Net Carbs 5.5g, Fat 12g

Soft Cabbage with Garlic and Lemon

Prep + Cook Time: 17 minutes | Servings: 4

INGREDIENTS

2 tsp minced Garlic
¼ cup Lemon Juice
1 tbsp Olive oil
2 cups chopped Cabbage
1 cup Veggie Broth
¼ tsp Onion Powder
Salt and Pepper, to taste

DIRECTIONS

Combine broth and cabbage in your instant pot. Seal the lid and cook on HIGH pressure for 5 minutes. When it goes off, do a quick pressure release. Open the lid gently and transfer the cabbage to a plate. Discard the broth and wipe the pot clean.

Set the Instant Pot to Sauté and warm the olive oil. Add the garlic and cook for 1 minute. Stir in the cabbage and all seasoning. Drizzle with the lemon juice before serving.

Nutrition facts per serving: Calories 83, Protein 3g, Net Carbs 2g, Fat 7g

Winter Vegetable Soup with Shirataki Rice

Prep + Cook Time: 30 minutes | Servings: 6

INGREDIENTS

½ cup grated Parmesan Cheese
6 cups Veggie Broth
1 Celery stick, chopped
2 Garlic cloves, minced
2 cups kale, shredded
1 Parsnip, chopped

1 leek, (green part removed) finely sliced, rinsed
2 Rosemary Sprigs
2 tbsp Butter
1 package Shirataki rice, cooked
Salt and Pepper, to taste

DIRECTIONS

Melt butter on Sauté, and add the leek. Cook for 3 minutes, until soft. Add the garlic and cook for another minute. Stir in the kale and cook for 3 minutes, until soft.

Pour in broth and add the rosemary, parsnip, and celery. Seal the lid, select SOUP/BROTH mode cook for 20 minutes on HIGH pressure.

When the timer goes off, do a quick pressure release. Discard the rosemary. Stir in the Parmesan cheese and shirataki rice, adjust the seasoning and serve immediately.

Nutrition facts per serving: Calories 181, Protein 11g, Net Carbs 2.5g, Fat 11g

Creamy Gingery Coconut "Rice"

Prep + Cook Time: 12 minutes | Servings: 4

INGREDIENTS

1 tsp minced Ginger
1 Cauliflower Head, riced in a food processor
3 tbsp shredded Coconut

10 ounces Coconut Milk
½ cup Water
Salt and Pepper, to taste

DIRECTIONS

Pour in milk and water and add the ginger. Let simmer on Sauté for a few minutes, until the milk becomes super fragrant.

Add in the cauliflower rice and cook for 2 minutes until soft and the liquid is absorbed. Stir in the coconut and season with salt and pepper. Serve immediately.

Nutrition facts per serving: Calories 110, Protein 9g, Net Carbs 4g, Fat 3g, Fiber 4g, Sodium 380mg

Cheesy Green Beans

Prep + Cook Time: 22 minutes | Servings: 4

INGREDIENTS

12 ounces Green Beans
2 cups Water
⅔ cup grated Parmesan Cheese
1 Egg
¼ tsp Garlic Powder
2 tbsp Olive oil
¼ tsp Onion Powder
Salt and Pepper, to taste

DIRECTIONS

Pour the water into the Instant Pot. Place the green beans inside the steamer basket and lower the basket into the water. Seal the lid and cook on HIGH pressure for 3 minutes.

When it goes off, release the pressure quickly. Remove the steamer basket using mittens. Discard the water and wipe the pot clean. Prepare an ice bath and add in the green beans.

Meanwhile, beat the egg and heat half of the olive oil on Sauté. Place all remaining ingredients in a bowl and stir to combine. Dip half of the green beans in egg first, then coat in Parmesan mixture. Place in the pot and cook for a minute per side. Cook in batches.

Nutrition facts per serving: Calories 151, Protein 11g, Net Carbs 3g, Fat 8g

Mock Grilled Onions

Prep + Cook Time: 25 minutes | Servings: 4

INGREDIENTS

4 Onions
½ cup Butter
4 Bouillon Cubes
1 ½ cups Water
Salt and Pepper, to taste

DIRECTIONS

Pour water in and lower the trivet. Cut 4 pieces of aluminum foil and place each onion on a piece of foil. Season onions with salt and pepper, and press a bouillon cube into each of them. Top the onions with equal amounts of butter.

Wrap the onions in foil and place them on a baking dish that can fit inside your Instant Pot. Place the dish on top and seal the lid. Cook on HIGH pressure for 15 minutes.

When ready, press Cancel and do a quick pressure release. Gently unwrap the onions and chop them up. Serve with barbecued meat, mayo, and ketchup.

Nutrition facts per serving: Calories 155, Protein 1.5g, Net Carbs 9g, Fat 11g

Kale "Pita Bread"

Prep + Cook Time: 25 minutes | Servings: 4

INGREDIENTS

1 cup chopped Kale
½ cup Almond flour
3 tbsp Butter
1 ½ tbsp Ground Flaxseed
¼ tsp Baking Powder
A pinch of Salt
A pinch of Cumin
2 tbsp grated Parmesan Cheese
1 ¼ cups Hot Water

DIRECTIONS

Place flour, flaxseed, cumin, salt, baking powder, and Parmesan, in a bowl; mix to combine.

Pour water gently while mixing, until dough is formed. Stir in kale and knead the dough within the bowl. Lightly flour a working surface and transfer the dough there.

Divide the dough into 4 equal pieces and roll out each of them into a circle. Set the pot to Sauté, and melt ¼ of the butter. Add one "bread" and cook until slightly browned on both sides.

Repeat with the remaining bread and butter.

Nutrition facts per serving: Calories 246, Protein 4g, Net Carbs 6g, Fat 18g

Caramelized Peppers and Onions

Prep + Cook Time: 1200 minutes | Servings: 4

INGREDIENTS

2 Bell Peppers
1 ½ Red Onions
1 tbsp Olive oil
1 tsp Basil
1 Garlic Clove, minced
1 tbsp Butter
Salt and Pepper, to taste
1 ½ cups Water

DIRECTIONS

Pour water in and lower the trivet. Add peppers and onions to a baking dish and place the dish on top of the trivet. Seal the lid, hit ManuAnd cook on HIGH pressure for 5 minutes.

When it goes off, do a quick pressure release. Transfer the veggies to a cutting board and chop them up. Meanwhile, heat the oil and butter on Sauté. Add garlic and cook for a minute.

Stir in the veggies and the remaining ingredients and cook for 4 minutes. Serve immediately.

Nutrition facts per serving: Calories 95, Protein 2g, Net Carbs 7g, Fat 7g

Soft and Cheesy Keto "Bread"

Prep + Cook Time: 27 minutes | Servings: 4

INGREDIENTS

¾ cup Coconut Flour
8 ounces shredded Mozzarella Cheese
A pinch of Cumin
A pinch of Garlic Salt
A pinch of Pepper
1 ½ cups Water

DIRECTIONS

Pour in water and lower the trivet. Arrange a baking dish with parchment paper and set aside. Place all remaining ingredients in a microwave-safe bowl; stir to combine.

Microwave for a few minutes, until the cheese melts. Stir the mixture once again and transfer to a lightly-floured working surface. With a rolling pin, roll out the dough, making a rectangle.

Cut that rectangle into 4 triangles. Arrange the triangles on the baking sheet. Place the baking sheet on top of the trivet and seal the lid. Cook on HIGH pressure for 13 minutes. When ready, do a quick pressure release. Serve with roast to enjoy.

Nutrition facts per serving: Calories 235, Protein 17g, Net Carbs 4g, Fat 12g

Squash Side

Prep + Cook Time: 17 minutes | Servings: 4

INGREDIENTS

1 Whole Spaghetti Squash
1 ½ cups Water

Salt and Pepper, to taste

DIRECTIONS

Cut the squash in half and remove the seeds with a spoon. Pour the water in the pot. Place the squash in the steamer basket and lower the basket into the water.

Seal the lid, hit Manual and cook for 7 minutes on HIGH pressure. When it goes off, do a quick pressure release. Transfer the squash to a cutting board. With a fork, pull of the flash to make spaghetti-like strings. Place in a bowl and season with salt and pepper.

Nutrition facts per serving: Calories 172, Protein 9g, Net Carbs 8g, Fat 5g

Chili Green Beans with Coconut

Prep + Cook Time: 20 minutes | Servings: 4

INGREDIENTS

¾ pound Green Beans, sliced crosswise
¾ cup shredded unsweetened Coconut
2 Chilies, seeded and diced
2 tsp minced Garlic
2 tbsp Butter

¼ tsp Cumin
½ tsp minced Ginger
½ cup Chicken Broth
Salt and Pepper, to taste

DIRECTIONS

Melt butter on Sauté. Add ginger, chilies, and garlic, and cook for a minute. Then, stir in the green beans and cumin, and cook for 2 minutes. Pour in broth and coconut; give it a stir.

Seal the lid and cook on HIGH pressure for 3 minutes. When ready, do a quick pressure release. For 'drier' beans, set to Sauté and cook for 3 minutes until the liquid evaporates.

Nutrition facts per serving: Calories 153, Protein 3g, Net Carbs 4g, Fat 15g

Soft Cumin Cabbage

Prep + Cook Time: 18 minutes | Servings: 4

INGREDIENTS

1 ½ pounds Cabbage, cut into wedges
¼ cup Chicken Broth
3 tbsp Butter

½ tbsp Cumin
Salt and Pepper, to taste

DIRECTIONS

Melt the butter on Sauté. Add the cabbage, season with cumin, salt, and black pepper, and cook for 3 minutes. Pour the broth over and stir to combine.

Cook until the broth is reduced by half. Stir well before serving and adjust the seasoning.

Nutrition facts per serving: Calories 123, Protein 2.6g, Net Carbs 5.5g, Fat 9g

Turmeric Squash Cubes

Prep + Cook Time: 33 minutes | Servings: 4

INGREDIENTS

1 Butternut Squash, peeled and cut in Half
1 cup Chicken Broth
¼ tsp Cumin
1 tsp Turmeric Powder
¼ tsp Garlic Powder
A pinch of Curry Powder
Salt and Pepper, to taste
2 tbsp Butter

DIRECTIONS

Pour in broth and lower the trivet. Place squash half on top of the trivet and seal the lid. Select Steam and cook for 5 minutes on HIGH pressure. When ready, release the pressure quickly.

Open the lid carefully and transfer the squash to a cutting board. Discard the broth and wipe the pot clean. Cut the squash into cubes. Set the pot to Sauté and melt the butter. Add squash cubes and sprinkle with spices. Stir to combine and cook for 3 minutes, or until caramelized.

Nutrition facts per serving: Calories 135, Protein 2g, Net Carbs 9.2g, Fat 6g

Curried Eggplant

Prep + Cook Time: 25 minutes | Servings: 4

INGREDIENTS

12 ounces Eggplants, sliced
1 tsp minced Garlic
1 tsp minced Ginger
1 Onion, diced
1 tsp Curry Powder
½ cup Tomato Sauce
⅔ cups Chicken Broth
2 tbsp Butter

DIRECTIONS

Melt half of the butter on Sauté. Add eggplants and brown on both sides. Remove to a plate. Melt the remaining butter, add the onions and cook for 3 minutes. Stir in garlic and ginger, and cook for another minute. Stir in the remaining ingredients and return the eggplant slices to the pot. Seal the lid and cook on HIGH for 7 minutes. Do a quick pressure release.

Nutrition facts per serving: Calories 145, Protein 2g, Net Carbs 8g, Fat 14g

Creamy Spinach

Prep + Cook Time: 15 minutes | Servings: 4

INGREDIENTS

1 pound Baby Spinach
¾ cup Heavy Cream
1 Tomato, diced
1 tsp Onion Powder
2 Garlic Cloves, minced
1 tbsp Butter
¼ cup Water
Salt and Pepper, to taste

DIRECTIONS

Melt butter on Sauté. Add garlic and cook for a minute. Stir in the tomato and cook for 2 more minutes. Pour the remaining ingredients and give the mixture a good stir to combine. Seal the lid and cook on HIGH pressure for 2 minutes. When ready, do a quick release.

Nutrition facts per serving: Calories 95, Protein 5g, Net Carbs 3g, Fat 8g

Tofu & Tomatoes

Prep + Cook Time: 19 minutes | Servings: 4

INGREDIENTS

- 14 ounces Tofu, cubed
- 2 tsp minced Garlic
- 14 ounces canned diced Tomatoes
- ¼ cup Chicken Broth
- 1 tbsp Olive oil
- 1 Celery Stalk, diced
- ½ Onion, diced

DIRECTIONS

Warm olive oil on Sauté. Add the onions and celery, and cook for 3 minutes. Stir in garlic and sauté for a minute. When fragrant, stir in tomatoes and tofu; cook for 2 minutes.

Stir in broth and seal the lid. Cook on HIGH pressure for 3 minutes. When it goes off, release the pressure quickly. Serve chilled.

Nutrition facts per serving: Calories 223, Protein 13g, Net Carbs 6g, Fat 18g

Low Carb Taco Soup

Prep + Cook Time: 30 minutes | Servings: 4

INGREDIENTS

- ½ tbsp Onion Flakes
- 2 cloves Garlic, minced
- 1 tbsp Chili Powder
- 1 tsp Cumin Powder
- 1 cup Diced Tomatoes
- 4 cups Beef Broth
- Salt to taste
- Pepper to taste
- ½ cup Cream Cheese
- ½ cup Heavy Cream

Toppings:

- Sliced Jalapenos
- Cheddar Cheese, grated
- Sliced Black Olives
- Chopped Avocados

DIRECTIONS

Add the ingredients, except heavy cream and cream cheese. Seal the lid and cook on High pressure for 5 minutes.

Once ready, let the pot sit uncovered for 5 minutes, then do a natural pressure release for about 10 minutes. Stir in cream cheese and heavy cream, and serve hot.

Nutrition facts per serving: Calories 386, Protein 27g, Net Carbs 5g, Fat 28g

Cauliflower Bacon Soup

Prep + Cook Time: 30 minutes | Servings: 6

INGREDIENTS

- 1 cup Butter, shared into 2
- 2 medium Onion, diced
- 2 Celery Stalks, diced
- 4 cloves Garlic, minced
- 2 large heads Cauliflower
- 2 tsp dried Parsley
- 5 cups Chicken Broth
- 1 ½ cups Almond Milk
- 2 ½ tsp Garlic Powder
- Salt to taste
- Black Pepper to taste
- 1 ½ cup Sour Cream
- 10 oz Cheddar Cheese
- 14 slices Bacon, chopped

DIRECTIONS

Melt half of the butter on Sauté, and add onion, garlic, and celery. Cook until tender. Add parsley, broth, and cauliflower. Stir lightly. Seal the lid, and cook on Low Pressure for 3 minutes.

Once ready, quickly release the pressure. Add the remaining butter and puree the ingredients inside the pot with a stick blender. Add milk, garlic powder, pepper, and salt.

Puree further until smooth. Select Keep Warm, add sour cream and some cheddar cheese. Simmer for 4 minutes. Serve sprinkled with bacon crumbles and extra cheddar cheese.

Nutrition facts per serving: Calories 269, Protein 12.9g, Net Carbs 7g. Fat 15.7g

Broccoli Soup

Prep + Cook Time: 50 minutes | Servings: 4

INGREDIENTS

1 tbsp Olive oil
2 Shallots, chopped
1 medium Yellow Onion, sliced thinly
1 lb Broccoli, cut into florets
⅓ tsp Thyme
15 oz Chicken Broth
¼ tsp Oregano

¼ tsp Turmeric
1 tsp Curry Powder
¼ tsp Cinnamon
7 oz Coconut Milk
Salt to taste
Black Pepper to taste

DIRECTIONS

Set on Sauté. Heat the oil, add the onions and shallots. Cook for 3 minutes until translucent. Add the broccoli, and cover with broth; stir. Add the remaining ingredients except for the coconut milk, pepper, and salt. Stir evenly.

Seal the lid, and cook on High Pressure for 10 minutes. Once ready, quickly release the pressure. Add the coconut milk, pepper and salt, and puree the ingredients inside the pot using a stick blender. Dish into a soup bowl and serve warm or cold.

Nutrition facts per serving: Calories 206, Protein 8.1g, Net Carbs 5.6g, Fat 11.9g

Broccoli "Slaw"

Prep + Cook Time: 14 minutes | Servings: 4

INGREDIENTS

4 Broccoli Stalks
1 ½ cups Water
1 tsp Celery Seeds
1 ½ tbsp Apple Cider Vinegar

⅓ cup Mayo
1 tbsp Sweetener
½ tbsp Dijon Mustard
Salt and Pepper, to taste

DIRECTIONS

Pour the water into the Instant Pot and place the broccoli stalks inside the steamer basket. Lower the basket in the pot and seal the lid. Cook on HIGH pressure for 4 minutes.

When ready, press Cancel and do a quick pressure release. Remove broccoli stalks to a cutting board and slice thinly. Transfer to a bowl. In another bowl, whisk together the remaining ingredients. Pour the mayo mixture over the broccoli and toss well to coat.

Nutrition facts per serving: Calories 120, Protein 6g, Net Carbs 3.5g, Fat 16g

Chili and Zesty Brussel Sprouts

Prep + Cook Time: 16 minutes | Servings: 4

INGREDIENTS

4 cups Brussel Sprouts
1 ½ cups Water
¼ tsp Salt
¼ tsp Pepper
½ Lemon Juice
¼ tsp Lemon Zest
1 Jalapeno, seeded and sliced
2 tbsp grated Parmesan Cheese
2 tbsp Olive oil

DIRECTIONS

Pour the water into the Instant Pot. Place the Brussel sprouts inside a steamer basket and then lower the basket into the pot. Seal the lid and cook on HIGH pressure for 6 minutes.

When it goes off, do a quick pressure release. Transfer the Brussel sprouts to a bowl. In another bowl, whisk together the remaining ingredients. Pour over sprouts and toss to coat.

Nutrition facts per serving: Calories 183, Protein 4g, Net Carbs 4.2g, Fat 12g

Squash and Zucchini Soup

Prep + Cook Time: 55 minutes | Servings: 2

INGREDIENTS

1 tbsp Olive oil
1 tbsp Butter
1 small Yellow Onion, chopped
1 clove Garlic, minced
2 tsp Italian Herb Blend
2 tsp Rosemary Leaves, chopped
4 cups mixed Green and Yellow Squash, chopped
4 cups Zucchini, chopped
4 cups Vegetable Stock
Salt to taste
Black Pepper to taste
Parmesan Cheese, freshly grated

DIRECTIONS

Set on Sauté. Melt olive oil and butter, and cook the onions for 3 minutes. Add the Italian herb blend, garlic, and rosemary. Stir and cook for 10 minutes.

Add the squash and zucchinis, stir and the vegetable stock. Seal the lid, select Manual and cook on High Pressure for 5 minutes. Once ready, quickly release the pressure.

Season with salt and pepper, then puree the ingredients with a stick blender. Select Sauté and simmer for 20 minutes. Serve soup in bowls and sprinkle cheese on top.

Nutrition facts per serving: Calories 45, Protein 1.5g, Net Carbs 3.2g, Fat 2.8g

Herbed Portobellos

Prep + Cook Time: 33 minutes | Servings: 4

INGREDIENTS

12 oz Portobello Mushrooms, sliced
2 tbsp Olive oil
1 tbsp chopped Basil
1 Garlic Clove, minced
2 tbsp Balsamic Vinegar
1 tsp dried Thyme
1 tbsp chopped Cilantro
1 tsp dried Rosemary
½ small Onion, diced

DIRECTIONS

Warm olive oil on Sauté. Add and cook the onions for 3 minutes. Add garlic; cook for 1 more minute. When fragrant, add the portobellos and cook for 3-4 minutes, stirring occasionally.

Pour in the rest of the ingredients and give it a good stir. Cook for another 2 minutes. Serve as a side dish to a meat meal.

Nutrition facts per serving: Calories 83, Protein 4g, Net Carbs 2g, Fat 4g

Tomato & Celery Okra

Prep + Cook Time: 20 minutes | Servings: 4

INGREDIENTS

1 pound Okra
14 ounces canned diced Tomatoes
2 Celery Stalks, diced
½ tsp Italian Seasoning
½ small Onion, diced
½ tsp Garlic Powder
1 tbsp Butter
1 ½ cups Water

DIRECTIONS

Pour the water inside the Instant Pot. Place the okra inside the steamer basket and lower the basket into the pot. Seal the lid and, pres Steam and cook on HIGH pressure for 4 minutes.

After the beep, do a quick pressure release and remove okra to a cutting board. Slice thinly.

Discard the water from the pot and wipe clean. Set to Sauté and melt the butter. Add the onions and celery; cook for 3 minutes. Stir in tomatoes and spices; cook for 2 minutes. Stir in the okrAnd cook for 2 more minutes.

Nutrition facts per serving: Calories 95, Protein 5g, Net Carbs 6g, Fat 5g

Cheesy Cauliflower

Prep + Cook Time: 12 minutes | Servings: 4

INGREDIENTS

1 Cauliflower Head, broken into florets
½ cup shredded Mozzarella Cheese
2 tbsp grated Parmesan Cheese
¼ cup Heavy Cream
Salt and Pepper, to taste
1 ½ cups Water

DIRECTIONS

Pour the water in the pot and lower the trivet. Place the florets in a baking dish and pour in heavy cream. Season with salt and pepper; stir to combine. Top with the cheeses.

Lower the baking dish on top of the trivet and seal the lid. Hit Manual and cook on HIGH pressure for 7 minutes. When it goes off, do a quick pressure release.

Nutrition facts per serving: Calories 180, Protein 5g, Net Carbs 2g, Fat 8g

Creamed Kale with Bacon

Prep + Cook Time: 20 minutes | Servings: 4

INGREDIENTS

2 cups Kale Leaves
8 Bacon Slices, chopped
½ cup Heavy Cream
⅔ cup Chicken Broth

½ tbsp Arrowroot mixed with 1 tbsp Water
1 Garlic Clove, minced
Salt and Pepper, to taste
¼ cup grated Parmesan Cheese

DIRECTIONS

Set to Sauté and add the bacon. Cook for 3-4 minutes, or until crunchy. Add the garlic and cook for a minute. When fragrant, stir in the kale and broth.

Seal the lid and cook on HIGH pressure for 2 minutes. After the beep, do a quick pressure release and open the lid carefully. Stir in the arrowroot mixture, heavy cream, and Parmesan

Set to Sauté and cook for 2 minutes, or until thickened. Serve immediately.

Nutrition facts per serving: Calories 175, Protein 8.5g, Net Carbs 1.5g, Fat 19.5g

Herbed Zucchini Flatbread

Prep + Cook Time: 33 minutes | Servings: 4

INGREDIENTS

1 Zucchini, peeled and shredded
1 cup Almond flour
1 tbsp chopped Parsley
1 ½ tsp chopped Cilantro
1 Egg

1 tbsp Coconut Oil, melted
½ cup Almond Milk
2 tbsp Butter
Salt and Pepper, to taste

DIRECTIONS

Melt butter on Sauté. Meanwhile, in a bowl, whisk together the melted coconut oil, milk, and egg. Whisk in flour gradually until the mixture becomes smooth. Stir in the herbs and season with salt and pepper.

To the pot, add half of the batter and cook for 3 minutes; then flip the flatbread over. Cook for another 2-3 minutes When ready, set the flatbread aside and melt the remaining butter.

Repeat the process with the rest of the dough. Serve with some pulled meat to enjoy.

Nutrition facts per serving: Calories 85, Protein 2.5g, Net Carbs 1.7g, Fat 11g

Cabbage Soup

Prep + Cook Time: 15 minutes | Servings: 3

INGREDIENTS

1 tbsp Olive oil
1 lb Mushrooms
1 small Red Onion, diced
1 clove Garlic, minced
1 tsp Cumin Powder
1 small Cabbage, chopped roughly

1 cup Beef Broth
3 Tomatoes, diced
2 Green Chilies, minced
2 cups Water
Salt to taste
Pepper to taste

DIRECTIONS

Set on Sauté. Add the oil and onion; sauté for 2 minutes. Add the remaining ingredients and stir. Seal the lid, select Manual and cook on Low Pressure for 4 minutes. Once ready, quickly release the pressure. Stir and serve soup.

Nutrition facts per serving: Calories 261, Protein 17g, Net Carbs 4g, Fat 18g

Fried Parmesan Cauliflower

Prep + Cook Time: 16 minutes | Servings: 4

INGREDIENTS

1 Cauliflower Head, chopped
1 ½ cups Water
½ tsp Curry Powder
½ cup grated Parmesan Cheese
2 tbsp Butter
¼ tsp Garlic Powder
¼ cup Heavy Cream
Salt and Pepper, to taste

DIRECTIONS

Pour the water into your Instant Pot. Place the cauliflower inside the steamer basket and lower the basket into the pot. Seal the lid and cook on HIGH pressure for 3 minutes.

When ready, release the pressure quickly. Remove the basket and discard water. Wipe the pot clean. Melt butter on Sauté. Add cauliflower, salt, pepper, curry powder, and garlic powder. Cook for a minute; stir in the heavy cream and Parmesan cheese. Cook for another 2 minutes.

Nutrition facts per serving: Calories 92, Protein 6g, Net Carbs 2g, Fat 12g

Broccoli Lemongrass and Cilantro Soup

Prep + Cook Time: 40 minutes | Servings: 3

INGREDIENTS

1 Brown Onion, roughly sliced
3 Lemongrass Sticks, halved
½ lb Broccoli, cut in florets
3 Celery Sticks, cut in 3 chunks
1 cup Cilantro
3 cloves Garlic
3 cups Vegetable Broth
1 Green Chili, minced
2 tbsp Fish Sauce
Salt to taste
1 Lime, juiced
Fresh Cilantro, chopped to garnish

DIRECTIONS

Place all ingredients, except the lime juice, in the Instant Pot. Seal the lid, select Manual and cook on High Pressure for 8 minutes. Once ready, do a natural pressure release for 10 minutes, then quickly release the remaining pressure.

Puree the ingredients inside the pot using a stick blender; add lime juice and keep blending until desired consistency. Garnish with chopped cilantro and serve.

Nutrition facts per serving: Calories 180, Protein 2g, Net Carbs 0g, Fat 2.5g

Spiced Radishes

Prep + Cook Time: 18 minutes | Servings: 4

INGREDIENTS

16 Radishes, halved
2 tsp minced Garlic
¼ cup Olive oil
1 tsp chopped Rosemary
½ tsp Red Pepper Flakes
Salt and Pepper, to taste

DIRECTIONS

Set to Sauté and dump all ingredients inside, and stir well to combine. Cook the radishes until roasted, slightly brown color and caramelized.

If you want radishes to be softer, remove them to a baking dish and pour 1 ½ cups of water into the pot. Place the dish on the trivet and cook the radishes for 3 minutes on HIGH pressure.

Nutrition facts per serving: Calories 105, Protein 1g, Net Carbs 1g, Fat 14g

Onion Soup

Prep + Cook Time: 35 minutes | Servings: 3 to 4

INGREDIENTS

2 tbsp Coconut Oil
6 cups Yellow Onions, sliced thinly
1 tbsp Plain Vinegar
4 cups Vegetable Stock
Salt to taste
1 Bay Leaf
2 sprigs Thyme

DIRECTIONS

Set on Sauté. Heat the coconut oil until translucent; constantly stirring. Add the vinegar and stir while scraping the pot's bottom to deglaze it. Stir in the remaining ingredients.

Seal the lid, select Manual and cook on High Pressure for 10 minutes. Once ready, quickly release the pressure. Remove and discard the thyme and bay leaf. Blend the soup using a stick blender until smooth. Adjust the taste and dish into soup bowls to serve.

Nutrition facts per serving: Calories 123, Protein 4.3g, Net Carbs 3g, Fat 8.7g

Mixed Vegetable Soup

Prep + Cook Time: 20 minutes | Servings: 4

INGREDIENTS

1 Onion, diced
3 cups Broccoli, chopped
2 cups Squash, diced
2 large Carrots, sliced
2 cups Water
2 cups Beef Broth
Salt to taste
1 cup Kale leaves
Chopped Parsley for garnishing

DIRECTIONS

Add all ingredients, except parsley, to the Instant Pot. Seal the lid and cook on High pressure for 5 minutes. Once ready, quickly release the pressure. Sprinkle with parsley to serve.

Nutrition facts per serving: Calories 68, Protein 1.9g, Net Carbs 4.9g, Fat 0.3g

Pumpkin Puree

Prep + Cook Time: 33 minutes | Servings: 4

INGREDIENTS

1 lb Pumpkin, chopped, seeds removed
¼ tsp Turmeric
¼ cup Almond Milk
A pinch of Nutmeg
Salt and Black Pepper, to taste
2 tbsp Butter

DIRECTIONS

Pour 1 cup of water into the Instant Pot. Place the cubes inside the steamer basket and then lower the basket into the pot. Seal the lid, select Steam and cook on HIGH pressure for 9 minutes.

When ready, release the pressure quickly. Remove the pumpkin to a bowl. Stir in the remaining ingredients, and puree the mixture until smooth and silky.

Nutrition facts per serving: Calories 83, Protein 1.5g, Net Carbs 5.7g, Fat 5g

Carrot Ginger Soup

Prep + Cook Time: 20 minutes | Servings: 2

INGREDIENTS

1 medium Onion, chopped
1 tbsp Olive oil
4 large Carrots, cut in large chunks
1 cup Vegetable Stock
1 tbsp Ginger Paste
1 cup Water
6 tbsp Full Milk
Salt to taste
Black Pepper to taste
Chopped Parsley for garnishing

DIRECTIONS

Set on Sauté. Add oil and onions; sauté for 2 minutes. Add carrots, stock, and water. Seal the lid, and cook on Low Pressure for 4 minutes. Once ready, quickly release the pressure.

Add salt, ginger paste and black pepper, puree the ingredients using a stick blender. Add the milk and puree further for a minute. Dish into soup bowls and garnish with parsley.

Nutrition facts per serving: Calories 70, Protein 0.9g, Net Carbs 7.2g, Fat 0.2g

Creamed Spinach Soup

Prep + Cook Time: 20 minutes | Servings: 3

INGREDIENTS

3 lb Spinach, washed
3 tbsp Butter
3 tbsp Cream Cheese
¼ cup Heavy Cream
1 medium White Onion, chopped
1 tsp Garlic Powder
Salt and Pepper to taste
3 cups Water

DIRECTIONS

Place spinach, onion, and water in the Instant Pot. Seal the lid, select Manual and cook on Low Pressure for 6 minutes. Once ready, quickly release the pressure. Add garlic powder, butter, cream cheese, and salt. Puree using a stick blender. Select Sauté and stir in heavy cream; cook for 5 minutes.

Nutrition facts per serving: Calories 148, Protein 7g, Net Carbs 0g, Fat 9g

Celeriac Pumpkin Soup

Prep + Cook Time: 15 minutes | Servings: 4

INGREDIENTS:

1 Celeriac, peeled and cubed
16 oz Pumpkin Puree
5 stalks Celery, chopped
1 White Onion, chopped
1 lb Green Beans, cut in 5 to 6 strips each
2 cups Vegetable Broth
3 cups Spinach Leaves
1 tbsp chopped Basil Leaves
¼ tsp dried Thyme
1/8 tsp rubbed Sage
Salt to taste

DIRECTIONS:

Open the Instant Pot and pour in the celeriac, pumpkin puree, celery, onion, green beans, vegetable broth, basil leaves, thyme, sage, and a little salt.

Close the lid, secure the pressure valve, and select Steam mode on High pressure for 3 minutes. Once ready, do a quick pressure release. Add the spinach and stir in using a spoon. Cover the pot and let the spinach sit in for 3 minutes or until it wilts. Use a soup spoon to fetch the soup into serving bowls. You may serve this with a low carb crusted bread as desired.

Nutrition facts per serving: Calories 98, Protein 4.1g, Net Carbs 2.5g, Fat 4.5g

Stuffed Mushrooms with Parmesan

Prep + Cook Time: 30 minutes | Servings: 4

INGREDIENTS:

10 large White Mushrooms, stems removed
¼ cup Roasted Red Bell peppers, chopped
1 Red Bell pepper, seeded and chopped
1 Green Onion, chopped
1 small Onion, chopped
¼ cup grated Parmesan Cheese
1 tbsp Butter
½ tsp dried Oregano
Salt and Black Pepper to taste

DIRECTIONS:

Turn on the Instant Pot, open the pot, and select Sauté. Put in the butter to melt and add the roasted and fresh bell peppers, green onion, onion, parmesan cheese, oregano, salt, and pepper. Use a spoon to mix them and cook them for 2 minutes. Spoon the pepper mixture into the mushrooms and use a paper towel to wipe the pot and place the stuffed mushrooms in it, 5 at a time.

Close the lid, secure the pressure valve, and select Steam mode on High pressure for 5 minutes. Once ready, do a quick pressure release.

Use a set of tongs to remove the stuffed mushrooms onto a plate and repeat the cooking process for the remaining mushrooms. Serve them hot with a side of steamed green veggies and a sauce of your choice.

Nutrition facts per serving: Calories 210, Protein 5g, Net Carbs 2g, Fat 14g

SNACKS & APPETIZERS

Barbecue Chicken Wings

Prep + Cook Time: 30 minutes | Servings: 6

INGREDIENTS:

3 lb Chicken Wingettes
3 tbsp Cajun Garlic Powder
Salt to taste
¼ cup sugar free Barbecue Sauce

½ cup Hot Sauce
¼ cup Butter, melted
½ cup Water

DIRECTIONS:

Pat the wingettes with a paper towel and put them in a bowl. Season them with the Cajun garlic powder and salt.

Open the Instant Pot, pour the water into it, and fit the steamer rack in it. Arrange the wingettes on the steamer rack. Close the lid, secure the pressure valve, and select Poultry mode for 5 minutes. Once ready, do a natural pressure release for 10 minutes, and then a quick pressure release to let out any more steam. Open the lid.

Remove the wings with tongs into a bowl and add the butter, half of the hot sauce and half of the barbecue sauce to it. Stir the chicken until is well coated in the sauce.

Arrange the chicken on a wire rack and put in an oven to broil at 350 F for 10 minutes. Remove the chicken into a bowl and add the remaining barbecue and hot sauces to it. Stir and serve the chicken with a cheese dip of your choice.

Nutrition facts per serving: Calories 61, Protein 5.7g, Net Carbs 0g, Fat 3.6g

Buffalo Chicken

Prep + Cook Time: 30 minutes | Servings: 4

INGREDIENTS:

1 lb Ground Chicken
Salt and Pepper to taste
2 tbsp Minced Garlic
2 tbsp Olive oil

½ cup Almond Meal
5 tbsp Hot Sauce
2 tbsp chopped Green Onions + extra for garnish

DIRECTIONS:

Add the ground chicken, salt, garlic, two tablespoons of green onions, and almond meal. Mix with your hands. Rub your hands with some oil and form bite-size balls out of the mixture.

Turn on the Instant Pot and select Sauté mode. Add the remaining oil, once heated fry the meatballs in the oil in batches to brown. Meanwhile, add the hot sauce and butter to a bowl and microwave them until the butter melts. Mix the sauce with a spoon.

Return all the meatballs to the Instant Pot and add the hot sauce mixture. Close the lid, secure the pressure valve, and select Poultry mode on Low Pressure for 10 minutes. Once ready, do a quick pressure release. Dish the meatballs, garnish with green onions, and serve the sauce with a dip of your choice.

Nutrition facts per serving: Calories 124, Protein 16g, Net Carbs 0g, Fat 28g

Bacon Wrapped Cheese Bombs

Prep + Cook Time: 25 minutes | Servings: 4

INGREDIENTS:

8 Bacon Slices, cut in Half
16 oz Mozzarella Cheese, cut into 8 pieces
3 tbsp Butter, melted

DIRECTIONS:

Wrap each cheese string with a slice of bacon and secure the ends with toothpicks. Set aside. Turn on the Instant Pot, open the lid, and select Sauté mode. Add the butter to melt and add then add the cheese wrapped bacon to it. Fry them to brown and then remove them with a slotted spoon onto a paper-lined plate. Serve them with a tomatoes dip.

Nutrition facts per serving: Calories 70, Protein 4g, Net Carbs 0g, Fat 5g

Cheesy Chicken Dip

Prep + Cook Time: 1 hour 20 minutes | Servings: 4

INGREDIENTS:

1 lb Chicken Breast
½ cup Low Carb Breadcrumbs
10 oz Cheddar Cheese
½ cup Sour Cream
10 oz Cream Cheese
½ cup Water

DIRECTIONS:

Open the Instant Pot and add the chicken, water, and cream cheese. Close the lid, secure the pressure valve, and select Meat/Stew mode on High Pressure for 10 minutes. Once ready, do a quick pressure release, and open the pot.

Add the cheddar cheese and shred the chicken with two forks. Spoon the dip into a baking dish, sprinkle the breadcrumbs on and place in a broiler to brown the top for 3 minutes. Serve warm with veggie bites or crunchies.

Nutrition facts per serving: Calories 287, Protein 17g, Net Carbs 2g, Fat 20g

Tomato Basil Dip

Prep + Cook Time: 20 minutes | Servings: 5

INGREDIENTS:

1 cup chopped Tomatoes
¼ cup chopped Basil
10 oz shredded Parmesan Cheese
10 oz Cream Cheese
¼ cup Heavy Cream
6 tbsp Water

DIRECTIONS:

Open the Instant Pot and pour in the tomatoes, basil, heavy cream, cream cheese, and water. Seal the lid, select Steam mode for 3 minutes. Once ready, do a natural pressure release for 10 minutes, then a quick pressure release to let out any remaining steam, and open the pot.

Stir the mixture with a spoon while mashing the tomatoes with the back of the spoon. Add the parmesan cheese and stir in until melts. Dish the dip into a bowl and serve with low carb chips or veggie bites.

Nutrition facts per serving: Calories 35, Protein 3g, Net Carbs 3g, Fat 2g

Avocado Paste Snack

Prep + Cook Time: 25 minutes | Servings: 2

INGREDIENTS:

2 Avocados, sliced
¼ cup green Bell Pepper, diced
2 cup cucumber, diced
Salt and Pepper, to taste

2 tbsp Lime juice
2 tbsp Cilantro
1 cup Water
¼ cup white Vinegar

DIRECTIONS:

Add avocados and green bell pepper into the pot on Sauté mode. Mix in the cucumber and water. Cook for 5 minutes. Transfer the mixture to a blender.

Blend the mixture for 2 minutes. Then, bring the mixture back to the pot. Stir in lime juice, white vinegar, and salt and pepper. Seal the lid. Cook for another 15 minutes on High pressure. When ready, do a quick pressure release. Garnish with cilantro to serve!

Nutrition facts per serving: Calories 355, Protein 6g, Net Carbs 5.6g, Fat 31g

Eggs in Sausage

Prep + Cook Time: 30 minutes | Servings: 4

INGREDIENTS:

4 Eggs
2 cups Water

1 lb ground Sausage
4 tbsp Olive oil

DIRECTIONS:

Put the trivet at the bottom of the Instant Pot. Place the eggs on top of the trivet. Add the water and seal the lid. Set to Manual mode and cook for 6 minutes on High pressure.

When boiled, allow 5 minutes of natural pressure release. Take the eggs out and place in an ice bath for 5 minutes. Then, peel off the skin. Take each egg, cover with the ground sausage, and shape it into a ball.

Lightly brush the egg ball with olive oil. Place inside the pot. Repeat with all eggs. Seal the lid and cook for 10 minutes on High pressure. When it beeps, do a quick release.

Nutrition facts per serving: Calories 512, Protein 46g, Net Carbs 1.7g, Fat 37g

Stir Fried Garlic Zest Spinach

Prep + Cook Time: 25 minutes | Servings: 3

INGREDIENTS:

2 cups baby Spinach
3-4 Garlic cloves, thinly sliced
¼ tbsp Salt

½ cup Chicken stock
4 tbsp Butter

DIRECTIONS:

Melt the butter on Sauté mode, and fry the garlic for 40 seconds. Add the spinach and stir-fry for 10 minutes. Add in the stock and mix well. When the water is dried out, season with salt and pepper.

Nutrition facts per serving: Calories 105, Protein 1.5g, Net Carbs 1.3g, Fat 11.5g

Sweet Potato Wedges

Prep + Cook Time: 20 minutes | Servings: 4

INGREDIENTS:

3 Sweet potatoes, cut into wedges
1 tbsp Garlic powder
½ tbsp Cinnamon powder
½ tbsp Cumin powder

2 tbsp Lemon juice
1 cup Olive oil, for frying
Salt and black Pepper, to taste

DIRECTIONS:

In a bowl, combine potatoes, garlic powder, cumin powder, and cinnamon powder and toss. Heat oil on Sauté mode. Add the potatoes and fry until golden, for 10-15 minutes.

Remove to a plate on a paper towel to soak up excess oil. Season with salt and pepper. Transfer to a serving dish, drizzle some lemon juice on top and serve.

Nutrition facts per serving: Calories 176, Protein 3g, Net Carbs 8.8g, Fat 9g

Fried Mushrooms

Prep + Cook Time: 10 minutes | Servings: 4

INGREDIENTS:

2 oz. Mushrooms, sliced
Salt and Pepper, to taste

¼ Garlic powder
4 tbsp Olive oil

DIRECTIONS:

Heat oil on Sauté mode. Fry mushrooms until golden, about 5-6 minutes. Transfer to a paper towel to drain excess oil. Season with garlic, salt and pepper; drizzle lemon juice.

Nutrition facts per serving: Calories 131, Protein 0.9g, Net Carbs 0.9g, Fat 14g

Easy Cauliflower Hummus

Prep + Cook Time: 50 minutes | Servings: 4

INGREDIENTS:

2 cups Cauliflower, chunks
1 pinch Salt
¼ tbsp Chili powder
3 cups Water

2 tbsp Olive oil
1 Onion, chopped
2 Garlic cloves, minced

DIRECTIONS:

Place water, cauliflower, salt, onion and garlic in the Instant Pot. Seal the lid and cook for 15 minutes on High pressure. When done, allow for a naturally release for 5 minutes.

Let it cool a little then transfer into a blender and pulse to a puree. Add olive oil gradually and blend. Put to a serving dish and sprinkle chili powder on top.

Nutrition facts per serving: Calories 98, Protein 2g, Net Carbs 3.5g, Fat 8g

Carrot Broccoli Stew

Prep + Cook Time: 55 minutes | Servings: 3

INGREDIENTS:

1 cup Broccoli, florets
1 cup Carrots, sliced
½ tbsp Salt
1 tbsp black Pepper
3 cups Chicken broth
1 cup Heavy Cream

DIRECTIONS:

Add florets, cream, carrots, salt, and chicken broth; toss well. Seal the lid and cook on Meat/Stew mode for 40 minutes on High. When ready, do a quick pressure release.

Transfer into serving bowls and sprinkle black pepper on top.

Nutrition facts per serving: Calories 145, Protein 1.5g, Net Carbs 1.2g, Fat 15.5g

Creamy Pumpkin Puree Soup

Prep + Cook Time: 55 minutes | Servings: 3

INGREDIENTS:

1 cup Pumpkin puree
2 cups Chicken broth
4-5 Garlic cloves
Salt and black Pepper, to taste
1 cup Heavy Cream
2 tbsp Olive oil

DIRECTIONS:

In the Instant Pot, add all ingredients. Seal the lid and cook for 40 minutes on Meat/Stew mode on High. When ready, press Cancel and do a quick pressure release.

Transfer to a blender and blend well. Pour into serving bowls to serve.

Nutrition facts per serving: Calories 465, Protein 15.4g, Net Carbs 6.2g, Fat 43.5g

Instant Pot Creamy Mushrooms

Prep + Cook Time: 30 minutes | Servings: 3

INGREDIENTS:

1 cup Mushrooms, sliced
1 cup Heavy Cream
½ cup Cream cheese
¼ tbsp black Pepper
½ tbsp Salt
2 Garlic cloves, minced
2 tbsp Olive oil

DIRECTIONS:

Set the Instant Pot on Sauté, add the oil and fry garlic for a minute. Add the mushrooms and cook for 4-5 minutes. Stir in the cream, broth, cream cheese, salt and pepper.

Seal the lid and cook for 20 minutes on High pressure. When ready, do a quick pressure release and serve immediately.

Nutrition facts per serving: Calories 358, Protein 5.5g, Net Carbs 4.5g, Fat 36g

Tomatoes Mix Recipe

Prep + Cook Time: 10 minutes | Servings: 3

INGREDIENTS:

1 tbsp Olive oil
1 Onion, chopped
2 Garlic cloves, minced
2 cup Vegetable stock
2 Tomatoes, diced

Salt and black Pepper, to taste
2 bay leaf
½ tbsp Oregano powder
½ tbsp Rosemary powder.
¼ cup Basil, chopped

DIRECTIONS:

Heat olive oil on Sauté. Add the onion and cook for 2 minutes until tender. Add the tomatoes, stock, bay leaf, rosemary powder, oregano powder, salt and pepper.

Seal the lid and set to Manual mode. Cook on High pressure for 5 minutes. When done, quick-release the pressure. Serve topped with basil.

Nutrition facts per serving: Calories 57, Protein 1.8g, Net Carbs 5.1g, Fat 2.3g

Hot Stir-Fried Chili Pepper

Prep + Cook Time: 20 minutes | Servings: 3

INGREDIENTS:

2 green Bell Peppers, sliced
2 red Bell Peppers, fried
1 Onion, sliced
½ tbsp Salt

½ tbsp Chili powder
½ tbsp Garlic paste
2 tbsp Olive oil

DIRECTIONS:

Heat oil and fry the onion and the garlic on Sauté mode. Add salt, chili powder, bell peppers and keep stirring. Stir-fry for 10-15 minutes with few splashes of water. Transfer to a serving dish and serve.

Nutrition facts per serving: Calories 107, Protein 1.6g, Net Carbs 4.1g, Fat 10g

Lemonade Pilaf

Prep + Cook Time: 15 minutes | Servings: 4

INGREDIENTS:

1 cup Cauliflower rice
1 cup Water
¼ tbsp Salt
3 tbsp Lemon juice

¼ tbsp black Pepper
1 Onion, chopped
2 tbsp Olive oil
4 Lime slices

DIRECTIONS:

Set the Instant Pot on Sauté mode. Heat oil and cook the onion until soft, for 2 minutes. Add the lemon juice, water, salt, pepper, cauliflower rice and let boil.

Seal the lid, set to Rice mode and cook for 5 minutes on High. Do a quick pressure release, and garnish with lime slices.

Nutrition facts per serving: Calories 91, Protein 1.4g, Net Carbs 5.1g, Fat 7.5g

Spiced Zucchini Fingers

Prep + Cook Time: 15 minutes | Servings: 5

INGREDIENTS:

2 large Zucchinis, sliced
1 tbsp Cumin powder
1 tbsp Cinnamon powder
¼ tbsp Garlic powder
¼ tbsp Salt
2 tbsp Almond flour
½ tbsp Chili powder
½ cup Olive oil

DIRECTIONS:

Roll out the zucchini slices into the flour and set aside. Set the Instant Pot on Sauté.

Heat oil and deep fry the zucchinis until lightly golden. Drain out the excess oil on a piece of paper. Sprinkle with salt, chili powder, cinnamon powder, and cumin powder.

Nutrition facts per serving: Calories 189, Protein 1g, Net Carbs 0.4g, Fat 22.4g

Zucchini Chips

Prep + Cook Time: 15 minutes | Servings: 4

INGREDIENTS:

3 large Zucchinis, thinly sliced
¼ tbsp Salt
¼ tbsp black Pepper
½ tbsp Olive oil

DIRECTIONS:

Heat oil on Sauté mode. Put a few slices of zucchini in the Instant Pot and fry until golden and crisp. Repeat the same steps for all zucchini chips. Remove onto a paper towel to drain out the excess oil. Season with salt and pepper.

Nutrition facts per serving: Calories 25, Protein 0.8g, Net Carbs 0.2g, Fat 2.3g

Asparagus Chowder

Prep + Cook Time: 45 minutes | Servings: 5

INGREDIENTS:

1 tbsp Olive oil
2 cups chopped Onion
2 tbsp grated Lemon rind
1 cup Cauliflower rice
3 cans fat-free, Chicken broth
2 cups sliced Asparagus
2 cups chopped Spinach
¼ tbsp ground Nutmeg
½ cup grated Parmesan cheese
½ tbsp Salt

DIRECTIONS:

Heat oil on Sauté mode. Add onion and cook for 5 minutes until transparent. Add the cauli rice, lemon rind, asparagus, spinach, broth, and salt. Seal the lid, press Manual and cook for 10 minutes on High pressure.

When ready, do a quick pressure release. Top with Parmesan and ground nutmeg.

Nutrition facts per serving: Calories 109, Protein 6g, Net Carbs 6.1g, Fat 8g

Ground Beef Zucchini Zoodles

Prep + Cook Time: 35 minutes | Servings: 4

INGREDIENTS:

¼ lb ground Beef
1 large Zucchini, spiralled
1 Onion, chopped
2 tbsp Olive oil
2 Tomatoes, chopped
2-3 Garlic cloves, minced
½ tbsp black Pepper
¼ tbsp Chili powder
2 tbsp Soy sauce
1 oz. Parmesan cheese, grated
¼ tbsp Salt

DIRECTIONS:

Heat oil on Sauté mode. Add the onion and garlic and cook for 2 minutes until tender. Add the beef and cook until brown, about 5-6 minutes. Add in the tomatoes, salt, chili powder, soy sauce and black pepper.

Transfer the beef to a bowl; set aside. In the same pot, add the zucchini zoodles and cook for 5-10 minutes. Stir in the ground beef; mix well. Sprinkle with cheese on top.

Nutrition facts per serving: Calories 186, Protein 10g, Net Carbs 4.2g, Fat 13g

Cauliflower Tots

Prep + Cook Time: 16 minutes | Servings: 4

INGREDIENTS

1 Cauliflower Head, chopped
1 ½ cups Water
⅓ cup shredded Cheddar Cheese
4 Egg Whites
2 tbsp Butter
2 tbsp Heavy Cream
Salt and Pepper, to taste

DIRECTIONS

Pour the water into your Instant Pot. Place the cauliflower pieces inside the steamer basket and lower the basket into the pot. Seal the lid and cook on HIGH pressure for 3 minutes.

After the beep, do a quick pressure release. Place the cauliflower florets in a bowl and allow to cool. Discard the water and wipe the pot clean. When the cauliflower is safe to handle, add the rest of the ingredients, except the butter, to the bowl.

Mash the mixture until well-pureed and wet your hands. Make small nuggets out of the mixture. Melt the butter on Sauté and cook the nuggets on both sides until golden, for a few minutes.

Nutrition facts per serving: Calories 255, Protein 10g, Net Carbs 2g, Fat 21g

Stir Fried Vegetables

Prep + Cook Time: 20 minutes | Servings: 4

INGREDIENTS:

3 Bell Peppers
1 Zucchini, sliced
1 Onion, sliced
½ cup Mushrooms, sliced
¼ tbsp Salt
¼ tbsp Chili powder
½ tbsp Garlic paste
2 tbsp Soy sauce
2 tbsp Vinegar
2 tbsp Olive oil

DIRECTIONS:

Heat oil on Sauté mode and stir fry all vegetables, about 4-5 minutes. Season with salt, pepper and soy sauce. Seal the lid, press Manual button and cook for 10 minutes on High pressure. When done, do a quick pressure release and serve immediately.

Nutrition facts per serving: Calories 110, Protein 1.8g, Net Carbs 5.1g, Fat 10g

Caulicheese Mini Bowls

Prep + Cook Time: 15 minutes | Servings: 4

INGREDIENTS

½ cup Half & Half
2 cups Cauliflower Rice
2 tbsp Cream Cheese

½ cup shredded Cheddar Cheese
Salt and Pepper, to taste
1 ½ cups Water

DIRECTIONS

Pour water in and lower the trivet. Place all ingredients in a baking dish. Stir to combine well and season with salt and pepper. Place the dish on top and seal the lid.

Select Manual and set the cooking time to 5 minutes. Cook on HIGH pressure. After the sound, allow for a natural pressure release, for 5 minutes. Divide between 4 bowls and serve.

Nutrition facts per serving: Calories 134, Protein 5g, Net Carbs 4g, Fat 10g

Stuffed Mini Peppers

Prep + Cook Time: 12 minutes | Servings: 4

INGREDIENTS

8 canned Piquillo Peppers
1 ½ Prosciutto Slices, cut into 8 pieces in total
½ tbsp Olive oil

Filling:
1 ½ tbsp Heavy Cream
½ cup grated Mozzarella Cheese
1 tbsp chopped Parsley

½ tbsp Balsamic Vinegar
1 ½ cups Water

½ tbsp Olive oil
A pinch of each Garlic and Onion Powder

DIRECTIONS

Pour the water into your Instant Pot and lower the trivet. Place all filling ingredients in a bowl and mix well. Stuff the peppers with the filling and arrange them on a greased baking dish.

Place the dish on top of the trivet and seal the lid. Cook on HIGH pressure for 2 minutes. When it goes off, do a quick pressure release. Arrange the peppers on a platter and drizzle with the olive oil and balsamic vinegar.

Nutrition facts per serving: Calories 115, Protein 6g, Net Carbs 2.5g, Fat 9g

Egg Brulee

Prep + Cook Time: 15 minutes | Servings: 4

INGREDIENTS:

8 large Eggs
1 tsp Swerve Sugar
Salt to taste

1 cup Water
Ice Bath

DIRECTIONS:

Open the Instant Pot, pour the water into it, and fit the steamer rack in it.

Put the Eggs on the steamer rack, close the lid, secure the pressure valve, and select Poultry mode on High Pressure for 4 minutes. Once ready, do a quick pressure release, and open the pot. Remove the Eggs into the ice bath and peel the Eggs.

Put the peeled Eggs in a plate and slice them in half with a knife. Sprinkle a bit of salt on them and then followed by the swerve sugar. Turn on the hand torch and carefully brown the sugar on the Eggs but not to burn the Eggs. Serve them as they are or with a spicy dip.

Nutrition facts per serving: Calories 77, Protein 6.3g, Net Carbs 1g, Fat 5.3g

Sausage Weenies

Prep + Cook Time: 20 minutes | Servings: 4

INGREDIENTS:

20 Hot Dogs, cut into 4 pieces
Salt and Black Pepper to taste
1 tsp Dijon Mustard
1 ½ tsp Coconut Aminos

1/6 cup Serve Sugar
1/6 cup Red Wine Vinegar
½ cup sugar free Tomato Puree
¼ cup Fresh Water

DIRECTIONS:

Add the tomato puree, red wine vinegar, swerve sugar, coconut aminos, Dijon mustard, salt, and black pepper in a medium bowl. Mix them with a spoon. Open the Instant Pot, put the sausage weenies in and pour the sweet sauce over it.

Close the lid, secure the pressure valve, and select Meat/Stew mode on High Pressure for 3 minutes. Once ready, do a quick pressure release, and open the pot. Serve the weenies and enjoy them as they are.

Nutrition facts per serving: Calories 180, Protein 10g, Net Carbs 0g, Fat 15g

Tropic Cauliflower Manchurian

Prep + Cook Time: 35 minutes | Servings: 4

INGREDIENTS:

2 cups Cauliflower florets
1 Onion, chopped
1 tbsp Salt
1 tbsp Chili flakes
½ tbsp Cumin powder
3 green Chilies, sliced
1 cup Tomato puree

3 tbsp Tomato Ketchup
½ tbsp Cinnamon powder
½ tbsp Garlic paste
¼ tbsp Turmeric powder
¼ cup Olive oil

DIRECTIONS:

Heat oil on Sauté mode. Add cauliflower florets and fry until lightly golden, set aside. In the same pot, sauté onion until transparent, about 2 minutes. Add in the tomato puree, tomato ketchup, salt, chili flakes, turmeric powder, and garlic paste.

Fy for another 5-6 minutes. Add in the cauliflower and fry again for 4-5 minutes. Sprinkle cinnamon powder, cumin powder, and green chilies on top.

Nutrition facts per serving: Calories 183, Protein 3g, Net Carbs 7.2g, Fat 15.5g

Tropic Sweet Potato Gravy

Prep + Cook Time: 25 minutes | Servings: 4

INGREDIENTS:

2 sweet potatoes, boiled, peeled, cut into cubes
1 Onion, chopped
1 tbsp Cumin seeds
1 tbsp Chili powder
½ tbsp Cumin powder
1 cup Tomato puree
½ tbsp Cinnamon powder
½ tbsp Garlic paste
½ tbsp Thyme
¼ tbsp Turmeric powder
2 tbsp Olive oil
½ cup Chicken broth

DIRECTIONS:

Heat oil in the Instant Pot on Sauté mode and cook the onion, cumin seeds and garlic for 2 minutes. Add the tomato puree, salt, chili powder, turmeric powder, and garlic paste and cook for another 5-6 minutes. Add the potatoes and mix thoroughly.

Stir in the chicken broth and cook for 10 minutes on medium heat. Sprinkle cinnamon powder, thyme and cumin powder on top.

Nutrition facts per serving: Calories 216, Protein 4.1g, Net Carbs 8.1g, Fat 8.4g

Pumpkin Pie Mini Pancakes

Prep + Cook Time: 20 minutes | Servings: 6-12

INGREDIENTS

½ cup Heavy Cream
1 Large Egg
¼ cup Pumpkin Puree
1 tsp Coconut Oil
½ tbsp Sweetener
⅔ cup Almond flour
½ tsp Baking Powder
¼ tsp Pumpkin Pie Spice
A pinch of Cinnamon
½ tsp Vanilla Extract
3 tbsp Butter

DIRECTIONS

Melt 1 tbsp butter on Sauté. Dump the dry ingredients in one bowl and stir to combine. In another bowl, whisk together all wet ingredients, except butter, and gently stir the wet mixture into the dry one.

When the butter is melted, add about 4 mini pancakes to the pot. Cook until set on both sides, for 2-3 minutes. Repeat the process with the remaining butter and batter. Serve chilled.

Nutrition facts per serving: Calories 99, Protein 5g, Net Carbs 2g, Fat 7g

Prosciutto Wrapped Asparagus

Prep + Cook Time: 10 minutes | Servings: 6

INGREDIENTS:

1 lb Asparagus, stalks trimmed
10 oz Prosciutto, thinly sliced
1 cup Water

DIRECTIONS:

Wrap each asparagus with a slice of prosciutto from the top of the asparagus to the bottom of it. Open the Instant Pot, pour the water into and fit the steamer basket in it. Put in the wrapped asparagus and then close the lid, secure the pressure valve, and select Steam mode on High Pressure for 4 minutes.

Once ready, do a quick pressure release, and open the pot. Remove the wrapped asparagus onto a plate and serve them with cheese dip.

Nutrition facts per serving: Calories 24, Protein 2.4g, Net Carbs 0g, Fat 2.4g

Bacon Cheeseburger Dip

Prep + Cook Time: 10 minutes | Servings: 6

INGREDIENTS:

½ cup chopped Tomatoes
10 oz shredded Cheddar-Monterey Jack Cheese
10 oz Cream Cheese
10 Bacon Slices, chopped roughly
4 tbsp Water

DIRECTIONS:

Turn on the Instant Pot, open the pot, and select Sauté mode.

Add the bacon pieces and cook them to brown. Use a spoon to fetch out the grease and add the water, cream cheese, and tomatoes. Do Not Stir.

Close the lid, secure the pressure valve, and select Steam mode on High pressure for 4 minutes. Once ready, do a quick pressure release. Add the cheddar cheese and stir until is well combined. Serve the dip with a side of low carb chips.

Nutrition facts per serving: Calories 53, Protein 3.9g, Net Carbs 0.5g, Fat 5.3g

Garlic Fried Mushrooms

Prep + Cook Time: 15 minutes | Servings: 3

INGREDIENTS:

2 cups Mushrooms, sliced
¼ tbsp Salt
1 tbsp black Pepper
½ tbsp Garlic paste
2 tbsp Soy sauce
1 tbsp Basil, chopped
2 tbsp Olive oil

DIRECTIONS:

Heat oil on Sauté mode. Add the garlic and cook for 30 seconds. Stir in the mushrooms and fry for 5-10 minutes on low heat. Stir in the soy sauce and season with salt and pepper. Cook for 5 more minutes, stirring occasionally. Sprinkle basil on top and serve.

Nutrition facts per serving: Calories 115, Protein 1.5g, Net Carbs 2.5g, Fat 12g

Pao de Queijo

Prep + Cook Time: 35 minutes | Servings: 4

INGREDIENTS:

2 cups Almond flour
1 cup Full Fat Milk
A pinch to taste
2 Eggs, cracked into a bowl
2 cups grated Parmesan Cheese
½ cup Olive oil

DIRECTIONS:

Grease the steamer basket with cooking spray and set aside. Put a pot on medium heat on a stove top. Add the milk, oil, and salt; let them boil. Add the almond flour and mix vigorously with a spoon.

Turn off the heat and let the mixture cool. Once it has cooled, use the hand mixer to mix the dough very well and then add the Eggs and cheese while still mixing. The dough will be thick and sticky after. Use your hands to make 14 balls out of the mixture and put them in the steamer basket and cover the basket with foil.

Open the Instant Pot, pour the water in, and place the steamer basket in and cover. Seal the lid, select Steam on High Pressure for 20 minutes. Once ready, do a quick pressure release, and open the pot. Put the balls in a baking tray and brown them in a broiler for 3 minutes.

Nutrition facts per serving: Calories 225, Protein 6g, Net Carbs 2.6g, Fat 14g

Mini Biscuits

Prep + Cook Time: 20 minutes | Servings: 8

INGREDIENTS

½ cup Coconut Flour
2 small Eggs
¼ cup Butter
⅓ plus 2 tbsp Milk
1 tbsp Gluten-Free Baking Mix
A pinch of Xanthan Gum
½ tbsp Sugar-Free Vanilla Protein Powder
¼ tsp Salt
1 ½ cups Water

DIRECTIONS

Pour the water into your Instant Pot and lower the trivet. Grease a baking tray and set aside. Place all dry ingredients in a bowl and stir to combine well. Add the butter to the bowl and rub it into the mixture with fingers, until a crumbly texture forms.

Add the wet ingredients and stir well to combine. Lightly flour your working surface and transfer the dough there. With a rolling pin, roll out the dough. Cut into 8 small pieces and arrange the mini biscuits on the greased tray. Place the tray on top of the trivet and seal the lid.

Select Manual and cook on HIGH pressure for 10 minutes. After the beep, turn the pressure handle to "Venting" for a quick pressure release and open the lid carefully. Serve chilled.

Nutrition facts per serving: Calories 105, Protein 2.5g, Net Carbs 2g, Fat 8g

Ham & Cheese Puffs

Prep + Cook Time: 20 minutes | Servings: 16

INGREDIENTS

½ pound Ham, cubed
2 ¼ tbsp Butter
¼ tsp Garlic Powder
½ tbsp Yogurt
2 Eggs
½ cup shredded Mozzarella Cheese
½ cup shredded Cheddar Cheese
¼ tsp Baking Powder
¼ cup Almond flour
½ tbsp Coconut Cream
Salt and Pepper, to taste
1 ½ cups Water

DIRECTIONS

Pour water in and lower the trivet. Line a baking tray with a piece of parchment paper and set aside. Place all ingredients in a large bowl.

Mix well until is well-combined. Roll the mixture into 16 balls and arrange them on the prepared baking sheet. Place the baking sheet on top of the trivet and seal the lid. Slect Manual and cook on HIGH pressure for 10 minutes. Do a quick pressure release and serve warm.

Nutrition facts per serving: Calories 65, Protein 2.2g, Net Carbs 0.5g, Fat 4g

Broccoli & Cheddar Nuggets

Prep + Cook Time: 20 minutes | Servings: 4

INGREDIENTS

2 Egg Whites
1 cup shredded Cheese
¼ cup Almond flour
2 cups Broccoli Florets
Salt and Pepper, to taste
1 ½ cups Water

DIRECTIONS

Pour in water and lower the trivet. Place the broccoli inside the steamer basket and then lower the basket into the pot. Seal the lid. Select Steam and cook on HIGH pressure for 4 minutes.

After the beep, do a quick pressure release. Transfer the broccoli to a bowl and mash them with a potato masher. Add the rest of the ingredients and stir to combine.

Line a baking sheet with parchment paper and arrange scoops of broccoli and cheese mixture inte the dish. Place the dish on top of the trivet. Seal the lid, select Manual and cook on HIGH for 6 minutes. Do a quick pressure release again. Serve warm.

Nutrition facts per serving: Calories 140, Protein 10g, Net Carbs 4g, Fat 9g

Basil Cheese Balls

Prep + Cook Time: 20 minutes | Servings: 20

INGREDIENTS

2 Eggs
3 tbsp Heavy Cream
⅓ cup grated Parmesan Cheese
⅓ cup crumbled Feta Cheese
4 tbsp Butter, melted
1 cup Almond flour
⅓ cup chopped Basil Leaves
¼ tsp Pepper
¼ tsp Salt
1 ½ cups Water

DIRECTIONS

Pour in water and lower the trivet. Place all ingredients in a food processor, and pulse until smooth. Transfer the mixture to a bowl and let sit in the freezer for 10 minutes, to set.

Line a baking sheet with parchment paper. Take the bowl out of the freezer and make 20 balls out of the mixture. Arrange the balls on the sheet. Place the sheet on top of the trivet.

Seal the lid, select Manual and set the cooking time to 7 minutes. Cook on HIGH pressure. When it goes off, do a quick pressure release. Serve immediately.

Nutrition facts per serving: Calories 65, Protein 2g, Net Carbs 0.8g, Fat 5g

Chili Tortilla Chips

Prep + Cook Time: 11 minutes | Servings: 12

INGREDIENTS

6 Keto Tortillas
1 tsp Chili Powder
¼ tsp Garlic Powder
¼ tsp Smoked Paprika
¼ tsp Salt
¼ tsp Pepper
3 tbsp Butter

DIRECTIONS

Melt 1 tbsp of butter on Sauté. Cut the tortillas into small pieces. Place about a third of the tortilla pieces in the pot and fry them for a minute per side. Transfer to a bowl.

Melt another tbsp of butter and fry the second third of the tortilla. Repeat the process with the remaining butter and tortillas. Finally, sprinkle with the spices and to coat well. Serve hot.

Nutrition facts per serving: Calories 45, Protein 1g, Net Carbs 0.3g, Fat 4g

Chili Party Meatballs

Prep + Cook Time: 20 minutes | Servings: 4

INGREDIENTS

½ pound ground Beef
1 small Egg
2 tbsp grated Parmesan Cheese
2 tbsp Hot Sauce
½ tsp Chili Powder
¼ tsp Garlic Powder
¼ tsp Onion Powder
1 tbsp Olive oil
1 ½ cup Water

DIRECTIONS

Heat oil on Sauté. Meanwhile, prepare the meatballs by mixing all ingredients together, except the water, in a bowl. Mix with hands until well combined, and then shape into meatballs.

When the oil is hot and sizzling, add the meatballs and cook for 2 minutes per side, until slightly browned. Transfer to a greased baking dish and pour the water into the Instant Pot.

Lower the trivet and place the dish on top. Seal the lid and cook on HIGH pressure for 6 minutes. After the beep, do a quick pressure release. Serve immediately.

Nutrition facts per serving: Calories 140, Protein 13g, Net Carbs 1g, Fat 10g

Carrot and Pumpkin Stew

Prep + Cook Time: 60 minutes | Servings: 4

INGREDIENTS:

1 cup Pumpkin, chopped
1 Onion, chopped
4 Carrots, peeled, chopped
1 tbsp Salt
1 tbsp black Pepper

½ tbsp Cumin powder
3 Garlic cloves, minced
2 tbsp Olive oil
2 cups Chicken broth
1 cup Vegetable broth

DIRECTIONS:

In the Instant Pot, add pumpkin, carrots, broth, onion, oil, salt, garlic, cumin powder, broth, and black pepper; mix well. Seal the lid and cook on High pressure for 20 minutes.

Transfer to a blender and blend to puree. Pour the stew into serving bowls and serve.

Nutrition facts per serving: Calories 262, Protein 10g, Net Carbs 6.8g, Fat 23.2g

Zucchini Ham and Cheese Rolls

Prep + Cook Time: 10 minutes | Servings: 4

INGREDIENTS

4 Zucchinis, cut Lengthwise
4 Ham Slices

⅓ cup Cheddar Cheese, grated
1 tbsp Butter

DIRECTIONS

Melt butter on Sauté. Lay out the zucchini slices on a working surface. Arrange a ham slice over and sprinkle with the cheese on top. Roll them up carefully and secure with toothpicks.

When the butter is melted, place the zucchini rolls inside your Instant Pot. Cook for 2-3 minutes, until the zucchinis brown and the cheese melts. Serve immediately.

Nutrition facts per serving: Calories 79, Protein 3g, Net Carbs 1g, Fat 6g

Pepperoni Pizza Bites

Prep + Cook Time: 14 minutes | Servings: 6

INGREDIENTS

24 Pepperoni Slices
¼ cup Low-Carb Pizza Sauce
¼ cup sliced Black Olives

1 ½ cups shredded Cheese
1 ½ cups Water

DIRECTIONS

Pour water in and lower the trivet. Arrange the pepperoni slices in a baking dish and place it on top of the trivet. Seal the lid, select Manual and cook on HIGH pressure for 2 minutes.

When it goes off, do a quick pressure release. Pour the pizza sauce over and sprinkle the olives on top. Top with the cheese. Return the dish on the trivet. Seal the lid again and cook for 2 more minutes on High pressure. When ready, do a quick pressure release.

Nutrition facts per serving: Calories 135, Protein 3g, Net Carbs 0g, Fat 9g

Mini Quesadillas

Prep + Cook Time: 11 minutes | Servings: 4

INGREDIENTS

2 Low-Carb Tortillas (made with Nut flour)
1 Stick of Butter

¼ cup shredded Cheddar Cheese

DIRECTIONS

Melt half of the butter on Sauté. Lay one of the tortillas and sprinkle all over with cheese; cover with the other tortilla. Put the butter on top. Cook for 2-3 minutes then flip quesadilla over.

Cook for 2 more minutes, or until it is golden on both sides. Cut into four and serve.

Nutrition facts per serving: Calories 81, Protein 3g, Net Carbs 0.5g, Fat 7g

Cream Cheese & Salami Snack

Prep + Cook Time: 15 minutes | Servings: 6

INGREDIENTS

4 ounces Cream Cheese
¼ cup chopped Parsley

7 ounces dried Salami
1 cup Water

DIRECTIONS

Pour water in and lower the trivet. Grab a baking sheet and arrange the salami slices in it. Place the baking sheet on top of the trivet and seal the lid.

Select Manual and cook on HIGH pressure for 3 minutes. When ready, do a quick pressure release. Remove the salami to a platter, top with cream cheese and sprinkle with parsley.

Nutrition facts per serving: Calories 176, Protein 9g, Net Carbs 1g, Fat 15g

Stuffed & Wrapped Meaty Jalapenos

Prep + Cook Time: 18 minutes | Servings: 4

INGREDIENTS

8 Jalapenos, sliced lengthwise, deseeded
8 Bacon Slices, sliced lengthwise
2 ounces Cream Cheese

6 ounces ground Beef
1 tbsp Olive oil
Salt and Pepper, to taste

DIRECTIONS

Warm the olive oil on Sauté. Add the beef and season with salt and black pepper. Cook for 4 minutes, or until browned. Transfer to a bowl. Stir in the cream cheese.

Divide the filling between the peppers. Wrap with the bacon. Arrange the stuffed and wrapped jalapenos on a baking dish. Pour 1 cup of water in and lower the trivet.

Place the baking dish on top and seal the lid. Select Manual, and cook on HIGH pressure for 4 minutes. After the beep, do a quick pressure release. Serve warm.

Nutrition facts per serving: Calories 143, Protein 9g, Net Carbs 2g, Fat 8g

Gorgonzola Chicken Dip

Prep + Cook Time: 14 minutes | Servings: 8

INGREDIENTS

½ cup Gorgonzola Dressing
1 ½ cups cooked and shredded Chicken
¼ cup shredded Mozzarella Cheese
2 tbsp grated Parmesan Cheese

2 tbsp Hot Sauce
8 ounces Cream Cheese
1 ½ cups Water

DIRECTIONS

Pour in water and lower the trivet. Place all ingredients in a baking dish and stir to combine.

Place the baking dish on top of the trivet and seal the lid. Press Manual, and cook on HIGH pressure for 4 minutes. After the beep, do a quick pressure release.

Nutrition facts per serving: Calories 115, Protein 8g, Net Carbs 1g, Fat 10g

Cheddar Crisps

Prep + Cook Time: 20 minutes | Servings: 10

INGREDIENTS

1 cup shredded Cheddar Cheese
¼ tsp Chili Powder

¼ tsp Garlic Powder
2 tbsp Butter

DIRECTIONS

Melt the butter on Sauté. Divide the cheddar cheese into 10 equal servings. When butter melts, add 5 of these portions to the top, making sure to leave some space between them.

Cook for 2 minutes per side, or until the cheese is melted and crispy. Transfer to a plate. Melt the other tbsp of butter and repeat the process with the remaining cheese. Combine the chili powder and garlic powder, and sprinkle the mixture on top of the cheddar crisps. Serve hot.

Nutrition facts per serving: Calories 88, Protein 7g, Net Carbs 2g, Fat 7g

Sausage and Cheese Dip

Prep + Cook Time: 16 minutes | Servings: 24

INGREDIENTS

1 pound Ground Sausage
½ Red Onion, diced
1 pound Sour Cream
15 ounces diced canned Tomatoes

8 ounces Cream Cheese
8 ounces shredded Cheddar Cheese
1 tbsp Olive oil

DIRECTIONS

Heat the oil on Sauté. Add the sausage and cook for 4-5 minutes. When browned, add the onions and cook for 2 minutes, until softened. Stir in the diced tomatoes. Cook for about 4 minutes. Stir in the cheeses and sour cream and cook for 2 more minutes.

Nutrition facts per serving: Calories 145, Protein 5.5g, Net Carbs 2.5g, Fat 12g

Prosciutto Wrapped Chicken Sticks

Prep + Cook Time: 20 minutes | Servings: 4

INGREDIENTS

8 Strips of Provolone Cheese
12 ounces Chicken Tenders
8 Prosciutto Slices

DIRECTIONS

Pound the chicken with a meat pounder until it becomes ½-inch thick. Cut it into 8 equal pieces. Place a provolone strip on top of each stick and wrap with a prosciutto slice.

Set the pot on Sauté and add the chicken wraps inside. Cook for about 4 minutes per side, or until the chicken is no longer pink in the middle. Serve immediately.

Nutrition facts per serving: Calories 125, Protein 12g, Net Carbs 0.7g, Fat 15g

Green Devilled Eggs

Prep + Cook Time: 20 minutes | Servings: 4

INGREDIENTS

6 Eggs
1 ½ tbsp Green Tabasco
⅓ cup Mayonnaise
Salt and Pepper, to taste
1 cup Water

DIRECTIONS

Pour the water into the Instant Pot. Place the eggs inside the steamer basket and lower it into the pot. Seal the lid, select Manual and cook on HIGH pressure for 7 minutes.

Do a quick pressure release. Prepare an ice bath and drop in the eggs. When safe to handle, peel the eggs. Then, cut in half and scoop out the yolks. Place the yolks in a bowl along with the remaining ingredients. Mix to combine and fill the egg holes with the yolk/tabasco mixture.

Nutrition facts per serving: Calories 153, Protein 6g, Net Carbs 3g, Fat 15g

Simple Almond-Buttered Walnuts

Prep + Cook Time: 15 minutes | Servings: 8

INGREDIENTS

1 ½ cups Walnut Halves
4 tbsp Sugar-Free Almond Butter
1 cup Water

DIRECTIONS

Add the water into the Instant Pot and lower the trivet. Place the walnuts in a baking dish and pour the almond butter over. Toss them a few times until the walnuts are well coated.

Seal the lid and select Manual. Set the cooking time to 4 minutes and cook on HIGH pressure. Do a quick pressure release. Stir once again, and allow for the butter to set before serving.

Nutrition facts per serving: Calories 90, Protein 1g, Net Carbs 3g, Fat 12g

Eggplant Spread

Prep + Cook Time: 30 minutes | Servings: 3 to 5

INGREDIENTS

3 tbsp Olive oil
1 ½ Eggplants, head removed, halved
2 cloves Garlic, skin on
1 clove Garlic, peeled

To Garnish:
3 sprigs Fresh Thyme
Extra Virgin Olive oil

Salt to taste
⅓ cup Water
½ Lemon, juiced
2 tsp Tahini

¼ cup Black Olives, pitted and unpitted

DIRECTIONS

Peel skins off the eggplants and set the cooker to Sauté mode. Add and heat the olive oil; add half of the eggplants face down and 2 unskinned garlic cloves. Caramelize for 5 minutes and turn eggplants over. Add the remaining eggplant, water, and salt; stir.

Seal the lid, select Manual mode and cook on High Pressure for 3 minutes. Once ready, quickly release the pressure, and strain the eggplants through a colander. Reserve a little of the brown liquid and remove the garlic's skin.

Put the eggplant and garlic in the pot. Add tahini, fresh garlic, lemon juice and some pitted black olives. Puree with a stick blender. Dish into serving bowls, drizzle extra virgin olive oil and garnish with thyme leaves and the remaining black olives.

Nutrition facts per serving: Calories 157, Protein 6.6g, Net Carbs 3.8g, Fat 13.9 g

Mushroom Pate

Prep + Cook Time: 3 hours | Servings: 3

INGREDIENTS

2 oz dried Porcini Mushrooms, washed
2 cups boiling Water
2 tbsp Butter, unsalted
2 tbsp Olive oil + 2 tbsp Olive oil
2 Shallots, sliced
2 lb Cremini Mushrooms, washed

⅓ cup Dry White Wine
Salt to taste
1 tsp White Pepper
2 Bay Leaves
5 tbsp Parmigiano Reggiano cheese, grated

DIRECTIONS

Place porcini mushrooms in a bowl, and cover with boiling water. Set aside. Select Saute mode, melt 2 tbsp of oil with butter, add the shallots; sauté for 3 minutes. Add mushrooms and sauté for 8 minutes.

Stir in wine, and let evaporate completely. Add the porcini mushrooms with liquid, pepper, bay leaves, and salt. Seal the lid, select Manual and cook on High Pressure for 13 minutes. Once done, quickly release the pressure and discard bay leaves. Add the remaining oil and puree the ingredients in the pot with a stick blender.

Add the cheese and pulse 3 to 4 times until fully incorporated. Dish in serving ramekins, and let chill.

Nutrition facts per serving: Calories 140, Protein 4.5g, Net Carbs 2.3g, Fat 5g

Mini Haddock Bites

Prep + Cook Time: 15 minutes | Servings: 8

INGREDIENTS

1 pound Haddock, chopped
3 Eggs
Juice of 1 Lemon
½ cup Half and Half
3 tbsp Olive oil

1 tsp Coriander
2 tbsp ground Almonds
1 tsp Lemon Zest
A pinch of Pepper

DIRECTIONS

In a bowl, whisk together the eggs, flour, zest, and spices. Set the pot on Sauté and add the oil. Dip the haddock pieces in egg mixture and then fry in the Instant Pot for a minute per side.

Pour the half and half and lemon juice over and stir to combine. Seal the lid and cook on HIGH pressure for 2 minutes. After the beep, do a quick pressure release. Serve chilled.

Nutrition facts per serving: Calories 160, Protein 15g, Net Carbs 2.3g, Fat 10g

Au Jus Dip

Prep + Cook Time: 20 minutes | Servings: 2

INGREDIENTS

¼ cup Soy Sauce
1 tbsp Worcestershire sauce
½ tsp Monk Fruit Powder
1 cup Keto Beef Broth
1 Shallot, minced

⅓ tsp dry Oregano
⅓ tsp dried Thyme
½ bay Leaf
1 clove Garlic, minced

DIRECTIONS

Select Saute mode. Add the liquid ingredients with the shallot and garlic. Sauté for 5 minutes. Stir in the remaining ingredients and let simmer for 10 minutes. Strain the sauce through a strainer.

Nutrition facts per serving: Calories 30, Protein 1g, Net Carbs 1g, Fat 1g

Chicken Ranch Dip

Prep + Cook Time: 20 minutes | Servings: 4

INGREDIENTS

1 pound Chicken Breasts
16 ounces shredded Cheddar Cheese
1 cup Hot Sauce
1 packet Ranch Seasoning

1 Stick of Butter
8 ounces of Cream Cheese
Salt and Pepper, to taste

DIRECTIONS

Place all ingredients in your Instant Pot and give the mixture a stir. Seal the lid and cook on High for 15 minutes. When ready, release the pressure quickly. Grab two forks and shred the chicken.

Nutrition facts per serving: Calories 115, Protein 11g, Net Carbs 1g, Fat 15g

Cauliflower Alfredo Dip

Prep + Cook Time: 20 minutes | Servings: 4

INGREDIENTS

1 ½ cup Cauliflower Florets
¼ cup Heavy Cream
2 tbsp Butter
A pinch of Nutmeg

Salt and Pepper, to taste
2 tbsp grated Parmesan Cheese
1 ½ cups Water

DIRECTIONS

Pour in water in the pot. Place the cauliflower florets inside the steamer basket and lower the basket into the pot. Seal the lid, select Steam mode and cook on HIGH pressure for 4 minutes.

Do a quick pressure release. Transfer the florets to a bowl and mash them with a potato masher until pureed. Add the rest of the ingredients and mix everything. Serve chilled.

Nutrition facts per serving: Calories 105, Protein 4g, Net Carbs 1.5g, Fat 8g

Spicy Chicken Dip

Prep + Cook Time: 20 minutes | Servings: 6 to 8

INGREDIENTS

1 ½ Chicken Breast
1 ½ (16 oz) pack Ranch Dip
1 ½ cup Hot Sauce

3 tbsp Butter
18 oz Cheddar Cheese
12 oz Cream Cheese

DIRECTIONS

In the Instant Pot, add all ingredients, except the cheddar cheese. Close the lid, secure the pressure valve, and select Manual on High Pressure for 15 minutes.

Once ready, quickly release the pressure, open the lid and shred the chicken using a fork. Add the cheddar cheese. Stir evenly as it melts. Serve with a side of julienned veggies.

Nutrition facts per serving: Calories 360, Protein 37g, Net Carbs 2g, Fat 40g

Spicy Queso Dip

Prep + Cook Time: 10 minutes | Servings: 4

INGREDIENTS

16 oz American Cheese
1 cup Cotija
1 ½ cups Full Milk
3 Jalapenos, minced
3 cloves Garlic, minced

3 tsp Paprika
2 tsp Cayenne Pepper
1 tsp Salt
Chopped Cilantro

DIRECTIONS

Place all ingredients, except the cilantro, in the Instant Pot. Seal the lid, and cook on High Pressure for 5 minutes. Once ready, quickly release the pressure and stir in cilantro, to serve.

Nutrition facts per serving: Calories 235, Protein 12g, Net Carbs 4g, Fat 17.5g

Veggie Tomato Dip

Prep + Cook Time: 20 minutes | Servings: 8

INGREDIENTS

1 cup chopped Broccoli
1 cup chopped Cauliflower
¼ Onion, diced
1 cup diced canned Tomatoes

1 tbsp Butter
¼ cup shredded Cheddar Cheese
¼ tsp Garlic Powder
Salt and Pepper, to taste

DIRECTIONS

Pour 1 cup of water into your Instant Pot. Place the cauliflower and broccoli inside the steamer basket and lower into the pot. Seal the lid, and cook on High pressure for 4 minutes.

Do a quick pressure release and transfer the veggies to a bowl. Mash finely with a potato masher. Discard the water from the pot and wipe clean. Melt the butter on Sauté. Add onions and cook for 3 minutes. Pour in tomatoes and spices; cook for 2 minutes. Stir in the mashed veggies and cheese.

Nutrition facts per serving: Calories 120, Protein 4g, Net Carbs 4g, Fat 5g

Homemade Ricotta Cheese

Prep + Cook Time: 4 hours 10 minutes | Servings: 6

INGREDIENTS

5 cups Full-Fat Milk
3 tbsp Plain Vinegar

A pinch of Salt

DIRECTIONS

Pour the milk into the pot and seal the lid. Select Yogurt mode and press adjust up to see the milk to start boiling. Allow the pot to complete the boil process; once it beeps, quickly release the pressure.

Add the vinegar, stir and let sit for 10 minutes. Line a strainer with cheesecloth and strain the milk through the cheesecloth. Let the whey strain out of the milk for 1 hour. Sprinkle with salt. Store cheese in an airtight container and refrigerate for 2 hours.

Nutrition facts per serving: Calories 174, Protein 11g, Net Carbs 3g, Fat 13g

Beef and Bacon Dip

Prep + Cook Time: 10 minutes | Servings: 3

INGREDIENTS

½ lb Ground beef
6 slices Bacon, chopped
1 cups Tomatoes, diced

1 cup Cream Cheese
1 cup Cheddar Cheese
5 tbsp Water

DIRECTIONS

Select Saute. Add the bacon and fry until crispy. Remove onto a paper towel. Add and brown the beef in the same fat for 4 minutes. Press Cancel; pour out excess grease.

Add water, tomatoes, bacon and cream cheese; don't stir. Seal the lid, and cook on High pressure for 4 minutes. Once ready, do a quickly release. Stir in cheddar and dish into bowls.

Nutrition facts per serving: Calories 131, Protein 5g, Net Carbs 1g, Fat 9g

BROTH, STOCK & SAUCES

Chicken Broth

Prep + Cook Time: 1 hour 35 minutes | Servings: 3 to 4 cups

INGREDIENTS

2 tbsp Olive oil
2 lb Chicken Carcass
4 Carrots, halved
4 Celery Stalks, halved
2 medium Onions, halved
1 Tomato, halved
1 cup fresh Parsley
1 cup fresh Thyme
Salt to taste
Water as desired

DIRECTIONS

Set on Sauté. Heat oil, and brown the chicken carcass for 10 minutes. Add carrots, onions, tomato, celery stalks, parsley, thyme, and salt. Pour the water over to cover the vegetables, about ⅔ of the pot. Stir.

Seal the lid, select Manual and cook on High Pressure mode for 1 hour. Once ready, quickly release the pressure. Strain the pot's content through a fine strainer and transfer the broth to a storage container. Let cool and use for your chicken soups or stews.

Tip: If refrigerated, after 6 hours, remove the solidified fat on top of the broth.

Nutrition facts per serving: Calories 12, Protein 0.9g, Net Carbs 1.5g, Fat 0.9g

Mixed Seafood Broth

Prep + Cook Time: 3 hours 20 minutes | Servings: 4 cups

INGREDIENTS

8 cups Seafood Bones and Shells, washed
4 tsp Olive oil
2 tsp Black Peppercorns
2 large Onion, halved
4 Carrots, halved
6 stalks Celery
4 cloves Garlic
1 cup Parsley
2 Bay Leaves
5 cups Water

DIRECTIONS

Set on Sauté. Heat oil, and add the onion, garlic, black peppercorns, celery, and carrots. Cook until fragrant. Add the seafood bones and shells; sauté them for 5 minutes. Stir occasionally.

Stir in the water, parsley and bay leaves. Seal the lid, select Manual and cook on High Pressure for 3 hours. Once ready, quickly release the pressure. Strain the content in the pot through a fine sieve, and discard the solids. Pour the stock into a storage bowl and leave to cool.

Nutrition facts per serving: Calories 10, Protein 2g, Net Carbs 0g, Fat 0g

Mixed Bone Broth

Prep + Cook Time: 3 hours 20 minutes | Servings: 8 cups

INGREDIENTS

4 Celery Sticks
3 small Carrots, halved
1 lb Chicken Bones, washed
1 lb Beef Bones, washed
1 lb Pork Bones, washed
10 cups Water
3 tbsp Fish Sauce

DIRECTIONS

Add the ingredients, except fish sauce, and pour the water over. Add the fish sauce. Give it a good stir. Seal the lid, select Manual and cook on High Pressure for 3 hours.

Once ready, quickly release the pressure. Remove the scum from the top of the broth using a ladle. Strain the broth through a fine strainer and transfer to a storage container. Let cool.

Nutrition facts per serving: Calories 31, Protein 4.7g, Net Carbs 0g, Fat 0.2g

Mushroom and Pork Broth

Prep + Cook Time: 2 hours 25 minutes | Servings: 3 cups

INGREDIENTS

4 - 5 cups Water
1 tsp Plain Vinegar
1 White Onion, halved
1 finger Ginger, washed and sliced into rounds
1 cup dried Mushrooms
2 lb Pork Bones, washed

DIRECTIONS

Add water and vinegar to the pot; cook on Sauté. Once the liquids start to boil, add ginger, mushrooms, bones, and onion. Seal the lid and cook on High Pressure for 2 hours.

Once ready, quickly release the pressure. Strain the content through a fine strainer and transfer broth to a storage container. Leave to cool before serve.

Nutrition facts per serving: Calories 85, Protein 3.5g, Net Carbs 2.3g, Fat 4.3g

Perfect Hard Boiled Eggs

Prep + Cook Time: 15 minutes | Servings: 3

INGREDIENTS

6 Eggs
1 cup Water
Ice Bath

DIRECTIONS

Place the trivet in the Instant Pot. Pour in water and arrange the eggs on the trivet. Seal the lid, secure the pressure valve and select Manual mode on High Pressure for 5 minutes.

Once it goes off, quickly release the pressure. Remove the eggs and place in ice bath to cool, for 3 minutes. Peel the eggs, slice and serve.

Nutrition facts per serving: Calories 155, Protein 13g, Net Carbs 1.1g, Fat 11g

Octopus Broth

Prep + Cook Time: 30 minutes | Servings: 3

INGREDIENTS

1 lb frozen Octopus, cleaned and chopped
8 cups Water
2 Bay Leaves
1 tsp Black Peppercorns
2 tsp White Vinegar
1 cup Porcini Mushrooms, chopped
⅓ cup Sea Beans, halved
2 sprigs Garlic Greens, chopped
1 Chive, thinly sliced
1 Lemon, squeezed
2 tsp Smoked Paprika
Salt to taste

DIRECTIONS

Place all ingredients in the Instant Pot. Seal the lid and cook on High Pressure for 15 minutes. Once ready, do a natural pressure release for 5 minutes. Remove octopus and veggies, and strain broth through a strainer. Cool broth and store it in an airtight bottle (s).

Nutrition facts per serving: Calories 46, Protein 8.3g, Net Carbs 1.2g, Fat 0.5g

Lemon Flavored Fish Broth

Prep + Cook Time: 65 minutes | Servings: 4

INGREDIENTS

2 large Salmon Heads (with tails), gills removed
1 tbsp Olive oil
1 medium Onion, chopped
1 large Carrot, halved
1 Celery Stalk, halved
2 sprigs Parsley
1 Bay Leaf
2 sprigs Thyme
2 Lemons, zested
2 tbsp Plain Vinegar
1 tsp Salt
5 cups Water

DIRECTIONS

Set on Sauté. Heat oil, and stir in onion and fish; cook for 3 minutes. Add the remaining listed solid ingredients, and cook for 3 minutes, stirring occasionally. Pour water and seal the lid.

Cook on High Pressure for 10 minutes. Once ready, do a natural pressure release for 15 minutes, Remove fish and veggies. Strain broth through a fine strainer. Store in airtight bottles.

Nutrition facts per serving: Calories 39, Protein 4.8g, Net Carbs 0.9g, Fat 1.4g

Anchovy Stock

Prep + Cook Time: 15 minutes | Servings: 3 cups

INGREDIENTS

1 lb dried Anchovies, washed
4 small Seaweed Kelps
3 cups Water

DIRECTIONS

Place all ingredients in the Instant Pot. Seal the lid and cook on High Pressure for 5 minutes. Once ready, do a natural pressure release for 5 minutes. Strain the stock through a strainer, cool and store in storage bottles. Use the anchovies for other dishes or discard them.

Nutrition facts per serving: Calories 42, Protein 6g, Net Carbs 0g, Fat 1g

Strawberry Jam

Prep + Cook Time: 15 minutes | Servings: 8

INGREDIENTS

6 oz Strawberries, diced
1/6 cup Xylitol
1/6 cup Water
⅓ tbsp Lemon Juice
¼ tsp Gelatin powder

DIRECTIONS

Add all ingredients to the Instant Pot. Seal the lid and cook on High Pressure for 1 minute. Once ready, do a natural pressure release for 5 minutes. Mash inside the pot to your desired texture. Select Sauté mode and let the jam thicken a bit.

Once sticking at the bottom starts, press Cancel. Scoop the jam into jars and allow to cool. It will thicken further as it cools. Refrigerate for up to 3 months.

Nutrition facts per serving: Calories 87, Protein 0.7g, Net Carbs 8g, Fat 0.3g

Pressure-Cooked Coconut Milk

Prep + Cook Time: 25 minutes | Servings: 5 to 6 cups

INGREDIENTS

10 oz Shredded Coconut
11 cups Water

DIRECTIONS

Add everything in the Instant Pot. Seal the lid and cook on High Pressure for 15 minutes. Once the timer goes off, do a natural pressure release for 10 minutes.

Transfer the content to a blender and pulse on high for 2 minutes. Strain the liquid through a fine strainer. Repeat straining 2-3 times. Transfer to storage bottles and use for up to 2 weeks.

Nutrition facts per serving: Calories 230, Protein 2.3g, Net Carbs 4.2g, Fat 24g

Keto Porridge

Prep + Cook Time: 10 minutes | Servings: 4

INGREDIENTS

½ cup grated Dried Coconut, unsweetened
1 cup Coconut Milk
1 ½ cups Water
1/6 cup Coconut Flour
1/6 cup Psyllium Husks
½ tsp Vanilla Extract
¼ tsp Cinnamon Powder
⅛ tsp Nutmeg Powder
15 drops Stevia Liquid
10 drops Monk Fruit Liquid

DIRECTIONS

Set on Sauté. Add the grated coconut and toast until golden brown. Do not burn it. Add water and coconut milk; stir well. Seal the lid and cook on High Pressure for 10 minutes.

Once ready, quickly release the pressure and add the remaining listed ingredients; stir evenly. Dish into serving bowls and serve.

Nutrition facts per serving: Calories 303, Protein 3g, Net Carbs 6g, Fat 25g

Cauliflower Mash

Prep + Cook Time: 15 minutes | Servings: 4

INGREDIENTS

2 small heads Cauliflower, cut into florets
1 cup Water
2 tbsp Butter
Salt to taste
Pepper to taste
⅓ tsp Garlic Powder

DIRECTIONS

Place the trivet in the Instant Pot and add the cauliflower florets and water. Seal the lid, and cook on High Pressure for 4 minutes. Once ready, quickly release the pressure and remove the inner pot; drain out the water.

Return to pot with steamed cauliflower in and partially mash the cauliflower with a stick blender. Add the seasonings and butter. Continue mashing until desired consistency. Serve with meat.

Nutrition facts per serving: Calories 130, Protein 2g, Net Carbs 5g, Fat 11g

Barbecue Sauce

Prep + Cook Time: 25 minutes | Servings: 3 cups

INGREDIENTS

2 tbsp Peanut Oil
2 Onion, chopped
1 cup Tomato Puree
1 cup Water
3 tbsp Monk Fruit Syrup
4 tbsp White Vinegar
2 tsp Salt
1 tsp Garlic Powder
2 tsp Hot Sauce
2 tsp Liquid Smoke
¼ tsp Clove Powder
¼ tsp Cumin Powder
2 tbsp Worcestershire Sauce, sugarless

DIRECTIONS

Add peanut oil and onion, and stir until the onion browns. In a bowl, add water, monk fruit syrup, tomato, and vinegar; mix well. Add garlic, salt, hot sauce, cumin powder, clove powder, Worcestershire sauce, and liquid smoke. Mix to dissolve everything.

Add the mixture to the pot and stir while scraping the bottom to remove stuck onions. Seal the lid, and cook on High Pressure for 10 minutes. Once ready, quickly release the pressure. Puree the ingredients with a stick blender. Dish into an airtight container. Use up for a week.

Nutrition facts per serving: Calories 131, Protein 7g, Net Carbs 4.2g, Fat 5g

Gouda Cheesy Vegan Sauce

Prep + Cook Time: 45 minutes | Servings: 2 cups

INGREDIENTS

2 cups Yellow Onion, diced
2 small Zucchinis, chopped
⅓ cup Daikon, chopped
1 small Cauliflower, cut into florets
4 clove Garlic, peeled
2 ½ cups Water, shared in 2
1 cup raw Cashews, soaked for 10 minutes in Water
1 cup Nutritional Yeast
Salt to taste
2 tbsp Smoked Paprika
3 tbsp Plain Vinegar

DIRECTIONS

Add all ingredients to the Instant Pot, seal the lid, select Manual and cook on High Pressure for 4 minutes. When ready, quickly release the pressure. Allow to cool for 10 minutes; then puree using a stick blender. Scoop into an airtight container.

Nutrition facts per serving: Calories 90, Protein 2g, Net Carbs 1g, Fat 8 g

Starfruit Sauce

Prep + Cook Time: 25 minutes | Servings: 1 cup

INGREDIENTS

2 ripe Star Fruit, skin removed
1 cup Water

1 tsp Monk Fruit Powder

DIRECTIONS

Add all ingredients to the Instant Pot. Seal the lid, select Manual and cook on Low Pressure for 10 minutes. Once done, press Cancel, and quickly release the pressure. Puree the ingredients in the pot using a stick blender. Scoop into an airtight container.

Nutrition facts per serving: Calories 25, Protein 0g, Net Carbs 3g, Fat 0g

Homemade Marinara Sauce

Prep + Cook Time: 30 minutes | Servings: 2 cups

INGREDIENTS

1 tbsp Olive oil
1 medium Onion, chopped
1 small clove Garlic, minced
1 Carrot, chopped
1 (25 oz) can Tomatoes, diced
¾ tsp Dried Basil

¾ tsp Dried Oregano
Salt to taste
Pepper to taste
½ tbsp Butter, unsalted
1 sprig fresh Parsley, to garnish

DIRECTIONS

Add oil, garlic, and onion, and cook until translucent, on Sauté. Stir in tomatoes, oregano, salt, and basil. Seal the lid, secure the pressure valve and select Manual mode on High Pressure for 10 minutes.

Once ready, quickly release the pressure. Use a stick blender to puree the content in the pot. Select Saute mode, add butter and some more salt.

Once the butter has melted, give it a good stir and select Cancel mode. Season with black pepper and sauce. Garnish with parsley leaves and serve.

Nutrition facts per serving: Calories 80, Protein 2g, Net Carbs 0g, Fat 2g

Keto Choc Mousse

Prep + Cook Time: 15 minutes | Servings: 6

INGREDIENTS

½ cup Cacao
1 cup Almond Milk
6 Egg Yolks
½ tsp Sea Salt
1 tsp Vanilla Extract
1 ½ cup Whipping Cream
½ cup Water
½ cup Erythritol Sweetener

DIRECTIONS

In a bowl, add the egg yolks and beat it. In a pan, add sweetener, cacao, and water. Whisk until the sweetener has fully melted. Add almond milk, and cream and whisk until fully combined.

Transfer to the pot and set on Sauté. Heat up but do not boil. Press Cancel. Add the vanillAnd salt. Mix evenly. Add a tablespoon of the chocolate mixture to the yolk, mix it smooth and slowly mix in the remaining chocolate mixture. Pour the mixture into ramekins.

Wipe the pot clean, place a trivet inside and pour in the water. Arrange the ramekins on top and seal the lid. Select Manual and cook on High Pressure for 6 minutes. Once ready, quickly release the pressure and remove ramekins using a napkin. Let to cool and refrigerate for 5h.

Nutrition facts per serving: Calories 231, Protein 7.1g, Net Carbs 4.4g, Fat 12g

Bolognese Beef Sauce

Prep + Cook Time: 40 minutes | Servings Size: 6

INGREDIENTS

3 tbsp Olive oil
2 brown Onion, diced
3 Carrots, diced
3 Celery Sticks, diced
Salt to taste
3 (14-oz) cans Chopped Tomatoes
1 Red Chilli, finely diced
2 lb Ground beef
5 cloves Garlic, minced
2 tsp Paprika Powder
1 tsp Cinnamon Powder
2 tsp Onion Powder
3 tsp Soy Sauce
1 tsp Fish Sauce

DIRECTIONS

Add in oil, celery diced onion, carrot, and chili. Cook for 5 minutes on Sauté. Add the beef, stir evenly using a wooden ladle and stir in the remaining ingredients, except the tomatoes.

Cook until the meat browns, stirring occasionally. Add the tomatoes with juices and stir well. Seal the lid and cook on High Pressure for 20 minutes. Once ready, quickly release the pressure. Press Sauté. Let the sauce thicken for 8 minutes; press Cancel.

Nutrition facts per serving: Calories 183, Protein 16g, Net Carbs 2g, Fat 7.5g

Homemade Ketchup

Prep + Cook Time: 20 minutes | Servings: 2 cups

INGREDIENTS

1 lb Tomatoes, quartered
2 tsp Paprika
½ tsp Salt
A pinch of Cinnamon
A pinch of Clove Powder
A pinch of Garlic Powder

½ tsp Celery Seeds
½ tsp Heinz Dijon Mustard
2 tsp Monk Fruit Syrup
1 Shallot
4 tbsp Plain Vinegar

DIRECTIONS

Add all ingredients to the Instant Pot. Mash with a potato masher to extract all the juice from the tomatoes. Seal the lid, select Manual and cook on High Pressure for 5 minutes.

Once ready, quickly release the pressure. Select Saute mode and allow it to simmer for 10 minutes or until thickened. Puree the ingredients in the pot using an immersion blender. Turn off the Instant Pot and scoop into an airtight container.

NUTRITION FACTS PER SERVING

Nutrition facts per serving: Calories 6, Protein 1g, Net Carbs 0g, Fat 1g

Homemade Tabasco Sauce

Prep + Cook Time: 10 minutes | Servings: 1 cup

INGREDIENTS

14 oz red Chilies, stem removed, chopped
2 cups Plain Vinegar

2 ¼ tsp Salt or to taste
¼ cup water

DIRECTIONS

Add the peppers, vinegar, water, and salt to the Instant Pot. Seal the lid, and select Manual mode on High Pressure for 1 minute. Once ready, quickly release the pressure.

Puree the ingredients in the pot using an immersion blender. Pour the hot sauce into a clean bottle. No need to strain the seeds out. Refrigerate and use as desired.

Nutrition facts per serving: Calories 32, Protein 0.7g, Net Carbs 5g, Fat 0.5g

DESSERTS

Chocolate Cheesecake

Prep + Cook Time: 40 minutes+ 6 hours for cooling | Servings: 6

INGREDIENTS:

2 cups Water

Crust:

½ cup Coconut Flour
½ cup Almond flour
2 tbsp Swerve Sugar
3 tbsp Cocoa Powder, unsweetened
3 tbsp Butter, melted

Filling:

2 Eggs, room temperature and cracked into a bowl
2 Egg Yolks, room temperature and cracked into a bowl
20 oz Cream Cheese, room temperature
1 tsp Monk Fruit Powder
1 tsp Stevia Powder
½ cup Cocoa Powder, unsweetened
1 cup Heavy Cream
½ cup Sour Cream
2 tsp Vanilla Extract
8 oz Baking Chocolate, melted

DIRECTIONS:

Start off with the crust: Line an 8-inch springform pan with parchment paper and use kitchen scissors to trim the paper to fit the pan.

In a mixing bowl, add the coconut flour, almond flour, cocoa powder, and swerve sugar. Use a spoon to mix them evenly then add the melted butter and mix again until well incorporated.

Spoon the mixture into the springform pan and tap to firm using the spoon. Set aside.

Move on to the make the filling:

In an electric mixer, add the cream cheese, swerve powder, monk fruit powder, and cocoa powder. Press Start and mix the ingredients.

While still mixing, add the Eggs and egg yolks. Once combined and still mixing, add the sour cream, melted chocolate, heavy cream, and vanilla extract. Use a spatula to scrape the sides of the bowl as you mix.

Once well combined, turn off the electric mixer, and spoon the filling mixture onto the crust in the springform pan. Use the spatula to smoothen out. Open the pot, and fit the trivet at the bottom; pour in the water. Loosely cover the springform pan with foil and place on the rack.

Close the lid, secure the pressure valve, and select Steam mode on High pressure for 10 minutes. Once ready, do a quick pressure release to let out the remaining steam.

With napkins in both hands, hold the trivet's sling and lift out with the spring form pan. Let the cake sit for an hour to cool and then refrigerate for at least 5 hours. After the refrigeration is done, open the spring form pan and slice the cake. Serve the slices.

Nutrition facts per serving: Calories 413, Protein 8g, Net Carbs 3g, Fat 38g

Easy Crème Brulee

Prep + Cook Time: 30 minutes + 6 hours for cooling | Servings: 4

INGREDIENTS:

3 cups Heavy Whipping Cream
6 tbsp Swerve Sugar
7 large Egg Yolks

2 tbsp Vanilla Extract
2 cups Water

DIRECTIONS:

In a mixing bowl, add the yolks, vanilla, whipping cream, and half of the swerve sugar. Use a whisk to mix them until they are well combined. Pour the mixture into the ramekins and cover them with aluminium foil. Open the Instant Pot, fit the trivet into the pot, and pour the water in.

Place 3 ramekins on the trivet and place the remaining ramekins to sit on the edges of the ramekins below. Seal the lid, select Steam on High for 8 minutes. Once ready, do a natural pressure release for 15 minutes, then a quick release to let out the remaining pressure.

With a napkin in hand, remove the ramekins onto a flat surface and then into a refrigerator to chill for 6 hours. Remove the ramekins and remove the aluminium foil. Equally, sprinkle the remaining sugar on and use a hand torch to brown the top of the crème brulee.

Nutrition facts per serving: Calories 404, Protein 4.1g, Net Carbs 3.2g, Fat 32.1g

Hot Lava Cake

Prep + Cook Time: 40 minutes | Servings: 4

INGREDIENTS:

1 cup Butter
4 tbsp Milk, full fat
4 tsp Vanilla Extract
1 ½ cups Chocolate Chips, unsweetened

1 ½ cups Swerve Sugar + Extra to garnish
7 tbsp Almond flour
5 Eggs
1 cup Water

DIRECTIONS:

Grease the cake pan with cooking spray and set aside. Open the Instant Pot, fit the trivet at the bottom of it, and pour in the water. In a medium heatproof bowl, add the butter and chocolate and melt them in the microwave for about 3 minutes. Remove from the microwave.

Add the swerve sugar and use a spatula to stir well. Then, add the Eggs, milk, and vanilla extract and stir again. Finally, add the almond flour and stir until even and smooth. Pour the batter into the greased cake pan and use the spatula to level it.

Place the pan on the trivet in the pot, close the lid, secure the pressure valve, and select Steam mode on High pressure for 15 minutes. Once the timer has gone off, do a natural pressure release for 12 minutes, then a quick pressure release.

Remove the trivet with the pan on and place the pan on a flat surface. Put a plate over the pan and flip the cake over into the plate. Pour the extra swerve sugar in a fine sieve and sift it over the cake. Use a knife to cut the cake into 8 slices and serve immediately.

Nutrition facts per serving: Calories 360, Protein 5g, Net Carbs 5g, Fat 23g

Vanilla Pudding

Prep + Cook Time: 35 minutes+ 6 hours for cooling | Servings: 4

INGREDIENTS:

1 cup Heavy Cream
4 Egg Yolks
4 tbsp Water + 1 ½ cups Water
½ cup Almond Milk
1 tsp Vanilla
½ cup Swerve Sugar
4 Strawberries, sliced
4 Blueberries

DIRECTIONS:

Open the Instant Pot, and fit the trivet at the bottom; pour in one and a half cup of water. In a small pan set over low heat on a stove top, add four tablespoons for water, and the swerve sugar. Stir constantly until dissolves. Turn off the heat.

Add the almond milk, heavy cream, and vanilla. Stir with a whisk until evenly combined. Crack the Eggs into a bowl and add a tablespoon of the cream mixture. Whisk and then very slowly add the remaining cream mixture while whisking.

Pour the mixture into the ramekins and place them on the trivet in the Instant Pot. Seal the lid of the pot, secure the pressure valve, and select Steam mode on High Pressure for 4 minutes.

Once the timer has gone off, do a quick pressure release. With a napkin in hand, carefully remove the ramekins onto a flat surface. Let them cool for about 15 minutes and then refrigerate them for 6 hours. Remove from the fridge and garnish with strawberry slices and blueberry.

Nutrition facts per serving: Calories 83, Protein 4g, Net Carbs 8g, Fat 9g

Blackberry Smash

Prep + Cook Time: 40 minutes | Servings: 4

INGREDIENTS:

1 cup blackberries
2 tbsp Almond flour
1 cup Almond Milk
1 cup Cream
½ cup Stevia
2 tbsp Butter

DIRECTIONS:

Melt butter on Sauté. Add flour and stir well. Pour in the milk and stir continuously. Add in cream, blackberries and stevia. Seal the lid and cook on Manual mode for 30 minutes on High pressure. Once ready, press Cancel, and do a quick release and serve chilled.

Nutrition facts per serving: Calories 245, Protein 4.9g, Net Carbs 5.5g, Fat 17.1g

Fruit Mix Dessert

Prep + Cook Time: 17 minutes | Servings: 2

INGREDIENTS:

2 cups Almond flour
2 tbsp Baking powder
1 pinch Salt
2 cups Stevia
2 tbsp Butter
2 tbsp Vanilla extract
2 Eggs
1 kiwi, sliced
2 cups strawberries, sliced
2 cups whipped Cream

DIRECTIONS:

Add flour and baking powder into a bowl. Mix in the salt, stevia, butter, vanilla extract and eggs. Pour the batter into a greased round baking tray.

Place the baking tray inside, then seal the lid and cook on high for 15 minutes. Once the timer beeps, allow the pressure to release naturally for 10 minutes.

Remove the cake from the Instant Pot and leave to cool slightly. Spread with whipped cream on the cake. Top with kiwi and strawberries to serve!

Nutrition facts per serving: Calories 587, Protein 15g, Net Carbs 7.1g, Fat 47g

Pumpkin Cake

Prep + Cook Time: 10 minutes | Servings: 10

INGREDIENTS

- 3 cups Almond flour
- 1 tbsp Baking powder
- 2 tsp Baking soda
- 2 tsp ground Cinnamon
- 1 tsp ground Nutmeg
- ½ tsp ground Cloves
- 1 tsp ground Ginger
- 1 tsp Salt
- 4 beaten Eggs
- 2 cup Stevia
- 1 can Pumpkin
- 1 cup Coconut oil

DIRECTIONS

Pour in 2 cups of water and lower the trivet. Grease a heat-proof baking tray with butter. Then, sift the flour, baking powder, soda, salt, and spices all together in a bowl, and set aside. In a deep bowl, beat the eggs until you obtain a foamy mixture.

Add the stevia and beat until thick. Add the pumpkin and oil; beat until smooth. Blend the dry ingredients into the pumpkin mixture.

Pour the batter into the already greased pan, lower the pan on top of the trivet. Seal the lid and cook on High pressure for 10 minutes. When the timer beeps, naturally release the pressure, for 10 minutes, and serve warm.

Nutrition facts per serving: Calories 250, Protein 3.8g, Net Carbs 1.3g, Fat 26g

Vanilla Bean Cheesecake

Prep + Cook Time: 20 minutes | Servings: 8

INGREDIENTS

- ½ cup Swerve
- 2 Eggs
- 1 Vanilla Bean, scraped
- 16 ounces Cream Cheese
- 1 tsp Vanilla Extract
- 1 ½ cups Water

DIRECTIONS

Pour water in and lower the trivet. Place all ingredients in a food processor, and process until smooth. Grab a cake pan (a 7-inch one), grease it with cooking spray and pour the batter in.

Cover the pan with a piece of foil and place on top of the trivet. Seal the lid and cook on HIGH pressure for 20 minutes. After the beep, press Cancel and do a quick release. Serve chilled.

Nutrition facts per serving: Calories 245, Protein 9g, Net Carbs 3g, Fat 8g

Lemon Ricotta Cheesecake

Prep + Cook Time: 35 minutes | Servings: 5

INGREDIENTS:

10 oz Cream Cheese
¼ cup Swerve Sweetener + 1 tsp Swerve Sweetener
½ cup Ricotta Cheese
One Lemon, zested and juiced

2 Eggs, cracked into a bowl
1 tsp Lemon Extract
3 tbsp Sour Cream
1 ½ cups Water

DIRECTIONS:

In the electric mixer, add the cream cheese, quarter cup of swerve sweetener, ricotta cheese, lemon zest, lemon juice, and lemon extract. Turn on the mixer and mix the ingredients until a smooth consistency is formed. Adjust the sweet taste to liking with more swerve sweetener.

Reduce the speed of the mixer and add the Eggs. Fold in at low speed until is fully incorporated. Make sure not to fold the Eggs in high speed to prevent a cracked crust.

Grease the spring form pan with cooking spray and use a spatula to spoon the mixture into the pan. Level the top with the spatula and cover with foil.

Open the Instant Pot, fit the trivet in it, and pour the water in it. Place the cake pan on the trivet. Seal the lid, select Steam mode on High pressure for 15 minutes. Meanwhile, mix the sour cream and one tablespoon of swerve sweetener. Set aside.

Once the timer has gone off, do a natural pressure release for 10 minutes. Place the spring form pan on a flat surface, and open it. Use a spatula to spread the sour cream mixture on the warm cake and refrigerate the cake for 8 hours. Slice into 6 pieces and serve.

Nutrition facts per serving: Calories 181, Protein 5g, Net Carbs 2g, Fat 25g

Lemony Ricotta Cake

Prep + Cook Time: 40 minutes | Servings: 6

INGREDIENTS

8 ounces Cream Cheese
⅓ cup Ricotta Cheese
¼ cup Sweetener (Xylithol)
1 tsp Lemon Zest

Juice of 1 Lemon
2 Eggs
1 ½ cups Water

Topping:

1 tsp Sweetener

2 tbsp Sour Cream

DIRECTIONS

Pour in water and lower the trivet. Add cream cheese, ricotta, sweetener, zest ,and juice, in a bowl, and mix with an electric mixer until well-combined and with no lumps.

Then, add in the eggs and mix them briefly, until fully combined. Otherwise, your crust will be cracked at the end. Pour the batter into a greased springform pan that fits in the Instant Pot.

Cover with a piece of aluminum foil. Place the pan on top of the trivet and seal the lid. Select Manual and set the cooking time to 30 minutes. Cook on HIGH pressure. After the beep, do a quick pressure release. Whisk together sour cream and sweetener, and spread over the cake.

Nutrition facts per serving: Calories 183, Protein 5g, Net Carbs 2 g, Fat 16g

Very Chocolate Cheesecake

Prep + Cook Time: 40 minutes | Servings: 8

INGREDIENTS

¼ cup Coconut Flour
¼ cup Almond flour
1 ½ tbsp Sweetener

Filling:

16 ounces Cream Cheese, softened
1 Egg plus 2 Egg Yolks
⅓ cup Cocoa Powder, unsweetened
½ tsp Stevia Powder
¾ cup Heavy Cream

2 ½ tbsp Cocoa Powder, unsweetened
2 tbsp Butter, melted
1 ½ cups Water

1 tsp Vanilla Extract
¼ cup Sour Cream
½ tsp Monk Fruit Powder
6 ounces Dark Chocolate, melted

DIRECTIONS

Pour the water into the Instant Pot, and line a cake pan with a piece of parchment paper. Lower the trivet. Combine all crust ingredients in a bowl, and press the mixture into the pan.

Place all filling ingredients in a blender, and pulse until smooth. Pour the filling over the crust. Grab a piece of aluminum foil and cover the pan. Make a sling with the foil and place the pan over the sling so you can easily remove it from the Instant Pot afterwards.

Place the pan on top of the trivet and seal the lid. Select Manual and cook on HIGH pressure for 20 minutes. After the beep, release the pressure quickly and serve chilled.

Nutrition facts per serving: Calories 402, Protein 8g, Net Carbs 8g, Fat 38g

Chocolate Mini Cakes

Prep + Cook Time: 20 minutes | Servings: 2

INGREDIENTS

1 tsp Vanilla Extract
2 tbsp Splenda
2 tbsp Heavy Cream

¼ cup Cocoa Powder, unsweetened
2 Eggs
1 ½ cups Water

DIRECTIONS

Pour the water in the Instant Pot and lower the trivet. Grease 2 ramekins with cooking spray; set aside. Whisk the dry ingredients in one bowl, and the wet ones in another one.

Gently combine the two mixtures, making sure the batter is smooth and well-combined. Pour into the ramekins and place them on top of the trivet. Seal the lid and select Manual.

Cook on HIGH pressure for 9 minutes. After the beep, press Cancel and do a quick pressure release. Flip the cakes onto plates. Serve with whipped cream.

Nutrition facts per serving: Calories 230, Protein 6g, Net Carbs 3.5g, Fat 7g

Strawberry Cobbler Mock

Prep + Cook Time: 20 minutes | Servings: 4

INGREDIENTS

1 cup chopped Strawberries
2 tsp Lemon Juice
5 Egg Yolks
¼ tsp Baking Powder
½ tsp Lemon Zest

4 tbsp Sweetener
¼ cup Almond flour
2 tbsp Heavy Cream
2 tbsp Butter
2 cups Water

DIRECTIONS

Pour water in and lower the trivet. Grease a cake pan that fits inside the Instant Pot, with cooking spray; set aside. Place all dry ingredients in a bowl, and whisk until well-combined.

In another bowl, whisk the wet ingredients until smooth. Combine the two mixtures gently, until they are no more lumps visible. Stir in the strawberries and pour the batter into the prepared cake pan. Seal the lid, select Manual and ook on HIGH pressure for 15 minutes.

After the beep, press Cancel and release the pressure quickly. Serve chilled and enjoy!

Nutrition facts per serving: Calories 440, Protein 9g, Net Carbs 5g, Fat 42g

Lemon Curd

Prep + Cook Time: 30 minutes | Servings: 3

INGREDIENTS

3 ounces Butter, at room temperature
1 ½ tsp Lime Zest
⅔ cup Lime Juice

1 cup Sweetener
2 Eggs plus 2 Egg Yolks
1 ½ cups Water

DIRECTIONS

Place the sweetener and butter in a food processor; pulse for 2 minutes. Add in eggs and egg yolks, and mix for 1 more minute. Stir in the zest and juice until the mixture is well combined.

Divide the mixture between 3 half-pint mason jars. Pour the water in your Instant Pot and lower the trivet. Arrange the jars on top of the trivet and seal the lid. Select Manual and cook on HIGH pressure for 10 minutes. After the beep, allow for a natural pressure release.

Note: *The curd can be enjoyed for up to a week if kept in a fridge.*

Nutrition facts per serving: Calories 223, Protein 8g, Net Carbs 5.5g, Fat 4g, Fiber 1.5g

Cocoa Walnut Cake

Prep + Cook Time: 30 minutes | Servings: 6

INGREDIENTS

1 cup Almond or Coconut Flour
3 Eggs
¼ cup chopped Walnuts
¼ cup Coconut Oil
¼ cup Cocoa Powder, unsweetened
⅔ cup Sweetener

⅓ cup Heavy Whipping Cream
1 tsp Baking Powder
1 ½ cups Water

DIRECTIONS

Pour the water into your Instant Pot and lower the trivet. Place all ingredients in a large bowl, and mix with an electric mixer until well-combined and fluffy.

Grease a cake pan with cooking spray and pour the batter in. Cover the pan with a piece of aluminum foil. Place the pan on top of the trivet. Seal the lid and cook on HIGH pressure for 20 minutes. After the beep, press Cancel and release the pressure quickly.

Nutrition facts per serving: Calories 313, Protein 8g, Net Carbs 7g, Fat 28g

Lavender and Apple Cake

Prep + Cook Time: 35 minutes | Servings: 6

INGREDIENTS

⅓ cup Butter, melted
2 tbsp Coconut Flour
2 tbsp Lemon Juice
4 small GalApples, peeled, cut into slices
½ tsp dried Lavender flowers
1 tsp Vanilla Extract

⅔ cup Cassav Flour
¼ cup Almond flour
½ tsp Baking Powder
1 tbsp Gelatin Powder
A pinch of Salt
2 cups Water

DIRECTIONS

Pour water in and lower the trivet. Line a cake pan with a piece of parchment paper; set aside. Combine apples, lemon juice, and lavender, in a bowl, and then arrange the apple slices at the bottom of the lined pan.

Combine the dry ingredients in one bowl, and whisk together the rest of the ingredients in another bowl. Combine the two mixtures gently, and pour the batter over the apple slices.

Grab a piece of aluminum foil and cover the pan. Place the pan on top of the trivet and sel the lid. Select Manual and set the cooking time to 25 minutes. Cook on HIGH pressure. After the beep, allow the valve to drop on its own for a natural pressure release, for about 10 minutes.

Nutrition facts per serving: Calories 285, Protein 5g, Net Carbs 5.5g, Fat 4g

Pistachio Cake

Prep + Cook Time: 50 minutes | Servings: 4

INGREDIENTS:

2 tbsp Pistachio powder
4-5 tbsp Mint leaves, finely chopped
½ cup Stevia
1 cup Almond flour

1 tbsp Vanilla extract
1 tbsp Cocoa powder
2 Eggs
½ cup Butter

DIRECTIONS:

In a bowl, beat the eggs until fluffy. In a separate bowl, mix butter, stevia, add vanilla extract and beat for 1-2 minutes. Add it to the eggs mixture and flour, mint, and pistachio.

Pour butter into a greased baking dish. Lower the trivet in the pot and pour in 1 cup of water. Lay the baking dish on top, seal the lid and cook on High pressure for 45 minutes. Once ready, allow the pressure to release naturally for 10 minutes. Serve chilled.

Nutrition facts per serving: Calories 191, Protein 4.4g, Net Carbs 0.5g, Fat 18.4g

Chocolate Squares with Chia Seeds

Prep + Cook Time: 10 minutes | Servings: 4

INGREDIENTS

4 oz. dark Chocolate, chopped
1 ½ tsp Stevia
½ tsp Vanilla Extract
4 tsp dried, diced Mango
2 tsp chopped Almonds
¼ tsp Chia seeds
¼ tsp Sea Salt
Melted Butter to grease muffin cups

DIRECTIONS

Pour 2 cups of water and put the steaming basket inside. Grease 4 ramekins with butter. Add the chocolate, stevia, and vanilla in a bowl; then pour in the ramekins and sprinkle the rest of the ingredients. Line the ramekins in the steaming basket.

Seal the lid and cook on High pressure on Manual for 10 minutes. When the timer beeps, quick release the pressure and serve chilled.

Nutrition facts per serving: Calories 215, Protein 1g, Net Carbs 9.1g, Fat 14g

Rum Mug Cake

Prep + Cook Time: 20 minutes | Servings: 1

INGREDIENTS

1 Egg
⅓ cup Almond flour
A pinch of Salt
½ tsp Rum Extract
1 tbsp Sweetener
1 ½ cups Water

DIRECTIONS

Pour in water and lower the trivet. Place all ingredients in a bowl and whisk well to combine. Grab a mason jar and pour the batter in. Seal the jar and set it on top of the trivet.

Seal the lid, select Manual and cook on HIGH pressure for 10 minutes. release the pressure quickly. Allow the mug cake to cool before slicing.

Nutrition facts per serving: Calories 216, Protein 5g, Net Carbs 2g, Fat 6.5g

Orange-Flavored Cake

Prep + Cook Time: 23 minutes | Servings: 3

INGREDIENTS:

2 Eggs
2 tsp Stevia
¼ tbsp Salt
2 tbsp Orange zest

2 cups Heavy Cream
1 tbsp Vanilla extract
2 cups Almond flour

DIRECTIONS:

Beat eggs and stevia in a bowl. Mix in salt, orange zest, heavy cream, vanilla extract and flour. Pour the batter into a greased baking tray.

To your pot, add the trivet and pour in 1 cup of water. Place the baking dish inside, seal the lid and cook on High pressure for 20 minutes. Once ready, allow the pressure to release naturally for 10 minutes. Remove the cake and let cool slightly, before slicing.

Nutrition facts per serving: Calories 328, Protein 6.1g, Net Carbs 3.1g, Fat 32.8g

Chocolate and Applesauce Pudding Cake

Prep + Cook Time: 20 minutes | Servings: 4

INGREDIENTS

½ cup Sugar-Free Applesauce
1 tsp Vanilla Extract
⅔ cup chopped Dark Chocolate, melted
3 tbsp Cocoa Powder, unsweetened

2 Eggs
¼ cup Arrowroot
A pinch of Salt
1 ½ cups Water

DIRECTIONS

Pour water into the Instant Pot and lower the trivet. Grease a 6-inch baking pan with cooking spray; set aside. Place all ingredients in a bowl and whisk until smooth and with no lumps.

Pour the batter into the prepared baking pan. Grab a piece of aluminum foil and cover the pan with it. Place the pan on top of the trivet and seal the lid. Press Manual and cook on HIGH pressure for 10 minutes. When ready, do a quick pressure release and serve chilled.

Nutrition facts per serving: Calories 155, Protein 4g, Net Carbs 8.2g, Fat 9g

30-DAY MEAL PLAN

Standard Drink: 6 to 8 glasses of water daily

Day	Breakfast	Lunch	Dinner	Dessert/Snacks	Calories
1	Giant Pancakes	Mexican Chicken	Dill Spiced Salmon	Rum Mug Cake	1657
2	Salmon Veggie Cakes	Chicken Wings+ Coconut Cauli Rice	Beef Short Ribs+the remaining Cauli Rice	Chocolate Mini Cakes	1727
3	Two-Cheese Almond Bagels	Fall-Apart Pork Butt with Garlic Sauce	Beef Casserole with Veggies	Pistachio Cake	1701
4	Creamy Egg Casserole	Beef Burgers	Ground Beef with Peppers	Orange-Flavored Cake	1669
5	Fresh Veggies Mix	Creamy Asparagus Soup	Crack Chicken+Fake Mac and Cheese	Lemon Curd	1789
6	Mexican Chili Eggs	Beef Curry Stew+ Asparagus Gremolata	Hot Scrambled Eggs + Spicy Queso Dip	Rum Mug Cakes	1643
7	Creamy Egg Casserole	Mexican Chicken+ Stuffed Mushrooms with Parmesan	Green Chile Pork Carnitas	Pumpking Cake	1677
8	Bacon & Sausage Omelet	Crème de la Broc + Asparagus Gremolata	Sliced Meat with Mixed Mushrooms	Easy Crème Brulée	1677
9	Spinach Almond Torilla	Beef Curry Stew	Dill Spiced Salmon + Prosciutto-Wrapped Asparagus Canes	Chocolate Mini Cakes	1637
10	Giant Pancakes	Creamy Asparagus Soup	Ground Beef with Peppers+Spicy Queso Dip	Strawberry Cobbler Mock	1790
11	Salmon Veggie Cakes	Chicken Wings+ Coconut Cauli Rice	Beef Short Ribs+the remaining Cauli Rice	Lemon Curd	1720
12	Two-Cheese Almond Bagels	Healthy Taco Soup	Crack Chicken+Fake Mac and Cheese	Pistachio Cake	1705
13	Mexican Chili Eggs	Beef Burgers	Sliced Meat with Mixed Mushrooms	Orange-Flavored Cake	1741
14	Fresh Veggies Mix	Mexican Chicken	Green Chile Pork Carnitas	Rum Mug Cake	1667
15	Creamy Egg Casserole	Fall-Apart Pork Butt with Garlic Sauce	Dill Spiced Salmon	Chocolate Mini Cakes	1636

Day	Breakfast	Lunch	Dinner	Dessert/Snacks	Calories
16	Giant Pancakes	Mexican Chicken+ Stuffed Mushrooms with Parmesa	Green Chile Pork Carnitas	Pumpking Cake	1651
17	Creamy Egg Casserole	Chicken Wings+ Coconut Cauli Rice	Beef Casserole with Veggies	Orange-Flavored Cake	1736
18	Two-Cheese Almond Bagels	Fall-Apart Pork Butt with Garlic Sauce	Beef Casserole with Veggies	Pistachio Cake	1702
19	Bacon & Sausage Omelet	Healthy Taco Soup	Crack Chicken+Fake Mac and Cheese	Strawberry Cobbler Mock	1803
20	Salmon Veggie Cakes	Beef Burgers	Dill Spiced Salmon + Prosciutto-Wrapped Asparagus Canes	Lemon Curd	1790
21	Fresh Veggies Mix	Crème de la Broc	Sliced Meat with Mixed Mushrooms	Rum Mug Cake	1653
22	Creamy Egg Casserole	Chicken Wings + Coconut Cauli Rice	Beef Short Ribs+the remaining Cauli Rice	Chocolate Mini Cakes	1709
23	Mexican Chili Eggs	Beef Burgers	Ground Beef with Peppers	Orange-Flavored Cake	1716
24	Giant Pancakes	Creamy Asparagus Soup	Crack Chicken+Fake Mac and Cheese	Strawberry Cobbler Mock	1736
25	Spinach Almond Torilla	Beef Curry Stew+ Hot Scrambled Eggs	Sliced Meat with Mixed Mushrooms	Pumpking Cake	1705
26	Bacon & Sausage Omelet	Mexican Chicken+ Stuffed Mushrooms with Parmesa	Beef Casserole with Veggies+Spicy Queso Dip	Easy Crème Brulée	1780
27	Salmon Veggie Cakes	Fall-Apart Pork Butt with Garlic Sauce	Green Chile Pork Carnitas	Lemon Curd	1857
28	Two-Cheese Almond Bagels	Healthy Taco Soup	Crack Chicken+Fake Mac and Cheese	Pistachio Cake	1704
29	Fresh Veggies Mix	Crème de la Broc	Dill Spiced Salmon	Rum Mug Cake	1603
30	Giant Pancakes	Chicken Wings + Coconut Cauli Rice	Beef Short Ribs + the remaining Cauli Rice	Orange-Flavored Cake	1811

Made in the USA
Middletown, DE
28 April 2019